The Structure of English Clauses

The Structure of English Clauses

David J. Young

Lecturer in English,
University of Wales
Institute of Science and Technology

Hutchinson

London Melbourne Sydney Auckland Johannesburg

Hutchinson & Co. (Publishers) Ltd
An imprint of the Hutchinson Publishing Group
24 Highbury Crescent, London N5 1RX

Hutchinson Group (Australia) Pty Ltd
30–32 Cremorne Street, Richmond South, Victoria 3121
PO Box 151, Broadway, New South Wales 2007

Hutchinson Group (NZ) Ltd
32–34 View Road, PO Box 40-086, Glenfield, Auckland 10

Hutchinson Group (SA) (Pty) Ltd
PO Box 337, Bergvlei 2012, South Africa

First published 1980

© David J. Young 1980
Illustrations © Hutchinson & Co. (Publishers) Ltd 1980

The paperback edition of this book is sold subject to the conditions that it shall not, by way of trade or otherwise, be lent, resold, hired out or otherwise circulated without the publisher's prior consent in any form of binding or cover other than that in which it is published and without a similar condition including this condition being imposed on the subsequent purchaser

Set in VIP Times Roman by Preface Ltd, Salisbury, Wilts.

Printed in Great Britain by The Anchor Press Ltd
and bound by Wm Brendon & Son Ltd
both of Tiptree, Essex

British Library Cataloguing in Publication Data

Young, David J
The structure of English clauses.
1. English language – Clauses
I. Title
425 PE1385

ISBN 0 09 141450 4 cased
0 09 141451 2 paper

Contents

Preface

This is a textbook about English grammar, intended for students in higher education. It has several related aims. First, it aims to describe a large number of English grammatical structures, though it does not pretend to be comprehensive. The structures selected belong in general to units of higher rank than words, and have verbs rather than nouns as their nuclear elements. In accordance with recent developments in linguistic theory and description, much attention is given to the grammatical means that speakers have at their disposal with which to signal their communicative intentions. The material is also chosen so that it will make for a unified exposition that can be read straight through; the book is not intended primarily as a reference work.

Second, the book aims to encourage an investigative and exploratory attitude towards English text. Grammar is not to be seen as some sort of intellectual exercise indulged in merely for the sake of its formal beauty. It is of interest because it has to do with communication and co-operation and is necessary to the existence of societies and individuals. I hope that the reader will gain some insights into how a language achieves this by furnishing its speakers with a system for encoding meaning. (I am not claiming to have treated this topic in a developed way, but only to be helping the reader towards an understanding of what is involved.)

Third, it is intended that the reader will gain some understanding of the criteria used in grammatical studies for distinguishing one structure from another. There is little point in learning to attach grammatical labels without knowing what they mean.

All of the above-mentioned aims indicate that the book has a realistic and descriptive intent. It is not concerned with matters of taste and correctness, but with what English is like in some parts of the English-speaking world. I have included among the illustrative examples and exercises many sentences drawn from authentic English texts. Many of these are simplified or otherwise adapted to the purpose immediately in hand, and alongside them are also quite a large number of made-up examples. This is justified by the pedagogical aim of the book, since a pattern often gets obscured in its real-life context by masses of distracting detail. In the interests of realism, therefore, I have put into Appendix B two slightly longer pieces of unedited text. Reference is made to these periodically and often they furnish the examples in the book. I cannot claim that they illustrate everything that is talked about – they make too small a corpus for that – nor does the book elucidate everything found in the texts. Moreover, I have not aimed at providing the reader with a method of textual analysis; but at least the texts provide some living examples of some of the things talked about in the book. Many people nowadays, including language teachers, speech therapists and sociologists find they need to study text, and it is hoped this book will help to explain some of the things that go on in text at the grammatical level.

The description is necessarily based upon certain assumptions about the way a language may appropriately be described. Some space is devoted to these assumptions in the first two chapters and here and there throughout the book. Most of them are not controversial or peculiar to any highly formalised model of description. Others are more particularly characteristic of that theoretical model called systemic grammar. But no attempt is made to justify the choice of this model in preference to others. This is not a book about systemic grammar. I am of the opinion that it is possible for the elementary student of language to go a long way without commitment to any highly specific theoretical framework. This is not to say that he can manage without any theoretical work at all. We must have some conception of what to look out for when making our observations. But it may be a hindrance to him to have to give detailed attention to a formal model before he has enough insights into what it is that is to be modelled. This book is partly intended to help prepare the ground for those who wish to pursue the subject to more advanced levels.

The book naturally owes much to the writings of other grammarians, especially to those working in the systemic tradition. In particular, it is greatly influenced by J. McH.

Sinclair's *A Course in Spoken English: Grammar*, and by several of M. A. K. Halliday's works. No great originality is claimed for the ideas the book contains, which can mostly be found in published works, though not always in forms or places which are accessible to the non-specialist reader.

I owe many of the ideas on mood and modality to work done by Eirian Davies, which was, at the time this book was first drafted, as yet unpublished (see Davies 1979). I have also benefited from some suggestions made by J. McH. Sinclair, with whose encouragement I first started work on the book.

I have used earlier versions of the book with students for several years, and have introduced many revisions as a result of this experience. I have also received many detailed comments on recent drafts from Margaret Berry, Chris Butler and Eirian Davies, who have taken great pains and to whom I am very grateful. I am also grateful to Robin Fawcett and Dick Hudson for their encouragement.

Symbols

Grammatical

‖	clause boundary
(( ))	boundaries of clause enclosed by splitting
|	boundary of clause or group element
(. . .)	boundaries of clause or group element enclosed by splitting
F	free clause
B	bound clause
B^{cont}	bound contingent clause
B^{add}	bound adding clause
B^{rep}	bound reported clause
$\rightarrow$ / $\leftarrow$	relation between bound and dominant clause, with arrow pointing towards the bound clause
+	relation between joined clauses
P	predicator
P^{pass}	passive predicator
P^{act}	active predicator
P^{op}	predicator which is only an operator
S	subject
S^{x}	delayed subject
C	complement
C^{i}	intensive complement
C^{loc}	locative complement
C^{o}	object complement
C^{oi}	indirect object
C^{od}	direct object

C^{ob}	oblique object complement
C^{part}	particle complement
C^{o}/S	element which is simultaneously object complement and subject (see Chapter 11, 'Phase')
A	adjunct
A^{+}	listing adjunct
A^{l}	linking adjunct
A^{time}	adjunct of time
A^{place}	adjunct of place
A^{man}	adjunct of manner
A^{int}	intensifying adjunct
A^{act}	action adjunct
WH	the WH-element: 'unidentified element'
Voc	vocative element
Voc^{t}	vocative tag

Group structure

m	modifier
h	headword
q	qualifier
v	main verb
cop	copula
f	marker of finiteness
b	marker of non-finiteness
a	auxiliary
m	modal auxiliary
h	perfect auxiliary
c	continuous auxiliary
p	passive auxiliary
o	prepositional object
prep	preposition

Verb morphology: see section 14.3 (page 168)

Phonological

Intonation

//	tone group boundary
//ʌ	tone group beginning with silent beat

tonic syllable underlined

/	foot boundary

Phoneme symbols: enclosed between oblique strokes /. . ./

i	as in	sp*ee*d	ɔɪ	as in	b*oy*	f	as in	*f*in
ɪ	as in	r*i*d	əʊ	as in	*go*	v	as in	*v*ery
e	as in	s*e*nd	aʊ	as in	n*ow*	θ	as in	*th*in
æ	as in	s*a*nd	ɪə	as in	n*ea*r	ð	as in	*th*ough
ʌ	as in	m*u*ch	ɛə	as in	*ai*r	s	as in	*s*in
ɑ	as in	c*a*r	ʊə	as in	p*oo*r	z	as in	*z*oo
ɒ	as in	sp*o*t	p	as in	*p*in	ʃ	as in	*sh*in
ɔ	as in	c*au*ght	b	as in	*b*in	ʒ	as in	plea*s*ure
ʊ	as in	g*oo*d	t	as in	*t*in	h	as in	*h*ang
u	as in	f*oo*d	d	as in	*d*in	m	as in	*m*an
ɜ	as in	m*i*rth	k	as in	*k*in	n	as in	*n*ag
ə	as in	Chin*a*	g	as in	*g*ap	ŋ	as in	ha*ng*
eɪ	as in	w*ai*t	tʃ	as in	*ch*in	l	as in	*l*ip
aɪ	as in	r*i*ght	dʒ	as in	*g*in	r	as in	*r*ip
						j	as in	*y*es
						w	as in	*w*et

Phonetic symbols between [. . .].

General symbols

* example which is ill-formed either absolutely or from the point of view specified

Round brackets ( ) are also used in the ordinary conventional ways, and so is the oblique stroke / meaning alternatively. It is always clear in which way these signs are to be taken.

The chapters are divided into sections which are referred to by number. Thus the third section of Chapter 4 is referred to as section 4.3.

1 Levels of linguistic structure

1.1 Structure

The aim of this book is to show the reader how to find and describe certain kinds of pattern that occur in English text. 'Text' means any piece of language, long or short, spoken or written, complete or fragmentary. Text is language in action, which means that people are using language for some purpose in some real situation in which normally there are other people to communicate with.

Such verbal behaviour is obviously patterned, or structured; otherwise it would be unintelligible, random and purposeless. Text can be seen as the realization of a selection of patterns from a vast potential. It is meaningful only because the patterns it displays might have been other patterns but are not.

It is important to appreciate that pattern, or structure, in language behaviour is dependent on this contrast between what is actualized at some point in time and space and what is actualizable.

1.2 Levels of language

There are so many kinds of pattern in text that it is necessary to separate them into distinct levels of structure. The elements of the patterns on one level are of a different kind from those on the other levels. Of course, this division into various levels is a purely analytic procedure; language is a unity and its patterns of different types are simultaneous and interrelated. It is comparatively easy to study patterns on one level or another, but much more difficult to put all the levels together again and still be aware of how the whole system works. It is customary to think in terms of levels (or strata) ranging from low to high. The use of these terms is a figure of speech, but it seems to be helpful to think of the level of sound structure as low level patterning and of the level of discourse structure, in which people are acting towards each other within various types of social setting, as high level.

Between the low and the high comes the level of grammatical structure, part of which is the subject of this book. In order to see the grammatical level in its proper place, I shall spend a little time in this chapter describing the other levels: phonology, the level of patterned sound, and discourse, the level of patterned linguistic action.

1.3 Phonology

Phonology is the level of patterned sound, not simply the level of sound. Speech sound, considered as pure noise, does not belong to any particular language. In order to understand speech sound as belonging to one language or another, we must know how the language in question makes use of sound; that is, we must know what differences in sound are significant in the structure of that language. For instance, the difference between the initial consonants in *day* and *they* ([d] and [ð]) is distinctive in English, but not in French or Spanish. Conversely, there are two kinds of [l] sound in English, occurring in *limb* and *mill*, but native English speakers are not usually aware that there is a difference because it is not a distinctive difference; from the point of view of English sound pattern these two different sounds count as the same.

Even at this low level of language, therefore, we are already dealing not with physical, concrete sounds but with abstract units in a system of contrasts – not with sounds as such, but with patterns that are manifested in sound. The basic units in phonological patterns are known as phonemes.

It is a characteristic of language that at each level the basic units can combine with each other to form larger units. Phonemes combine to form syllables. For instance, *principles* has nine phonemes – one for each of the symbols in the phonological transcription / prɪnsɪplz /. But the phonological structure is not to be thought of as a simple row of nine units. The nine can be grouped into three syllabic units: / prɪn sɪ plz /. Each syllable has a structure. Typically, the English syllable has a vowel phoneme as its nucleus; this may be preceded and/or followed by a consonant phoneme or a cluster of consonants.

The last syllable in *principles* is of a different type; its nucleus is not a vowel phoneme but one of a small number of consonants that are able to function as a nucleus, namely / l /.

Even this brief description shows that syllables are patterned combinations of phonemes; that is, that syllables have structure. The types of syllable structure that occur in English can be described, and we can state that certain hypothetical patterns, like / pfun /, are un-English, not because there happens to be no such word in the language, but because there is no such syllabic structure. Compare this with / kus /, *koose*, which happens not to be an English word, but which, as far as phonological pattern goes, could very well be one.

Larger than the syllable is the rhythmical unit, or foot. The foot is constituted of syllables. For instance *principles and problems of religion* consists of three feet, as shown in the transcription in **1**, where the symbol / marks foot boundaries:

1 / prɪn sɪ pl zən / prɒb ləm zəv rɪ / lɪdʒ ən /

The structure of the foot can be described in terms of three factors. First, the number of syllables it contains; second, the various degrees of prominence, or salience, of the syllables; third, the relative length of time which the foot and its constituent syllables occupy. In the analysis of English rhythm on which the above transcription is based, each foot begins with a salient syllable.

Feet combine to form tone groups, which have a structure describable in terms of intonation, i.e. the fluctuations in the pitch of the voice and the place in the intonation contour where the most significant change in direction of pitch occurs. This place is called the tonic. For example, the most usual way of pronouncing *How do you do? Pleased to meet you*, has two tone groups with the boundary coming before *pleased*. The first tone group has the tonic on the last syllable and the second has it on the last but one. Tonics are underlined in **2**:

2 // how do you / <u>do</u> // pleased to / <u>meet</u> you //

The symbol // represents the boundaries of a tone group. (The rhythm and intonation can be represented satisfactorily without showing the precise syllable and phoneme structure; hence the above example is given in conventional orthography.) Both of these groups have the falling tone, Tone 1, on their tonics. That is to say, the pitch of the voice falls from a high or mid level to a low level on this syllable. Tone 1 can be contrasted with Tone 2, rising tone, which is the typical intonation in **3**:

3 // is there any / sugar in it //

In this book reference is fairly often made to the rhythm and intonation of grammatical structures. For this reason Appendix A gives a rather brief account of one analysis of English rhythm and intonation. (See Halliday 1970a.) The subject is a large one, and the appendix is not a substitute for a proper study of this part of English phonology. It is included so that the book will be a little more self-contained than it would otherwise be, and so that the reader will understand the notation employed.

1.4 Discourse

The distinction between discourse and grammar can be introduced with a simple example. Imagine that somebody utters *Where have you put your shoes?* Considered grammatically this is an interrogative clause. Moreover it is a kind of interrogative that begins with what is known as a WH-item such as *where? who? when? at what time? which car? how long?* etc. This is different from the other kind of interrogative that is often called the 'yes/no' type, such as *Have you put your shoes away?* The grammatical structures and their meanings will be discussed in detail in Chapter 5.

In the description of discourse we must take account not only of the grammatical form of the utterance but also of the social setting in which it is made, including the relationship between speaker and addressee. If the speaker is someone who is known to be about to clean everyone's shoes, the utterance of our example clause is to be interpreted as a request for information to assist the accomplishment of the task in hand. On the other hand, if the speaker is a parent addressing a child who has left his shoes in the middle of the kitchen floor, the utterance cannot be taken as a request for information. It is something more like a command combined with a rebuke. Grammatically the utterances are the same in each of the two cases we have considered, but from the point of view of discourse structure they are very different. In order to interpret the speaker's meaning at this level the addressee has to apply his knowledge not only of the grammatical system but of the social setting. If we use the terms *question*, *statement* and *command* for types of move which speakers make towards addressees in well-defined social settings, these terms belong to discourse analysis, not to grammar, where the appropriate terms are *interrogative*, *declarative* and *imperative*. Thus the grammatically declarative *I didn't catch your name* might be a question or a statement according to whether the expected response is:

Harold Millstone (responding to a request for information);
or
Didn't you? (responding to the giving of information)

There is no one-to-one correspondence between the discourse and the grammatical types. There is, however, a most literal (or most direct or neutral) function for the grammatical types. For instance, *What's your name?* is a more literal or direct way of asking someone's name than *I didn't catch your name*, which is somewhat indirect; in this lies its greater politeness. The literal meanings of the utterances are crucial in distinguishing the grammatical types to which they belong. (See the discussion of mood meanings in sections 6.2–6.7.)

It is evident that the description of structure at the discourse level has its own complexities. This is an area of study that is much less well developed than grammar and phonology. One study of discourse structure that has been published is Sinclair and Coulthard 1975. Their book aims to develop a general theory of discourse but is based upon a description of the language used in the schoolroom. This type of discourse was chosen because in it the roles of the participants (teacher and pupil), their aims and the steps towards fulfilling the aims are relatively well defined. It seemed necessary, at this stage in discourse study, to take some fairly restricted kind of discourse, rather than, say, casual conversation, where the roles of the participants and their aims are much less clear cut and hence the discourse structure is likely to prove much more subtle and complex.

Just as there is a hierarchy of units in phonology – phoneme, syllable, foot, tone group etc. – so in classroom discourse Sinclair and Coulthard set up a hierarchy of discourse units – act, move, exchange, transaction. A unit consists of one or more of the units next below it in the hierarchy; so in phonology a

<table>
<tr><td colspan="10">transaction</td><td>. . .</td></tr>
<tr><td colspan="9">exchange</td><td>. . .</td><td>. . .</td></tr>
<tr><td colspan="3">move</td><td colspan="2">move</td><td colspan="3">move</td><td>. . .</td><td>. . .</td><td>. . .</td></tr>
<tr><td>act</td><td>act</td><td>. . .</td><td>act</td><td>. . .</td><td>act</td><td>act</td><td>. . .</td><td>. . .</td><td>. . .</td><td>. . .</td></tr>
</table>

Figure 1

syllable consists of one or more phonemes, a foot consists of one or more syllables, etc. In discourse, a move consists of one or more acts, an exchange of one or more moves, etc. This hierarchy is illustrated in Figure 1.

Here are some examples of discourse units taken from Sinclair and Coulthard 1975 (pp. 104–5):

(a) Example of an exchange. This exchange consists of three moves which are classified and named as follows:

opening move:	What material would you use for a cake?
answering move:	Flour
follow-up move:	Yes, you'd use flour.

These three moves constitute one exchange. There are various classes of exchange. This one belongs to the class called 'elicit' because the teacher's aim is to elicit a verbal response from the pupils.

(b) In the above example each move was simple in structure, consisting of just one act. Here is another example of an opening move:

opening move:

elicitation act:	If your mummy was going to make a frock, what material would she use?
cue act:	Hands up
bid act:	(this is not a verbal act but is realized by volunteers raising their hands)
nomination act:	Marie

The opening move is now complete and then comes an

answering move and a follow-up, all of which, as in (a), constitute an exchange. It is important to notice that in discourse the units are not always realized by verbal behaviour. One of the acts in this example is the raising of hands, an act which is nevertheless a part of the structure of the discourse.

(c) Here is an example of a complex follow-up move, consisting of two acts:

follow-up move:
evaluate act: Good boy, two team points, yes
comment act: We call these materials

In the type of act called *evaluate* the teacher is judging the quality of, say, a pupil's reply. The *comment*, at least in this example, has a summarizing function.

This follow-up move is the last move in an exchange, which is now complete. The teacher now begins another exchange, thus adding one exchange to another and building up a transaction.

Discourse structure is seen by Sinclair and Coulthard as interpretable by reference to two kinds of factor, in addition to the linguistic form of what is uttered. First there are situational factors such as who the participants are, what they know about each other and about the universe in which they are placed, and what their norms of behaviour are (such as not leaving one's shoes in the middle of the floor). Secondly there are tactical factors. These are the functional and conventional stages or sequences of moves that characterize linguistic interactions and which vary from one kind of discourse to another, e.g. classroom interactions, telephone conversations, doctor–patient consultations, broadcast interviews, etc.

Exercise 1.1

(a) Attach a grammatical label to sentences **1–5**, either declarative, interrogative, imperative or moodless. *Moodless*, for present purposes, can be taken to mean whatever is not any of the others. I am assuming the reader has some familiarity with the other terms. *Declarative* is perhaps the least well known; sometimes *affirmative* is used in the same (or a similar) sense. The reader with no previous experience of the terms should return to this exercise when he has reached the end of Chapter 7.

1 Can you touch your toes?
2 Send it back to the maker
3 Victoria Station
4 Who wants to go for a walk?
5 I shall send for the police

(b) Referring to the examples given above, in what circumstances might **1** be taken as an instruction to act and in what circumstances as a request for information?

(c) What is the difference between a piece of advice and a command? Apply the difference to example **2**.

(d) When could **3** be an instruction to act and when an announcement?

(e) Suggest several different kinds of communicative intention that might be realized by uttering **4**. Explain how one would know what the intention was in the different cases.

(f) What makes a threat a threat? Is **5**, in itself, a threat or a promise, or neither?

1.5 Hierarchies

We have used the notion of a hierarchy of units at both the phonological and discourse levels. There is a minimum unit – phoneme or act – out of which higher units, syllable or move, are built. From these higher units in their turn still higher units are constructed. The top of the hierarchy is left open and indeterminate. It is often held that it is useful to see tone groups as combining to form some higher phonological unit, e.g. the phonological paragraph. Similarly, in discourse, transactions may be seen as combining to constitute 'lessons', though this term is obviously rather specialized to one type of discourse.

The units in a hierarchy are better thought of as higher and lower rather than larger or smaller since, as we have seen, a unit may consist of just *one* of the units next below it. Thus in phonology, / hu / (*who*) is a tone group consisting of one foot which consists of one syllable which in turn consists of two phonemes.

1.6 Grammar

This book is about grammar. Grammar is the level of structure that comes between discourse and phonology. It is the level of verbal pattern, or wording. It too can be seen as having a hierarchy of units. So this gives us three hierarchies, which are shown in Figure 2.

discourse	*grammar*	*phonology*
⋮		
transaction	⋮	
exchange		⋮
move		
act	clause	tone group
	group	foot
	word	syllable
	morpheme	phoneme

Figure 2

There is no very easy and direct correspondence between the units of the different hierarchies. Neither an act nor a move is necessarily co-extensive with a clause; a morpheme is not necessarily realized by one syllable, etc. The closest correspondence seems to be between act, clause and tone group, but even this is very approximate. The grammatical units will be explained in the next chapter.

1.7 A terminological note

We have distinguished three levels of language structure: discourse, grammar and phonology. Each level is seen as having its own hierarchy of units; for instance, syllables come above phonemes and below feet in the phonological hierarchy. It would be misleading to use the term *level* over again in a different sense. So we shall not say that syllable is on a higher level than phoneme, but that it has a higher *rank*. In Figure 2, the levels are arranged across the page, and the ranks are arranged in vertical columns.

Exercise 1.2
What types of information does a hearer (or reader) need in order to understand discourse?

Exercise 1.3
Suggest a plausible structure of tone groups and feet for the following. (The phonemes and syllables are given.)

> When the weather was fine we went for walks in the fields.
> / wen ðə weð ə wəz faɪn wɪ went fə wɔk sɪn ðə fildz /

2 Grammar and grammatical rules

2.1 Grammatical units

Towards the end of the last chapter there was a list of units in the grammatical hierarchy: clause, group, word and morpheme. Here are some examples analysed in terms of grammatical units of the various ranks. The vertical lines | represent the boundaries of grammatical units. (Slanting lines are used for phonological units.)

1 I can’t find the keys — *clause*
I | can’t find | the keys — *three groups*
I | can’t | find | the | keys — *five words*
I | can | n’t | find | the | key | s — *seven morphemes*

2 The caretaker mended the fuse last night — *clause*
The caretaker | mended | the fuse | last night — *four groups*
The | caretaker | mended | the | fuse | last | night — *seven words*
The | care | take | er | mend | ed | the | fuse | last | night — *ten morphemes*

3 Shoot — *clause*
Shoot — *one group*
Shoot — *one word*
Shoot — *one morpheme*

It will be remembered that, according to the theory of ranks, a unit of one rank consists of one or more of the units of the next lowest rank until one comes to the bottom of the scale.

2.2 Sentences

The term ‘sentence’ may be thought conspicuous by its absence from our grammatical hierarchy. Very often the sentence is presented as a unit of higher rank than the clause, so that a sentence consists of one or more clauses. In that case the three examples given above would be sentences consisting of one clause, and the following would be sentences consisting of two clauses:

4a If the caretaker mends the fuse | we'll be able to get on
4b I can't find the keys | but they've left a window open

There are certain problems, however, about regarding sequences of clauses as sentences. Among them is the fact that the term 'sentence' in popular usage is usually applied only to written text and is associated largely with punctuation. The theory of the grammatical relations between clauses, however, should be applicable to both written and spoken text. Further discussion of the problems is postponed until Chapter 18, under the heading of 'clause complexes'.

2.3 Groups

The reader will see that the rank 'group' is definable as that which comes below 'clause' and above 'word'. The traditional technical term that comes closest to this in sense is 'phrase', but this term is deliberately avoided here since traditional theory identifies as phrases many things that we shall not regard as groups.

There are various kinds of group, each having its own characteristic sort of structure. The most important are verbal groups, nominal groups, adjectival groups, adverbial groups and prepositional groups. It will be sufficient to illustrate these with the first two types; the others will be illustrated in Chapter 3 (pages 32–4).

1 Verbal groups are made up of one or more verbs: *sings*, *was*, *might move*, *is talking*, *have disappeared*, *having lasted*, *had been hoping*, etc. The structure of verbal groups is described in detail in Chapters 14 and 15.

2 Nominal groups of the principal type have a noun as headword and may also have other elements placed before or after the headword in a dependent relation to it. In **5a–f** the headword is in italics:

5a *Butter*
5b *Houses*

5c A *tree*
5d Two large *apples*
5e Those *clouds* in the sky
5f A *house* that expensive

2.4 Words and morphemes

The notion '(grammatical) unit' implies segmentability. In other words, it is normally the case that a clause can be segmented into a sequence of groups:

6 they | 've left | a window | open
/ ðeɪ | v left | ə̣ wɪndəʊ | əʊpən /

We can, with more or less precision, associate grammatical boundaries with places in the sequence of orthographical letters and spaces, or with places in the stretch of phonological structure. To put it another way, each grammatical unit is in principle realizable by a separate chunk of phonological (or graphological) material. In **7** the symbol + stands for the boundary of such a chunk, and not for a syllable boundary. (Syllables are purely phonological units, and are established without reference to grammatical structure; for instance, *tease* is one syllable and one morpheme, while *teas* is one syllable, but two morphemes: *tea* + *s*.)

7			
	reader:	read + er	/ rid + ə /
	stolen:	stol + en	/ stəʊl + ən /
	musical:	music + al	/ mjuzɪk + l /
	sending:	send + ing	/ send + ɪŋ /
	outspokenness:	out + spoke + en + ness	/ aʊt + spəʊk + ən + nəs /
	translation:	trans + late + ion	/ trænz + leɪʃ + ən /

The examples in **7** are all of words segmented into two or more morphemes. The segmentability is not seriously affected by the fact that here and there there is some mistiness or overlap at the borders of the graphological or phonological chunks. It should be stressed that we are not saying that the grammatical unit actually is a stretch of spelling or sound, but that it is represented (or realized) by a stretch of spelling or sound. There is thus no difficulty in seeing **8** as a string of five morphemes, even though there is some mistiness in the representation of the morphemes *do* and *you*.

> **8** How do you eat it?
> / haʊ dʒʊ it ɪt /

Morpheme theory, however, is complicated by facts such as the following. Although the plural of *book* (one morpheme) is *book+s* (two morphemes), the plural of *man* (one morpheme) is *men*. Now, shall we count *men* as two morphemes? The arguments in favour of this are:

1 It differs from the singular in its realization;
2 grammatically there is a proportion:
as *books* is to *book*
so *men* is to *man*

Most grammarians describe the word *men* as two morphemes which are fused in their realization. This is an irregular case; regular plurals are straightforwardly segmentable. The principle of segmentation is not abandoned but allowed to be overridden in special cases. But this does mean that there are certain embarrassing cases where the grammarian is faced with equally strong arguments for treating a word as one morpheme or more than one. Some forms of the verb *be* are among these as shown in Figure 3. A case can be made for treating *is* as *be* + *s* fused, on the analogy of *eats* as *eat* + *s*; but what of the words *am* and *are*? In no other verb is a similar distinction made, so that recourse to a regular pattern of segmentable units elsewhere in the language is weak. There are thus borderline cases where different grammars come up with different descriptive solutions.

This book is not much concerned with the structure of English words, but concentrates more on the higher ranks, clause and group. The theoretical and descriptive problems of English word structure are largely left on one side, not because they are unimportant or uninteresting but because it is necessary to limit the scope of the book.

be	*other verbs*
I am	I/you eat
you are	
he is	he eats

Figure 3

2.5 Items

One technical term that is frequently used in this book is *grammatical item*, or simply *item*. A grammatical item is any individual morpheme, or word, or group, or clause. Some examples of items are given in **9**:

9a De- (as in *decipher*)
9b Go
9c Philharmonic
9d The next three days
9e When he comes, send him in
9f Harold isn't there

Every item in the language belongs to some rank of unit.

2.6 Grammatical classes

Two English clauses are shown in **10** and **11**:

10 The car has broken down
11 Has the car broken down?

The first of these items is a declarative clause and the second is an interrogative clause. In other words, though both are clauses, they belong to different classes of clause. The different classes are established by reference to their different significance in discourse structure, though, as was pointed out above (page 5) there is no simple correspondence to discourse classes.

In describing the grammar of a language we set up a system of classes, so that each item can be described first in terms of the class to which it belongs, and second in terms of what signs it contains by which it shows that it belongs to that class rather than another. For example, what is the formal difference that enables us to recognize **10** as declarative and **11** as interrogative? Classification in our grammatical theory is organized by rank; that is, there is one system of classification for clauses, another for groups, another for words and another for morphemes. Classification can be thought of in another more psychological way; namely, that the speaker (or writer) is faced with choices. The language provides him with a system of classes that he must choose from when he speaks. He can only choose from what the language provides, but there is always a choice, otherwise what he has to say would be predictable and hence meaningless.

At various places in this book we use a method of diagramming classifications which is not confined to language. The following illustration is drawn not from grammatical classification but from something that is more familiar. Let us assume that for administrative purposes it is necessary to classify the people likely to be found in a university library. The following is a list of dimensions of classification that would be likely to be relevant:

1 library staff v. reader
2 male v. female
3 lecturer v. student

It will be noticed that these are exclusive systems of classification; a person is either library staff or reader, but not both. Further, while systems 1 and 2 apply to all the people inhabiting the library, the third system is not relevant to any but readers. So while systems 1 and 2 are a cross-classification (*x* may be both a reader and female), 3 is a subclassification of readers. These notions can be set out in the form shown in Figure 4, where the square brackets mean 'either . . . or' and the curly bracket means 'both . . . and'; thus anyone who is a library inhabitant is both (a) either staff or reader, and (b) either male or female. Figure 4 shows six classes: staff, male; staff female; reader lecturer, male; reader, lecturer, female; reader, student, male; and reader, student, female.

Let us assume that Harold Millstone belongs to the class reader, lecturer, male. Then he also belongs to the class 'reader', and to the class 'lecturer' and to the class 'male'. Another way of expressing it would be to say that we have assigned to him the features: 'reader', 'lecturer' and 'male'. Do not forget that all the people we are talking about belong to the class (or have the feature) 'library inhabitant'. This is the feature that distinguishes them from other people who do not come within the scope of Figure 4.

Each of the dimensions of classification, indicated by a square

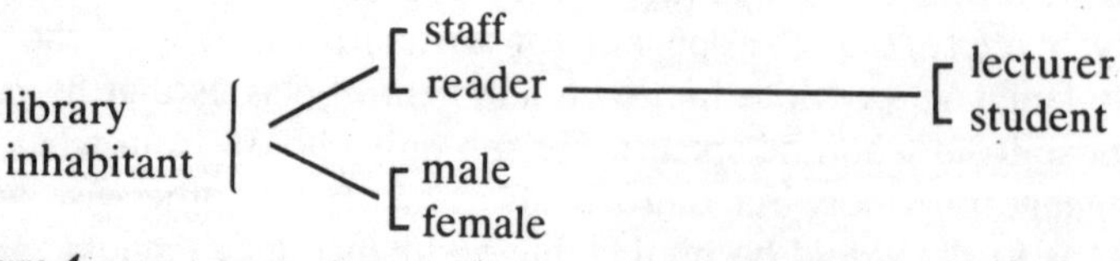

Figure 4

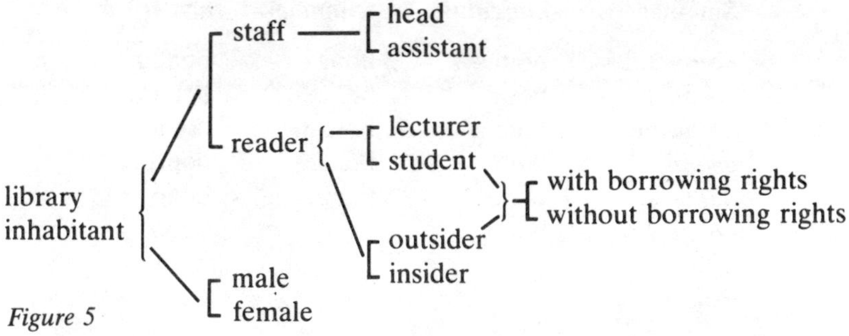

Figure 5

bracket, is called a *system*, and the whole diagram is a *system network*. The logic of classes allows for networks involving both cross-classifications and subclassifications combined in complex patterns. Some of the complexity can be illustrated by adding more systems to our network:

4 assistant (librarian) v. head (librarian)
5 (reader) with borrowing rights v. (reader) without borrowing rights
6 (reader) belonging to the university v. (reader) from another institution (insider v. outsider)

Let us assume further, that system 5 is applicable only to student outsiders; that is to say, that all others automatically have borrowing rights, and that only among student outsiders are there some to whom borrowing rights are denied. This situation is illustrated in Figure 5.

In this illustration of system networks all of the systems have a choice of two terms. This is not a logically necessary restriction; systems may have any number of terms that is greater than one.

Exercise 2.1
Incorporate into the network for library inhabitants the information that some student outsiders have to pay a returnable deposit, while others do not. Assume this has nothing to do with whether or not they have borrowing rights.

2.7 Paradigms

The reader will probably be familiar with the notion of the word paradigm from the study of such a language as Latin. Figure 6

Singular	*masculine*	*feminine*	*neuter*
nominative	bonus	bona	bonum
vocative	bone	bona	bonum
accusative	bonum	bonam	bonum
genitive	boni	bonae	boni
dative	bono	bonae	bono
ablative	bono	bona	bono

Plural			
nominative	boni	bonae	bona
vocative	boni	bonae	bona
accusative	bonos	bonas	bona
genitive	bonorum	bonarum	bonorum
dative	bonis	bonis	bonis
ablative	bonis	bonis	bonis

Figure 6

shows a typical textbook paradigm for one type of Latin adjective. This paradigm provides the reader with an example of the way this type of adjective varies in form according to its place in the construction in which it appears. The adjective *bonus* is chosen as the paradigm word and other adjectives of the same type vary in the same way. Thus the accusative feminine plural of *fidus* (faithful) is *fidas*. Some of the information contained in the paradigm can be expressed in the system network shown in Figure 7.

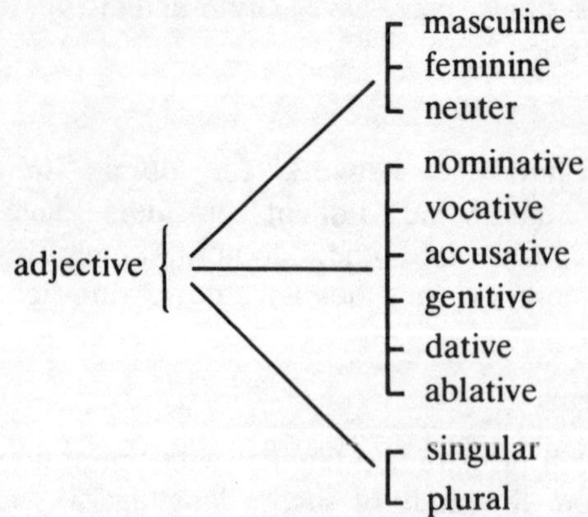

Figure 7

Exercise 2.2
According to the system network for Latin adjectives given in Figure 7, how many features does each word have?

The paradigm gives more information than the system network, but its method is for some purposes unsatisfactory. It gives more information, since it tells the reader not only that there are three genders, six cases and two numbers, but for each combination of features it tells him what difference it makes to the form of the word. In other words, it states both the meaningful choices that the speaker is faced with, and also the signs that one choice has been made rather than another; it says not only that there is an accusative, feminine, plural form, but that this form is modelled on the form of *bonas*.

But this is rather rough and ready; the reader really has to work out for himself from the various forms of the sample word what the rules are. He has to make his own division of the words into the parts *bon* plus an ending, he has to observe for himself that the endings including the vowel *-a* are associated chiefly with the feminine gender and so on. These rules are not explicitly stated. The paradigm is in many ways a useful language-learning device. But the student of Latin as a foreign language does not get very far if he merely learns the paradigms by heart. He must, among many other things, in some way deduce from the paradigms what the rules are and apply them to every new case. How he can be made to do this is a pedagogical problem; he perhaps does not need to be made conscious of the rules in order to be induced to behave in conformity with them. The student of language structure, on the other hand (including, presumably, the teacher of foreign languages), is very much concerned with the rules which the textbook paradigm merely hints at.

So the information in the system network has to be supplemented by a set of statements about 'what difference it makes' – about how the speaker signals to his addressees what options he has plumped for. That is, the system network has to be supplemented by a set of realization rules. The paradigm is a very informal way of doing this, and informality is sometimes a fault. But it is unsatisfactory in another way. The principles underlying the paradigm and the system network (supplemented by the realization rules mentioned above) can be applied to

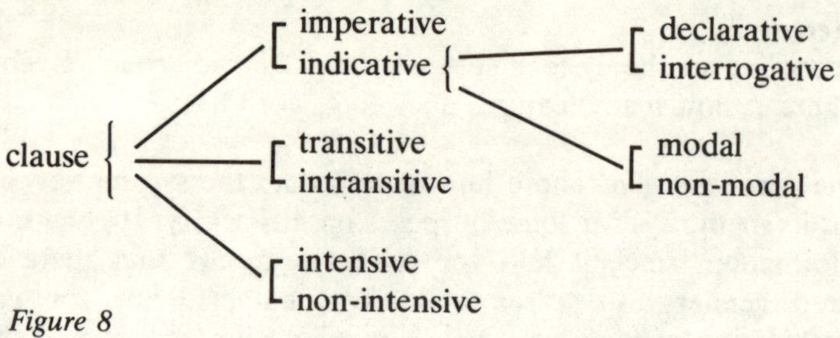

Figure 8

units of any rank, not just to words. The trouble with the paradigm is that with units of higher rank (and in some languages even with units of word rank) the number of different combinations of classificatory features is so great, and the examples take up so much more space on the page, that it would not be useful, or even possible, to display the facts in paradigm form. Figure 8 shows the system network for a very incomplete classification of English clauses. This network provides for twenty distinct types of clause. The list given in **12–31** includes one example of each type:

12 Run
13 Be careful
14 He ran
15 Did he run?
16 He is careful
17 Is he careful?
18 He would run
19 Would he run?
20 Mend the tyre
21 Make the box big
22 He must be careful
23 Must he be careful?
24 He is mending the tyre
25 Is he mending the tyre?
26 He would mend the tyre
27 Would he mend the tyre?
28 He is making the box big
29 Is he making the box big?
30 He would make the box big
31 Would he make the box big?

For instance, **24** has the features clause, indicative, declarative, non-modal, transitive, non-intensive. The feature indicative is realized by the presence of both a subject (*he*) and the verbal element (*is mending*). Declarative, as opposed to interrogative, is realized by the arrangement *he is mending* rather than *is he mending*. Non-modal is realized by the absence of any modal verb such as *may*, *might*, *will*, *would*, *must*, etc. Transitive is realized by the presence of an object (*the tyre*). Non-intensive is realized by the absence of any intensive complement such as *big* in **28** or *careful* in **16**.

As a further example, **23** has the features clause, indicative, interrogative (cf. the declarative **2**), modal (it contains the modal verb *must*), intransitive (there is no object), intensive (there is an intensive complement, *careful*). In this set of examples the intensive complements are adjectives.)

Exercise 2.3

Assign a set of features to each of the other eighteen clauses. (Again I am assuming familiarity with such basic concepts as *imperative* and *object*. The reader who is unable to understand these terms should return to this exercise after working through the first seven chapters of the book.)

2.8 Rules

The reader will by this time have noticed that in this book the attitude taken towards language and the study of language is different from that which is often taken in the schoolroom. The rules of grammar that we speak of here are not rules telling the speaker of a language what he ought to do, but descriptions of what the speakers of a language actually do.

At school it is often among the aims of the teacher to train the pupil either to use language for special purposes such as writing compositions or to speak a different dialect from the one he ordinarily uses, or both. In these circumstances the teacher acts prescriptively, telling the pupils what they ought to do that is different from what they have hitherto been inclined to do. Such aims may be praiseworthy, but the present book has no concern with them. It is worth pointing out, however, that one justification for these procedures that is often given to pupils – directly or by implication – is quite false. It is often said that one variety of the language (the literary standard) is correct English and is linguistically superior to other varieties, which are 'incorrect', or 'impure', or 'illogical' or 'unintelligible'. The various types of English and the necessity and desirability of varying the language according to the circumstances and the aims of language use are, in this situation, ignored. It should be stressed, first, that there is no standard of correctness that can be applied to a language other than what is inherent in the usage of those who use it; second, that there are many varieties of a language, which differ according to dialect and the purposes of communication, and that each variety has its own inherent usages that distinguish it from other varieties; third, that it is often desirable to teach people a command of some variety that they do not already have in their repertoire, but that it is not the case that this other variety is desirable because it is linguistically better, but only because social convention requires that this other variety be used for the purposes in question. What makes a standard variety widely accepted is not that it is better language, but that it is the language of some group with whom people want to identify themselves.

These facts have no bearing on the question whether it is desirable for people to change their language, but only on the two procedures of description and prescription. Both procedures are sometimes necessary, but the most efficient kind of prescription has a firm basis in accurate description. For example, teaching a foreigner to speak English entails prescribing to him the usages of that variety of English which has been selected as the kind he is to learn; this variety must first be described so that it can then be prescribed. For a further example, teaching a native speaker a command of literary standard requires a description of what that literary standard is like; it would be futile to prescribe to him usages which are not in fact included in that standard but which the teacher believes ought to be a part of it because they are what he calls correct. In order to find out what usages are included in some variety of language there is no method but observation and description of what has been observed.

Obviously this book is not going to attempt to describe English in all its varieties. The variety described is southern British standard and ranges from colloquial to literary. This is a rather vague statement. The variety itself is only partially different from other varieties. Moreover, it contains within it many subvarieties, so that usage is not entirely fixed and invariable. Most students are surprised to find other speakers of broadly their own kind of English speaking differently from themselves. Even more often a speaker is tempted, when questioned, to reject as unacceptable some form which he himself uses. The student is warned not to rely exclusively upon his own private judgements of acceptability, but to be objective and to be aware that the language is not one monolithic system, but an agglomeration of varieties.

3 Clauses: meanings and structures

3.1 Clauses: meanings

We will start by trying to characterize clauses from the point of view of their meanings. Typically a clause embodies a proposition; that is, an expression in language of some part of our experience of the world. Propositions are things that are capable of being asserted, or negated, or speculated about, or suggested as being desirable though not actual. There are many types of proposition. Miscellaneous examples are given in **1–4**.

1 The manager closed the shutters at 5 o'clock

This is a proposition of material action; it contains an actor (*the manager*) and a thing acted upon (*the shutters*) as well as circumstantial detail of time.

2 He didn't like the tone of the place

This is a proposition of mental activity involving a person (*he*) and a phenomenon (*the tone of the place*); it concerns the reaction of the person to the phenomenon.

3 Mary is a clever girl

This is a proposition of logical relation; it states a relation between an individual (*Mary*) and the class of individuals called clever girls; namely, that she is one of them.

4 He told a lie

This is a proposition of verbal action involving a speaker (*he*) and a verbalization (*a lie*).

The propositions given above are spoken of in such terms as material action, mental activity, logical relation and verbal action. These are different types of process. What process a proposition refers to depends to a large extent on what verb is chosen: eating is one process, while thinking is another.

However, it is not simply a question of what verb occurs, since many verbs have a range of different meanings. Thus telling the time is a different kind of process from telling a lie; it is a process of cognition in which a person knows or is able to distinguish a certain fact, and not a process of verbalization.

A proposition is capable of being asserted; we do not say that to count as a proposition it must actually be asserting something. Thus **4** does assert that he told a lie (or rather, it would do so if it were uttered by somebody on some real-life occasion), but the examples in **5**, which all embody the same proposition as **4**, do not assert it:

5a Did he tell a lie?
5b . . . after he told a lie . . .
5c . . . his telling a lie . . .
5d . . . for him to tell a lie . . .
5e Perhaps he told a lie
5f He might tell a lie
5g . . . if he told a lie . . .

The proposition could be given a kind of abstract representation with no indication of whether it is being asserted or not:

6 'he tell a lie'

In **5a** the speaker wants to know whether the proposition is true; in **5b** he presupposes it to be true without actually asserting it; in **5c** and **5d** the event is named without any commitment as to its actuality; **5e** and **5f** only admit the possibility of the event and do not assert it; **5g** supposes the truth of the proposition as a hypothesis.

What the abstract representation of the proposition, given in **6**, lacks as real English is any signal of what attitude the speaker is taking towards it; that is, whether his attitude is assertive, enquiring, presupposing, speculative, non-committal, etc. This attitudinal kind of meaning is of great importance. Since language is used for communication between people, it must not only be able to encode propositions, but must also be able to indicate what attitude the speaker is taking towards these propositions with respect to the question whether they are true. Otherwise the people addressed would not know whether they were being told or not, and if not, just how they were being expected to react. The aspect of clause grammar which reflects this kind of meaning is called mood.

Exercise 3.1
Here is a 'skeletal' proposition: *left-handedness be abnormal*. Make a list of genuine English wordings that embody this proposition and that register a variety of attitudes on the part of the speaker towards the truth of the proposition.

3.2 Clauses: structure

Clauses consist of various combinations of *elements*, or *elements of structure*. Thus **7** consists of three elements, a subject (S), a predicator (P) and a complement (C). The following example **8** also contains instances of the element called adjunct (A):

7	He	saw	the accident			
	S	P	C			
8	Bill	sold	the house	to John	last year	though
	S	P	C	C	A	A

Each element is a constituent of the clause and thus has relations with the other elements; they co-operate with each other, performing different functions in the work of the whole. The concept 'element of structure' can be compared with the concept 'member of a committee'. The committee members are, let us say, chairman, treasurer, secretary and ordinary member. Each performs a function in the work of the committee as a whole and so contracts different kinds of relations with the other members. It does not directly matter what the members are – men or women, fair or dark haired, teachers, shopkeepers or bank managers, and so on; it might be an advantage to have an accountant as treasurer, but John Smith, who happens to be an accountant, may turn out to be the chairman. Similarly in grammar, when speaking of *he* as S in **7** we are less concerned with the fact that *he* is a personal pronoun than with the relations it has with the other elements in the clause.

Recognizing elements of structure is a question of seeing what functions they have in the whole construction. The functions of an element can be investigated by pursuing two lines of enquiry, its meaning and its formal properties. The beginner in grammatical analysis usually has a tendency to underestimate the importance of formal properties, but it is important to keep as many formal checks on our semantic classifications as possible. Consider **9** and **10**:

9 He | saw | the accident
S P C
10 He | was | a witness
S P C

We will focus upon the last element in these constructions. In both cases we are dealing with a complement, in the sense that the element is an essential completion of the construction begun by the subject and predicator; but it is a different type of complement in the two cases. *The accident* is an object complement and *a witness* is an intensive complement. In the first example *the accident* names something distinct from the subject, *he*; the process of seeing involves two participants, each with a different role, one who sees and a thing seen. It is certainly possible for one person to be both seer and seen; but in that case the second mention has to be explicitly reflexive: *he saw himself* (where *himself* is a reflexive form). This does not alter the fact that seeing is essentially a two-role process in which the process carries over from one entity to the other. Such clauses as **9** are usually called transitive. In the second example *a witness* is not a distinct entity from the subject *he*; rather, it is a characterization of 'he', describing 'his' function in the situation being talked about. This is not a transitive clause. We conclude that *the accident* in **9** and *a witness* in **10** perform different functions in their constructions and are different types of element.

The argument has to this point been based on an analysis of meaning; but we need not rely only on meaning. We note that a clause like **9** has a regular formal correspondence with another clause of the following pattern:

11 The accident | was seen | by him

The formal correspondence between **9** and **11** is easily describable (see sections 13.1 and 13.2) and is not merely accidental, since we can find countless other pairs, such as:

12a The author | signed | the letter
12b The letter | was signed | by the author

It is customary to say that **9** and **12a** are in the active voice and that **11** and **12b** are in the passive voice. (The last element in the passive examples can be left out and quite often it reads more naturally like that. This is a point of detail that will be taken up later, but it does not affect the validity of the active-passive correspondence as a test for types of complement.)

Exercise 3.2

(a) What are the passive correspondences to the following active clauses?

1 The dog chased the cat.
2 Somebody is going to buy that house.
3 Harold addressed the crowd.
4 The fox can smell the chickens.

(b) What are the active correspondences to the following passive clauses?

1 Some of the grass was eaten by the goats.
2 The job must have been finished by another firm.
3 These articles were probably written by their regular correspondents.
4 The marks in the corner weren't noticed by the inspector.

We now observe that *he was a witness* is not in correspondence with any such passive-voice equivalent: **A witness was been by him*. (NB An asterisk is used to distinguish an example that is in some way ill-formed; it does not conform to the regular patterning of the language.) In short, there is not only a semantic difference between the two constructions under investigation, but there is a formal difference as well. In grammatical analysis we appeal wherever possible to both formal and semantic criteria. That this is important is a result of the fact that the object of the exercise is to show how a language manages to encode meaning in verbal constructions. This is not to say that differences of opinion might not arise on how much weight to give to the semantic and the formal criteria relative to each other.

Exercise 3.3

Decide which of the italicized elements are object complements and which are intensive complements:

1 Science | can calculate | *the price*.
2 Acton | quoted | *Mill*.
3 Disputes about property | became | *a cause of conflict*.
4 I | feel | *hungry*.
5 I | can feel | *the dampness of the floor*.
6 He | enclosed | *a cheque for £20*.
7 That dilapidated shack | may be | *the sports pavilion*.
8 The farmers | grow | *quite a lot of barley*.
9 The farmers | are growing | *prosperous*.
10 No contestant | can win | *more than two events*.

It has already been said that the function an item has as constituent of a clause – what sort of element it is – is a somewhat separate consideration from its own internal construction. For instance, in **13** the item *the man* has two different functions:

13a The man chased the dog
13b The dog chased the man

In **13a** *the man* is subject, while in **13b** it is object. This is a fact that is independent of the other fact that *the man* is a nominal group. The inherent nature of the item itself is a separate matter from what it is doing in the whole construction in which it is playing a part. Nevertheless, just as there is an affinity between being an accountant and the office of treasurer, so there is an affinity between nominal groups and the functions of subject and object. Similarly, verbal groups, such as *chased*, *can calculate* and *are growing*, function as predicators and do not occur as subjects or objects. So the internal economy of an item, though a secondary consideration, is not irrelevant to the task of identifying elements of structure.

We can now summarize the criteria that are used in establishing the elements of structure:

1 *semantics*: what contribution does the item make to the meaning of the whole construction?
2 *syntax*: what formal relations hold between the item and the other constituents of the construction?
3 *componence*: the internal economy of the item, i.e. what is its identity, or how is it, in its turn, constructed?

One of the objects of this book is to enlarge upon and illustrate these three types of analytical criterion. It is a feature of recent developments in grammatical tradition that the criteria for establishing the elements of grammatical structures have been sharpened up and made more explicit. This is true of all modern schools of linguistics; the methods of exploring the properties of linguistic constructions are not peculiar to particular models of language structure.

3.3 Elements of clause structure

The elements *subject* and *predicator* are largely definable by the part they play in signalling the mood of the clause. They will be given detailed attention in Chapters 5, 6 and 7. For the present it is sufficient to say that they are the elements whose relative position helps to distinguish whether a clause is declarative or interrogative, as example **14** makes clear:

14a The tractor | is coming | down this side
S P

14b Is(the tractor) coming | down this side?
P (S)

In **14b** the predicator *is . . . coming* is split, and the subject is enclosed within it. The brackets are a way of showing this; the formula P(S) means that the predicator begins before the subject and continues after it.

In this chapter we shall concentrate on the elements, if any, that make up the remainder of a clause after the S and P have been identified. The whole of the rest of the clause (if there is a remainder) will consist of complements (C) and adjuncts (A) or both. There may be more than one C and more than one A, which means that there are subtypes of each. The basis of the distinction between C and A is that a C is an element which is essential to the structure of the proposition, while an A is not, but can be detached without detriment to it. Needless to say, this description is not very precise. It turns out that the notion 'essential' is not simple, but can be broken down into several partially independent notions. Chapter 9 will give a detailed treatment of the various criteria that might be used to decide how essential an element is. For the time being we will use only examples where the decision is relatively easy to make in terms of the rather crudely expressed distinction between essential and inessential.

Exercise 3.4

Decide whether the unidentified elements in the following are C or A.

1 They | still | have to pay | their surcharge of £7000.
S P

2 They | deliberately | broke | the law.
S P

3 This | is not | a bad law.
S P

4 They | might issue | similar incitements | on this precedent.
S P

5 They | flouted | it | for party political reasons.
S P

6 It | isn't | normal.
S P

7 Obviously | a special leaflet | had to be produced | in a hurry.
S P

8 The sky | suddenly | grew | overcast.
S P

9 The clover | we | shall cut | next month.
S P

3.4 Adjuncts

Some adjuncts provide circumstantial details of the proposition. In many types of proposition, specifications of manner, time, place and reason are not essential to the sort of process being talked about; thus elements that provide answers to the questions *How?*, *When?*, *Where?* and *Why?* are usually adjuncts:

15a He cut the pieces *carelessly* (How? In what manner?)
15b Consternation was felt *in the villas and bungalows* (Where?)
15c They had a picnic *in the afternoon* (When?)
15d They came home early *because of the insects* (Why?)

Other adjuncts lie outside the proposition altogether. They do not answer any question because they do not add to the propositional content of the clause. Such adjuncts, illustrated in

16, inform the addressee how he is expected to connect the proposition with the context in which it is uttered:

16a *Obviously*, it won't do
16b It isn't any trouble, *however*
16c *Similarly*, the eagle preys on small mammals

In **16a** *obviously* gives the speaker's comment on the proposition, namely that its truth is obvious. In **16b** and **16c** the adjuncts show how the clause connects with what has already been said.

As for the syntactic properties of adjuncts, their main characteristic is that they are optional; leaving them out does not change the nature of the construction. In other respects adjuncts are rather diverse. There are many types of adjunct, as we would expect from the fact they are recognized by somewhat negative criteria; they are whatever elements are left over when S, P and C have been disposed of, i.e. whatever is not closely involved in the structure of the proposition. As a result of this diversity it is not possible to generalize very strongly about their position relative to other clause elements. The question of adjunct positions is discussed at length in sections 9.7–9.9. For the time being we may note that some kinds of adjunct are very much freer in the position they can take up in the clause than are complements.

17a It won't do, *obviously*
17b It *obviously* won't do
17c *Obviously* it won't do
17d I didn't notice those trees *this morning*
17e *This morning* I didn't notice those trees

In **17** the adjuncts are moved about from one position to another, not entirely without significance, but producing an effect that is far less striking than if we moved a complement:

18a I didn't notice *those trees*
18b *Those trees* I didn't notice

In **18b** an object complement has been put in initial position, which is quite clearly not a normal position for it.

One further point about the position of adjuncts is that where both a complement and an adjunct occur after the predicator, the usual sequence is for the complement to come first. This appears in **19** where the sequence A C is extraordinary in the prominence it gives to the complement:

19a I | didn't notice | those trees | this morning
S P C A
19b I | didn't notice | this morning | those trees
S P A C
19c I | didn't notice | this morning | all those dead trees
S P A C
19d She | is | quite well off | at the moment
S P C A
19e She | is | at the moment | quite well off
S P A C

There is thus a 'neutral' sequence of C and A, and departures from this sequence are in one way or another 'special effects'.

The classes of item that can function as adjuncts are various, but the most frequent are adverbial groups and prepositional groups. Adverbial groups have an adverb as headword. In **20** the headword is italicized:

20 *quickly* | so horribly *suddenly*
very *quickly* | *cunningly*
more *impatiently* than ever | as *cunningly* as that

Prepositional groups consist of two elements as shown in **21**. In each case, the first element is a preposition and the second is a prepositional object:

21 in | the morning | by | force
at | the end of the road | into | the street
with | some speed | through | your ingratitude

The prepositional function is realized by one of the class of items known as prepositions, and the function of prepositional object is realized by a nominal group.

Other classes which function as adjunct are:

1 Some classes of items which are not expandable:
(a) *however*, *perhaps*, *nevertheless*, *though*, etc.
(b) some items referring to time or frequency:
still, *sometimes*, *yet*, *already*
(There are no expansions such as **very however*; **more already than that*.)
2 Some-time expressions based upon the items *yesterday*,

today, *tomorrow*, *next week*, *last night* (expandable as *late yesterday*, *early today*, etc.) and other time and frequency expressions constructed according to various patterns: *the year after next*, *a week ago tomorrow*, *every month*, etc. Many of these are nominal groups of specially restricted types.

3 Miscellaneous formulaic expressions such as *a great deal* and *a lot*, (e.g. *He talks a lot*).

3.5 Complements

Complements are elements that are necessary for completion of the proposition after it has been begun by the subject and predicator. This is not to say that complements can never be left out, but that, if they are, the clause is rendered highly dependent for its interpretation on the context in which it occurs. Thus the complements in **22** might be left out if we contrived suitable contexts:

22a Harold | conducted | the orchestra
S P C

22b Harold | was | the conductor
S P C

23a (There was an orchestral concert and)
Harold conducted

23b (Who was the conductor?)
Harold was

Optionality of elements in such circumstances as these obviously does not count against their being considered complements.

Whereas adjuncts supply circumstantial detail and can usually be questioned with *where*, *when*, *how* or *why*, complements supply information on the people and things involved in the process and can be questioned with *who* or *what* as shown in **24**:

24a He | may fabricate | difficulties (What?)
S P C

24b She | seems | rather young (What?)
S P C

24c He | has brought | his secretary (Who?)
S P C

24d The instructor | could be | that girl with long hair (Who?)
S P C

We saw that adjuncts are realized by various classes of item. These did not include adjectival groups or nominal groups (except for certain restricted types with a time meaning such as *next week*, *the following day*, etc.). The following could therefore not function as adjuncts, but they occur readily in complement function. In the adjectival groups in **25** the headword, which is an adjective, is in italics. In the nominal groups in **26** the italicized headword is a noun:

25a *young*
25b rather *young*
25c a little *thinner* than me
25d *essential*
25e quite *normal*
25f *overcast*
25g more *necessary* than you would think
26a his *secretary*
26b that *girl* with long hair
26c *difficulties*
26d the *clover*
26e a certain *stigma*
26f a *cause* of conflict
26g the *girl* he was talking to just now

3.6 Object complements and intensive complements

The distinction between object complements and intensive complements has already been made (see pages 26–7). All we need do here is summarize and add a few supplementary points.

Semantically, objects (which might also aptly be called transitive complements) denote something different from the subject of the clause; the process which the proposition is about carries over from one thing or person to another. From now on the symbol C^O is used for object complements, as in **27**:

27a He | may fabricate | difficulties
S P C^O

27b They | don't believe | her statements
S P C^O

It is possible for there to be more than two participants in a transitive process, i.e. more than just a subject and a single object. The sentences in **28** have two objects:

28a We | are giving | the manager | more help
S P C^o C^o

28b The gardener | has dug | us | a good deep trench
S P C^o C^o

(These two objects are not absolutely alike; the difference between them will be taken up later, in section 10.3.)

Syntactically, a C^o has a systematic correspondence with the subject of a passive equivalent:

29a Difficulties | may be fabricated | (by him)
S P ?

29b The manager | is being given | more help
S P C^o

29c More help | is being given | to the manager
S P ?

(The function of the elements that are queried in these examples will be dealt with in Chapter 10.)

The class of item at C^o is normally a nominal group; and although the word 'normally' hints at certain complications to be dealt with later, at least we can say that a C^o cannot be an adjectival group.

Intensive complements, symbolized by C^i, have the property of providing some sort of characterization or description of either the subject, as in **30** or of an object as in **31**:

30a She | seems | rather young
S P C^i

30b The instructor | could be | that girl with long hair
S P C^i

30c Harold | is | an MP
S P C^i

31a They | made | the box | big
S P C^o C^i

31b He | found | the tractor | a great help
S P C^o C^i

The relation between the C^o and the C^i in **31** is comparable with that between the S and the C^i in *The box is big* and *The tractor is a great help*.

Unlike object complements, intensive complements have no correspondence with the subject of a passive equivalent, (e.g. **Rather young is seemed by her*; or **A great help was found the tractor by him*). Intensive complements can be either nominal or adjectival groups. For instance in **32**, the nominal group and the adjectival group are interchangeable without making much difference to the type of construction:

32a The tractor | is | a great help
S P C^i

32b The tractor | is | very useful
S P C^i

But the choice is not free in all cases; in **33** only nominal groups can occur at C^i:

33a The committee | elected | Harold | chairman
S P C^o C^i

33b That grey building | is | the Town Hall
S P C^i
(meaning That grey building and the Town Hall are the same thing)

Exercise 3.5

The patterns that occur in continuous real-life text are usually more elaborate than those we have studied so far. Not only are there far more patterns than we have yet looked at, but even those we have dealt with are sometimes greatly expanded, and they are also yoked together and worked into an integrated texture in complex ways. Nevertheless, it may be possible to focus upon the limited stretch of text in which some item occurs and to see that it fulfils some or all of the criteria for being identified as C^o, C^i or A. In the following passage, identify each of the items in italics as one of these three. Also note whether the item is a nominal group, an adjectival group or a prepositional group. (Where two items would otherwise run into each other, they are separated by an extended space.)

A great many amusements fulfil *all these conditions*. Watching games, going to the theatre, playing golf, are all *irreproachable* *from this point of view*. *For a man of a bookish turn of mind* reading unconnected with his professional activities is *very satisfactory*. However important a worry may be, it should not be thought about *throughout the whole of the waking hours*.

In this respect there is a great difference between men and women. Men *on the whole* find it very much easier to forget their work than women do. *In the case of women whose work is in the home* this is *natural*, since they do not have the change of place that a man has when he leaves *the office* to help them to acquire *a new mood*. But if I am not mistaken, women whose work is outside the home differ from men *in this respect* *almost as much as those who work at home*.

BERTRAND RUSSELL, *The Conquest of Happiness*

4 Structural recursion

4.1 Rankshift

For simplicity of presentation most of the examples given in the preceding chapters have been fairly short. We have been dealing with one clause at a time, and each element in the clause has been realized by an item of moderate length. When people use language, however, they are not usually so terse; it is clear that there is no set limit to the length of what someone might say. The rules of languages allow their speakers to go on and on. This property of languages has been called creativity.

A speaker can expand the structures he uses in two ways. The first is structurally simple: when he has said one thing he can go on and say another immediately afterwards. There are various ways of making plain what the nature of the connection is, but all that is really required is that the addressee be able to perceive the thread of connection running through what is said. The other way is structurally complex. This is the one that we shall begin with, returning later to the simpler, 'one thing after another' method of expansion. The more complex type of expansion can be illustrated diagrammatically as in Figures 9 and 10. In this kind of diagram the horizontal lines represent units and the vertical lines represent the elements of structure. In such diagrams just as much detail can be introduced as is needed. For instance, if it is not relevant for the matter in hand, the structure of the items that function as S and P need not be shown as in Figure 10. The diagram will then look like that in Figure 11.

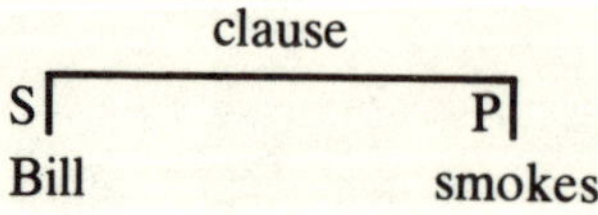

Figure 9

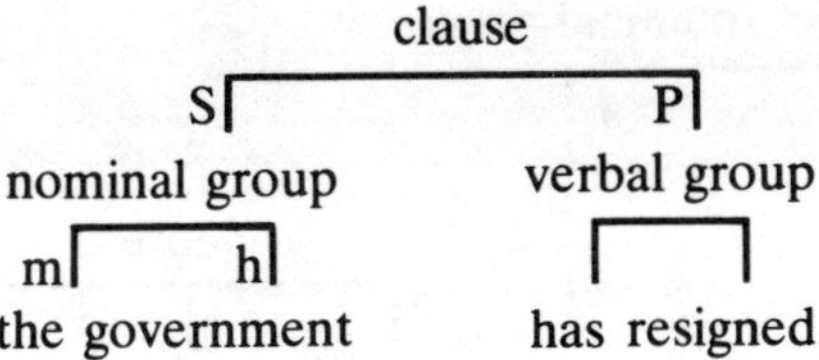

Figure 10

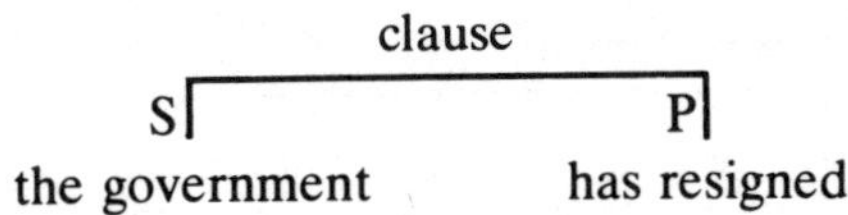

Figure 11

For the moment, however, we are interested in the structure of nominal groups. In Figure 10 the symbols m and h stand for *modifier* and *head* respectively. In **1** there are further examples of nominal groups, with the elements modifier and head identified:

1a | some | English | clauses
m m h

1b | his | three | happy | children
m m m h

It is possible for a nominal group to have modifying elements also coming after the head; they are then called *qualifiers* to distinguish them from the modifiers that come in front, and are identified by the symbol q:

2a | the | fact | that Bill smokes
m h q

2b | a | rumour | that the government has resigned
m h q

As nominal groups these constructions are capable of functioning as the subject in a clause like **3** or as object as in **4**.

3 The fact that Bill smokes | is | deplorable
S P C^i

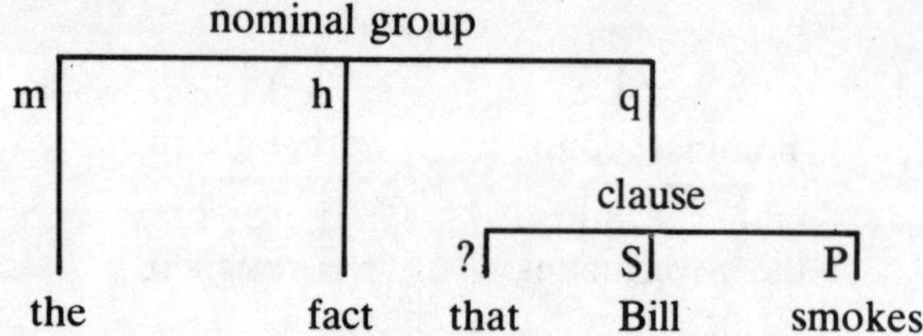

Figure 12

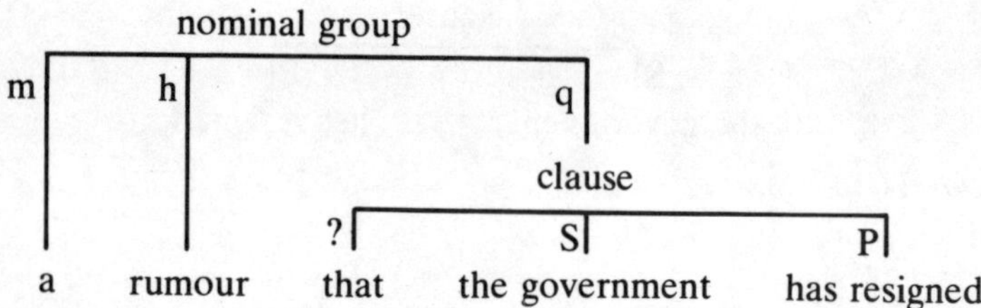

Figure 13

4 He | is spreading | a rumour that the government has resigned

S P C^{O}

But if we now analyse the nominal groups in **2** we come up with the result shown in Figures 12 and 13. In short, these nominal groups have a clause functioning as one of their elements. The fact that there is a slight structural adjustment from *Bill smokes* to *that Bill smokes*, does not alter the fact that in their essentials these two items are both the same. In fact virtually any clause, provided it has a *that* in front of it, could be embedded in a nominal group of this type. It follows from the analyses that have been presented, that in Figure 14, which shows the structure of **3**, a unit labelled 'clause' will occur somewhere within the total structure, which is itself labelled 'clause'. This structural phenomenon goes under the general name of *embedding*. In a model of structure which works with a fixed number of grammatical ranks such as 'clause', 'group', 'word' and 'morpheme', embedding has the more particular name of *rankshift*. A unit of some rank has been shifted down the scale so that it is implanted below the label for its own rank, as in Figure 14. Moreover, this phenomenon is recursive, which

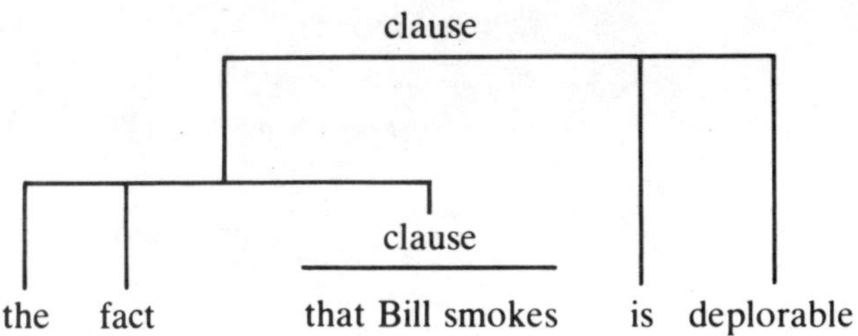

Figure 14

means that a unit containing embedded material can itself be embedded. Example **5** has three layers of embedding:

5 She deplored the fact (that Bill encouraged the belief (that the government had resigned))

The notion of rankshift has been illustrated with examples of just one kind of rankshifted structure. Here are a few others with brief explanations. A fuller discussion and justification of these and other types can be found in Chapter 23.

6 I resent *their having overlooked my claim*

The italicized portion is, with the exception of its having a special form for the first word and a different kind of verb form, paralleled by the clause: *they have overlooked my claim*. The rankshifted clause in **6** is functioning as C^{O}.

7 The person *that you spoke of* is over there

Here the adjustment of structure is from a pattern like that in **8** to one like that in **9**:

8 You | spoke | of somebody
9 That | you | spoke | of

This adjustment having been made, the clause is then embedded within the nominal group as in **10**:

10 The | person | that you spoke of
11 The administration of *the scheme*

In **11** we are dealing not with a rankshifted clause but with a rankshifted group; *the scheme* is a nominal group and so is *the administration of the scheme*. In fact *of the scheme* is also a group, namely a prepositional group, whose elements are a

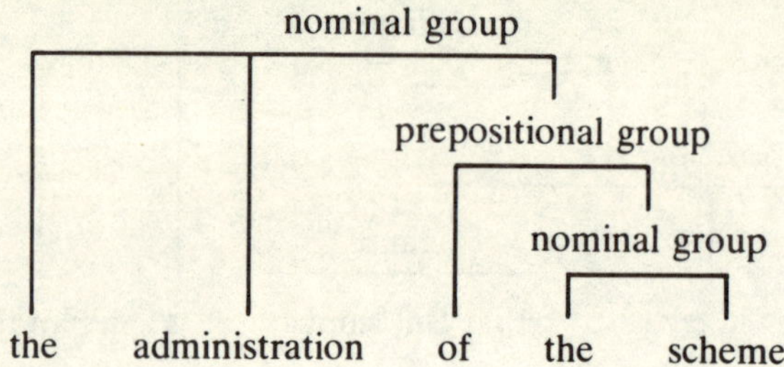

Figure 15

preposition *of* and a prepositional object *the scheme*. So the total structure of **11** is shown in Figure 15. Finally consider **12** which is another structure with a clause within a nominal group:

12 The scheme *for old-age pensioners to receive extra benefits*

There is an extra element introducing the clause, namely the word *for*. In other respects we can descern the same S P C^{O} pattern that is found in *old age pensioners* | *receive* | *extra benefits*. The total structure is shown in Figure 16.

Exercise 4.1
Draw the diagram which will show the layers of rankshifting in the following nominal group:

The administration of the scheme for old age pensioners to receive the benefits which they need.

Exercise 4.2
Find instances of rankshifted clauses in the following examples:

1 In the case of women whose work is in the home this is natural.

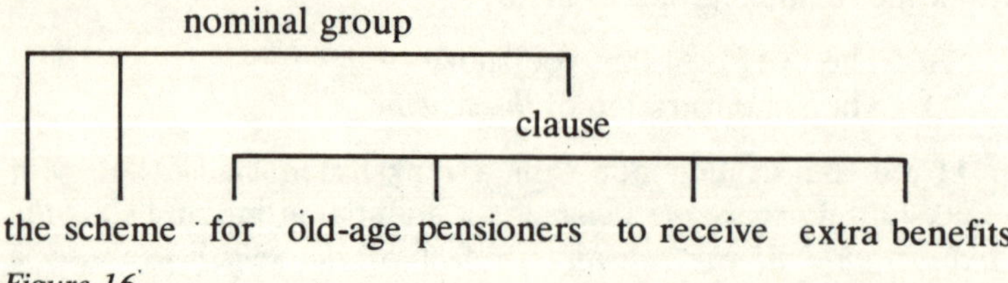

Figure 16

2 They differ from men almost as much as those who work at home.
3 The man who treats everything as a matter of principle cannot be happy with politics.
4 We do not understand the situation we are in.
5 The view that rational planning is prevented by the intrusion of politics is not based on a complete misunderstanding.
6 The possibility of their destroying an established order is largely absent.
7 That a valuable distinction was lost was not noticed.
8 What's wrong in one case must be wrong in every case.
9 I can't understand your preferring such expressions.

4.2 Tactic recursion

We now turn to the structurally simpler kind of expansion of structure; after a speaker has said one thing he can go on to say another, with or without giving his hearer specific help in perceiving the thread of his discourse. Let us assume that in some text we have the two clauses given in **13**, with a connection of cause and effect between them. The question is: what are the ways the speaker has available to him of yoking these clauses together?

13 It got dark. I couldn't see

14a It got dark; I couldn't see
14b It got dark. I therefore couldn't see
14c It got dark and I couldn't see
14d It got dark, so I couldn't see

15a It got dark, upon which I couldn't see
15b Because it had got dark, I couldn't see
15c If it got dark, I couldn't see
15d When it got dark, I couldn't see

16a Its getting dark prevented me from seeing
16b That it had got dark was the reason why I couldn't see

Example **14** contains what are usually regarded as co-ordinate structures; each clause has an equal status. (See also Chapter 18). It is clear that texts can be constructed by extending the string of co-ordinated clauses. At the other extreme, the examples in **16** have one or both of the original clauses rankshifted; each of these examples is, at first analysis, a single clause. Here the embedded clauses have been totally subordinated in an extreme way to form a single clause. The sentences in **15** are intermediate; there is subordination of one clause to another but the subordination is less severe. In this book the examples in **15** are treated not as instances of rankshift but rather more like those in **14**, as clauses in succession to each other where one clause is dominant and the other is bound to it in a subordinate relation which is not rankshift. The types in **15** are treated in much more detail in Chapters 17–21. We can see a similar progression from co-ordination, through a relatively simple type of subordination, to rankshift in the list in **17**:

17a The train was late. Nobody realized it
Nobody realized this: the train was late
17b Nobody realized that the train was late
It wasn't realized that the train was late
17c Nobody took in the fact that the train was late
The fact that the train was late escaped their notice

The bound clauses in **15** are dealt with later under the headings of *adding* clauses and *contingent* clauses; those in **17b** under the heading of *reported* clauses.

One last point about the stringing together of clauses is that sometimes a clause gets interrupted and another clause fills the gap before the first clause is completed as in **18**:

18a Democracy, if we give the word the fairest meaning we may want to give it, is still but one form of politics
18b The Act, which was often criticized, was still part of our legal system
18c The Act (and who would want to defend it?) must still be respected

This is clearly a different phenomenon from embedding; we are dealing here with two clauses, not with one clause which has another embedded within it. It is as though you interrupted your dinner to have a telephone conversation, the conversation not being part of the structure of your dinner. When a unit is made discontinuous in this way it is said to be *split*.

5 Mood

5.1 The meaning of mood

Mood is the name given to those grammatical systems that express the speaker's relation to a proposition, but this kind of meaning does not concern only the speaker and the proposition. Speakers take up attitudes towards what they are saying for the sake of communicating with other people; addressees are necessarily involved, and the speaker may impute to the addressee some relationship to the proposition. Thus if a speaker asserts **1** he will ordinarily believe that the addressee needs telling:

1 This is Bill's house
2 Is this Bill's house?

Similarly if he asks the question in **2** he is imputing to the addressee knowledge of whether or not this is Bill's house; otherwise he would not have asked. The speaker, in fact assigns roles in the process of communication to himself and the addressee. There are, of course, many other meaningful choices than simply that between declarative and interrogative. In the course of the next few chapters we shall see what these are. For the present we will look at the ways in which the most basic moods are signalled.

5.2 Basic moods

In section 2.7 there is a system network for the clause. The part of this that claims immediate attention is given again in Figure 17.

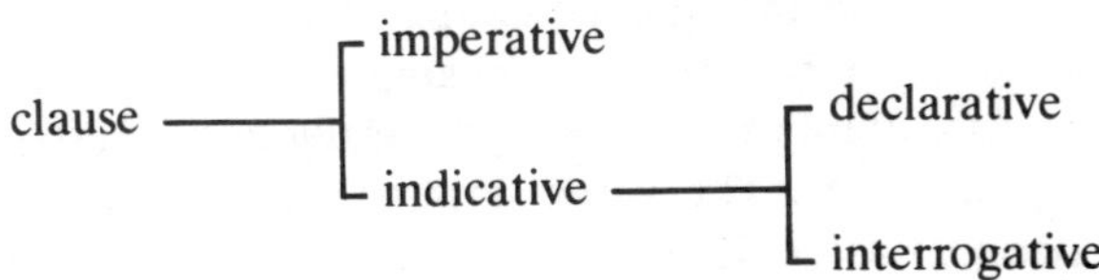

Figure 17

This network will later be elaborated, but this is sufficient as a basis for the simplest realizations of mood, which are:

1 *Indicative:* the clause contains both S and P
2 *Declarative:* the sequence is S P
3 *Interrogative:* the sequence is P (S)
4 *Imperative:* the clause contains P but not S

(The bracket means that the predicator is split and that the subject interrupts it, as in example **4**, below.) These types of clause are illustrated in **3–5**:

Indicative declarative

3a Bill | is asking | questions
S P C

3b Bill | comes | from Llanelli
S P C

Indicative interrogative

4a Is (Bill) asking | questions?
P (S) C

4b Does (Bill) come | from Llanelli?
P (S) C

Imperative

5a Be | quiet
P C

5b Look | at that
P C

5.3 Operators

The splitting of predicators, as in **4**, where the predicators are *is . . . asking* and *does . . . come*, is a matter of such importance in the structure of clauses that we need a name for that part of the verbal group that comes before the split. The term for this is *operator*. Here are more examples of indicative clauses. The reader's attention is drawn specifically to the verbal groups acting as predicators. The verbal groups are outside the brackets and operators are in italics:

6 (He) *has* sent (the letter)
7 (He) *is* being sent (the letter)
8 (He) knows (the way)
9 (He) *does* know (the way)
10 (He) *will* have been running (for hours)

It will be noticed that the interrogative equivalent of these clauses is formed by splitting the predicator after the operator, all except **8**, which has no operator. With respect to this clause, we could say either that it has no interrogative equivalent, or that its interrogative is formed by supplying the verb *do* in its appropriate form as in **9** and then splitting the predicator.

There are also interrogative clauses where the entire predicator comes before S, i.e. there is no splitting. The examples in **11–15** show the declarative form alongside the interrogative; again, operators are in italics:

11	(He) *is* (a Christian)	*Is* (he a Christian)?
12	(He) *has* (a new car)	*Has* (he a new car)?
13	(He) *does*	*Does* (he)?
14	(He) *might*	*Might* (he)?
15	(He) *has*	*Has* (he)?

Here again the operator is the significant word, since in these examples the verbal group consists of nothing but an operator.

We can now revise our statement of the realization of interrogative mood, as follows in **16**:

16 *Interrogative:* the sequence is *either* P (S), where P is a verbal group containing an operator, and is split after the operator; *or* P^{op} S, where P^{op} is a verbal group consisting only of an operator.

(Note that P^{op} is a type of P, namely the type that is realized by a verbal group that contains nothing but an operator. The converse of P^{op} is also a type of P, namely the type that is realized by a verbal group that does not consist only of an operator; either it has no operator or it has more than just an operator.)

The element 'operator' is set up chiefly in order to describe the differences between the realizations of the various moods.

However, operators have other characteristics, which are described below. It is here necessary to anticipate some of the description of the verbal group (see Chapters 14 and 15). The operator is:

1 The first word in a finite verbal group; ('finite verbal group' means a class of verbal group with tense or modality, e.g. *has gone*, *had gone*, *would go*, *would have gone*, *goes*, *went*, *would be going*, *is going*, *was going*, etc. Compare with the non-finite *having gone*, *to be going*, *to have been sent*, etc.)
2 Either an auxiliary verb (as opposed to a main verb) or the main verb *be* (or sometimes *have*, as in **12**). ('Main verb' is the last word in a full verbal group, e.g. *is being followed*, *am trying*, *eats*. *Be* (and sometimes *have*) stand apart from other main verbs, which are lexical verbs like *follow*, *try*, *eat* etc. In this sense, operators are non-lexical verbs.)
3 The word in a verbal group, if any, which carries a negative suffix, e.g. *isn't*, *doesn't*, *won't*; or precedes the word *not*, e.g. *is not*, *does not*, *will not*.

Exercise 5.1

In the following sentences, taken from Appendix BI, identify the predicators and the operator if there is one. Note which predicators are verbal groups that consist only of an operator.

1 They are encouraged in their migration by very thundery close conditions.
2 This electric field causes a glowing discharge.
3 How do insects produce light?
4 It is perfectly lively.
5 It will start to discharge electrons.
6 They glow.
7 It is quite possible.
8 They're all glowing.
9 We start from the UFO sightings.
10 There is no direct evidence.
11 Mariners have known this for centuries.

5.4 Theme

The theme of a clause is usually what the speaker has chosen to place first; it is the starting point of his argument. This is a different kind of meaning from mood, but choices of theme affect the way mood is realized, so it is necessary to say something about theme here. (See also Chapter 12.)

Ordinarily the speaker places first in the clause those elements that signal what mood the clause has, but quite often he can choose something else if he wishes to lay special emphasis upon it. Examples **17–19** each show two clauses which contrast in respect of thematic organization:

17a S P C
You | ought to wash | those curtains
THEME | RHEME

17b C S P
Those curtains | you | ought to wash
THEME | RHEME

18a S P C A
You | will find | a bucket | in the kitchen
THEME | RHEME

18b A S P C
In the kitchen | you | will find | a bucket
THEME | RHEME

19a S P C
The church | stands | in the square
THEME | RHEME

19b C P S
In the square | stands | the church
THEME | RHEME

These examples are all declarative clauses. In the (**a**) examples the theme is ordinary and consists of the subject plus the operator, if there is one. The (**b**) examples are unusual with respect to the choice of the theme; the speaker has opted to begin with some element other than the one that announces the mood of the clause. In **17** an object has been chosen as theme, in **18** the theme is an adjunct and in **19** it is a complement of a locational kind (for which see section 5.5, below). The remainder of the message, i.e. whatever is not the theme, is called the rheme.

The ordinary choice of theme – more technically, the neutral, or unmarked, choice – varies, therefore, according to the mood of the clause. In declaratives it is the subject (possibly with an operator); in interrogatives of the kind we have considered so far the neutral theme is the operator followed by the subject:

20a P (S) C
Do (you) want | these hairbrushes? (*neutral theme*)
THEME | RHEME

20b C P (S)
These hairbrushes | do (you) want? (*marked theme*)
THEME | RHEME

However, there is another type of interrogative that we have not yet looked at. Interrogatives can be divided into *polar* and *non-polar*. The polar interrogatives ask 'whether or not', and require a yes / no answer; hence the name 'polar'. Non-polar interrogatives are of the type exemplified in **21** and **22**:

21 When did he come?
22 Who did you see?

In **21** it is presupposed that he came, so the speaker is not asking whether or not; what he is asking for is the missing information as to when. The clause has a presupposition expressible as *He came at some time* and asks for the 'some' to be specified. The neutral theme for this type of interrogative is what is known as the WH-item (because so many of them, but not all, are spelt with the initial letters *wh*). Here are examples of non-polar interrogative clauses with neutral theme; the WH-items are thematic and are in italics:

23 *Which soprano* is the biggest?
24 *What* are the dangers?
25 *How many snails* has he eaten?
26 *Why* aren't they hurrying?

Exercise 5.2
Identify the theme of the following clauses, and state whether it is neutral or a marked choice of theme. If it is marked, what element of structure is it?

1 She's lost somewhere in the house.
2 Peter's taking them on a tour.
3 I came here for a rest.
4 Shorthand I learned at college.
5 All this winter I've been feeling off colour.

6 Who asked to come this weekend?
7 What work have you done today?
8 At dinner she talked about matters of daily interest.
9 I'll tell you in the morning.
10 Are you going to Berlin?
11 When are you going?
12 All those can you spare?
13 Nowadays where do you live?
14 A merry old soul was he.

5.5 Declaratives under special thematic conditions

In some circumstances a marked theme disturbs the ordinary realization of declarative mood. Among these are the following:

1 When the theme is of a negative character:

27 Not until eight | did (I) realize | the fact
A^{neg} P (S) C

28 Not only the curtains | did (she) wash
C^{neg} P (S)

29 Hardly even then | will (you) get | any results
A^{neg} P (S) C

2 When the theme contains an expression of result grading, generally with the word *so* and with a clause beginning with *that* following later:

30 So late | did (the performance) finish | that . . .
A P (S)

31 So rich | was | he | that . . .
C^{i} P^{op} S

32 So much porridge | did (he) eat | that . . .
C^{o} P (S)

(The term 'result grading' is explainable as follows: in **30**, the lateness of the finishing of the performance is graded, or measured, by reference to the result it produced.)

In both (1) and (2) declarative mood is realized in the same way as for interrogatives: *did the performance finish*; *was he*; *did he eat*. Note, however, that the structure is not ambiguous because thematic elements of these particular kinds render an interrogative interpretation impossible.

3 *The church stands in the square* is an instance of an SPC structure of a particular type: the complement is locational or directional and the verb leads one to expect a complement of just this kind. Further examples of this type of clause are given in **33–36**:

33 A girl came into the room
34 A herd of cattle were grazing in a field by the river
35 The body of Harold Millstone lies here
36 The jet screamed across the sky

When the locational complement (C^{loc}) of such a clause is thematic the subject is usually placed last as in **37**:

37 Across the sky | screamed | the jet
C^{loc} P S

Here the realization of declarative mood is PS. This end position of the subject is, however, not obligatory, it is just the ordinary thing to do when the locational complement comes first (in this type of clause). The speaker can, if he wishes to make a special point of the predicator, place it last, but the result is often somewhat extraordinary as in **38** and **39**:

38 Across the sky | the jet | screamed
C^{loc} S P

39 Here | the body of Harold Millstone | lies.
C^{loc} S P

We will call the optional end position of the subject 'S-arrest'.* The realization of declarative mood can now be stated more fully. (See figure 18.)

5.6 Non-polar interrogatives

The WH-item in non-polar interrogatives has a double function. First there is the WH-function, the function

*This term derives from J. McH. Sinclair (personal communication).

<table>
<tr><td colspan="5">declarative</td></tr>
<tr><td colspan="3">neutral theme</td><td>SP</td><td>Bill asked questions</td></tr>
<tr><td rowspan="4">Marked theme</td><td colspan="2">negative theme</td><td rowspan="2">P(S)
or
P^{op} S</td><td>Only occasionally did Bill ask questions</td></tr>
<tr><td colspan="2">result-grading theme</td><td>So often did Bill ask questions that . . .</td></tr>
<tr><td rowspan="2">C^{loc} theme</td><td>with S-arrest</td><td>PS</td><td>In the kitchen stood a new stove</td></tr>
<tr><td>without S-arrest</td><td>SP</td><td>In the kitchen a new stove stood</td></tr>
</table>

Figure 18

describable as 'unidentified element'. Secondly it has one of the functions S, C or A. What this second function is can be deduced from the structure of the proposition which the interrogative presupposes. For example, **40** presupposes **41**:

40 What did you say?
41 You | said | something
S P C

The *what* in **40** corresponds to the *something* in **41** so that the analysis of **40** is:

42 What | did (you) say?
WH–C P (S)

The symbol for the first of these elements shows that it has two functions in the structure of the clause. Here are further examples where the WH-function is combined with A or C:

43 Where | has (he) gone? (He | has gone | somewhere)
WH–C P (S) C

44 Why | are | you | late? (You | are | late | for some reason)
WH–A P^{op} S C A

45 What | is | Harold? (Harold | is | something, e.g. a politician)
WH–C P^{op} S C

In the examples **42–45** the WH-element is immediately followed by the usual realizations of interrogative mood: P (S) or P^{op} S. But none of these examples has an element labelled WH-S. When it is the subject that also has the WH-function there is a conflict between the theme rule, which places WH first, and the ordinary interrogative rule, which places an operator first. Examples **46–48** show that the theme rule takes priority and that the rule concerning operators is abandoned:

46 Who | said | that? (Somebody | said | that)
WH–S P C S P C

47 What | has happened?
WH–S P
(Something | has happened)
S P

48 Which contribution | surprised | you | most?
WH–S P C A
(Some contribution | surprised | you | most)
S P C A

The realization rules for interrogatives can now be stated more fully and are given in Figure 19.

Exercise 5.3

Assign functions to the italicized elements.

1 I have left my purse *somewhere.*

<table>
<tr><td colspan="4">interrogative</td></tr>
<tr><td rowspan="2">non-polar</td><td>S-questioned</td><td>WH–S P</td><td>Who said that?</td></tr>
<tr><td>not S-questioned</td><td>WH P(S)
or
WH P^{op} S</td><td>What did you say?

Where is it?</td></tr>
<tr><td colspan="2">polar</td><td>P(S)
or
P^{op} S</td><td>Did you say something?

Is it over there?</td></tr>
</table>

Figure 19

2 *Somebody* has just gone out.
3 He has been reading *some novel.*
4 Bill is *something* by profession.
5 *Where* did you put my sunglasses?
6 *What novel* has he been reading?
7 *Who* has just gone out?
8 *What* is Bill by profession?
9 *How* do insects produce light? (Appendix BI, ll. 12–13)
10 *Where in the world* looks like that?
11 *Who* did you see?
12 *What time on Thursday* shall I come to see you?

5.7 The system network for clauses

The dimensions for classifying clauses that have been discussed in this chapter can be summarized in the network in Figure 20. Neutral v. marked theme is introduced as a separate classification from the mood network, but as having its effect on declarative mood. The network can be read as follows: a clause must choose either neutral theme or marked theme, and at the same time it must choose either indicative or imperative mood. If the mood is indicative, it must then be either declarative or interrogative. If it is declarative and has neutral theme, there is nothing more to be chosen; but if it is declarative and has marked theme we can choose C^{loc} theme, negative theme or result-grading theme (or, of course, some other kind of marked theme that will make no difference to the arrangement of S

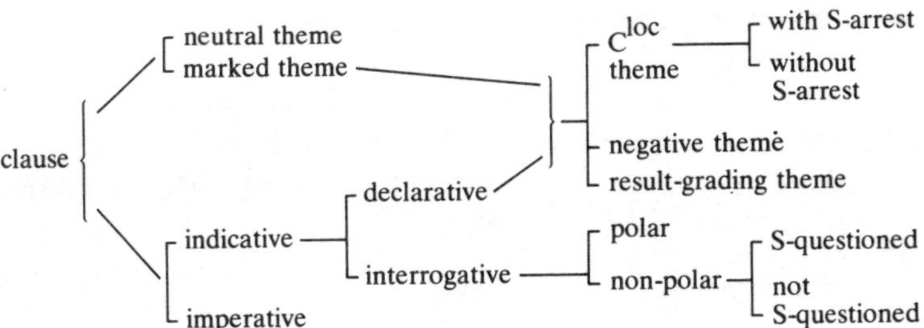

Figure 20

and P: e.g. *That result I didn't anticipate*). If the clause is interrogative, it must be either polar or non-polar, and if non-polar it must be either S-questioned or not S-questioned.

Now we can apply this network to particular examples, as in **49–51**.

49 Did you learn shorthand at college?
50 Yesterday where did you have dinner?
51 So ill was he that he collapsed

49 has neutral theme and indicative mood; the indicative mood is of the interrogative kind, and, more particularly, it is a polar interrogative. **50** is marked theme, indicative, interrogative, non-polar, not S-questioned. **51** is marked theme, indicative, declarative, result-grading theme.

Exercise 5.4

Write out structural formulae for the mood realizations in the following. Attach a feature specification to each clause by reference to the network in Figure 20. (Sample question and answer:
Have you been looking for me?
P (S); P = *have . . . been looking*; S = *you*; indicative, interrogative, polar, neutral theme.)

1 Did he become a Member of Parliament?
2 It is absolutely essential.
3 Is that what you mean?
4 When will you be ready?
5 Here comes the bus.
6 Who would have believed you?
7 What can?
8 Only in a special sense is it acceptable.
9 Are they?
10 This creed has accepted inequality for centuries.
11 Which of the examples haven't you analysed?
12 What you're talking about now is equality of power (Appendix BII, ll. 15–16)
13 Go to bed.

Exercise 5.5

In which of the following is *have*, *has* or *had* an operator? In which is it a main verb? (Remember that sometimes *have*, like *be*, is both a main verb and an operator at once.)

1 He has a new coat.
2 He has dinner at his digs.
3 He may have gone away.
4 He has got a new coat.
5 He had a nasty experience.

6 Mood tags

6.1 Structures

There are two types of indicative mood tag, checking tag and copy tag.

Checking tag

1 They've gone even further, *haven't they*?
2 They didn't want us to move, *did they*?

These occur with either falling or rising tone on the tag.

Copy tag

3 They've gone even further, *have they*?
4 They didn't want us to move, *didn't they*?

These always have rising tone on the tag.

The tags are here treated not as clauses in their own right but as elements within a clause; so each of the above four examples is one clause. However, the clause is divided into two parts as shown in Figure 21. The reason for taking these to be single clauses is that, apart from the choice between the two different kinds of tag, the form of the tag is determined by the form of the proposition. There are rules for tag-formation such that, if you write **5**, the tag could be filled in by anyone who knows the language:

5 Quite a lot of people are willing to listen (+ checking tag)

	PROPOSITION			TAG	
	They've gone even further			haven't they?	
Figure 21	S	P	. . .	P^{op}	S

Model 1

John is here, isn't he?	John	he
You're late, aren't you?	you	you
Everything has gone, hasn't it?	everything	it
What he said was shocking, wasn't it?	what he said	it
The teacher was absent, wasn't he/she?	the teacher	he/she
The tag pronoun subject is co-referential with the proposition subject, which need not be a pronoun.		

Model 2

This one is better, isn't it?	this one	it
isn't he?		he
isn't she?		she
Mine won't work, will it?	mine	it
will he?		he
will she?		she
will they?		they
Some is spilt, isn't it?	some	it
Some will come early, won't they?	some	they
won't it?		it
The proposition subject may itself refer back to something in the context, in which case it may not fully determine the tag pronoun, which is ultimately determined by the wider context.		

Model 3

Everybody likes him, don't they?	everybody	they
Indefinite human singular pronouns have the plural pronoun *they* in the tag.		

Model 4

There's a bird in that cage, isn't there?	there	there
The non-referential subject *there*, is simply repeated.		

Figure 22 Rules for specifying tag subject

Model 1

This a hard one, isn't it? Bill should come, shouldn't he? Bill didn't come, did he? Bill has been imprisoned, hasn't he? There isn't one, is there?	is should did has is	is should did has is
If the proposition has an operator it is repeated in the tag.		

Model 2

John takes the *Guardian*, doesn't he? They take the *Guardian*, don't they? John took the *Guardian*, didn't he?	takes take took	does do did
When the proposition has no operator *does/do/did* must be supplied. This parallel with the rule for interrogatives: *They take it* v. *Do they take it?*		

Figure 23 Rules for specifying tag P^{op}

Model 1

This is a hard one, isn't it? John takes it, doesn't he? They take it, don't they? They were Japanese, weren't they?	is it does he do they were they
Generally speaking the tense and concord of P^{op} is paralleled by that of P in the proposition.	

Model 2

Everybody has left, haven't they?	have they
When the proposition S and the tag S are different in number, the P^{op} is in concord with tag S.	

Figure 24 Rules for S: operator concord in the tag

The difference between the two types of tag is in the pattern of polarity – the contrast between positive and negative. With checking tags proposition and tag have opposite polarity: positive–negative or negative–positive. With copy tags they have the same polarity: positive–positive or negative–negative. Differences in meaning will be discussed later.

In other respects the two kinds of tag are formed in the same way. The S of the tag is controlled by the S of the proposition; the P of the tag is a P^{op} based upon the P of the proposition. In the simplest case we have something like *He has gone, hasn't he?* where *he* and *has* are simply repeated. But the rules cannot be stated as repetitions of pronoun subject and operator. In fact

Model 1

	Proposition negative	tag positive
negative P	He isn't here	is he?
negative S	Nobody came	did they?
	None of them arrived	did they?
negative S^x	There are no letters	are there?
negative C^o	He has no sense	has he?
	He found no excuse	did he?
negative A	He will never see it	will he?
	He hardly ever goes there	does he?
	He seldom tries	does he?
In the proposition negation may be located in various elements, not necessarily in the P. See note 1 below on S^x.		

Model 2

proposition positive	tag negative
He's here	isn't he?
Somebody came	didn't they?
When it is the tag that is negative there is, of course, no choice where to locate the negation.	

Figure 25 Rules for polarity in the tag: checking tags

Model 1

proposition positive	tag positive
You like it	do you?

Model 2

proposition negative	tag negative
He didn't come There are no letters He will never see it	didn't he? aren't there? won't he?
Again, the negation may be located in one of several places in the proposition. But see note 6, below.	

Figure 26 Rules for polarity in the tag: copy tags

there is quite a lot of detail to cover in specifying the way the proposition determines the tag, some of which is shown in Figures 22–26.

Notes on Figures 22–26:

1 The element that follows the verb *be* in the *there is/are/was/were* construction is a delayed subject. The normal functions of the subject are divided between *there* (which inverts with the operator and which I treat as S proper) and the delayed subject, which controls the concord of the verb: *There is/are no letter(s)*. See also the end of section 10.2.

2 The negative forms of some operators are anomalous: *will – won't* / wəʊnt /; *shall–shan't* / ʃɑnt /; *can–can't* / kɑnt /; *do–don't* / dəʊnt /.

3 Many speakers do not have a negative form of *may*, e.g. ?**He may come, mayn't he?* ?**He may come, mightn't he?*

4 Some speakers have *should* in the tag when *ought* is in the proposition, e.g. *They ought to try, shouldn't they?* This seems to indicate that they feel some disinclination to use *oughtn't*.

5 In tags *am + not* is realized as *aren't*/ ɑnt /, e.g. *I'm late, aren't I?*

6 The negative copy tag occurs much less commonly than the positive one, and with some speakers perhaps not at all.

Exercise 6.1

Identify the tags in the following as either checking or copy tags.

1 Hilda is a more complex character, isn't she?
2 You didn't go to Blackpool, did you?
3 The light's working again, is it?
4 She is unsympathetic, isn't she?
5 She is unsympathetic, is she?
6 Nothing matters, does it?
7 Nothing matters, doesn't it?
8 Few people have seen one, have they?

Exercise 6.2

In what circumstances do the operators *don't*, *doesn't* and *didn't* appear in checking tags?

6.2 Meanings

From the structural point of view tagged clauses are of declarative form in the proposition and interrogative form in the tag. Since, however, the proposition is the dominant part of the structure, one might argue that the whole clause is a kind of declarative. In that case one would say that declaratives may be either tagged or untagged. This conclusion is also supported by the following analysis of the meanings of tagged clauses.

It is clear that tagged clauses are in some way poised between the central types of interrogative and declarative. Perhaps it is less important what decision one reaches on the question of whether they are interrogatives or declaratives than to explore the meanings thoroughly.

In declaratives of the central type the speaker treats himself as one who knows his assertion to be true and the addressee as one who does not know (or at least needs reminding). In abbreviated form we could say 'speaker = knower, addressee ≠ knower'. (This does not mean that the speaker always knows the truth, but that he sets himslf up as one who knows the truth; similarly it does not mean that the addressee does not know, but that the speaker is treating him as one who does not know.) In the interrogatives of the central type, these roles are reversed: speaker ≠ knower, addressee = knower.

People do not always speak to each other in this clear-cut way; they have other motives for speaking than simply giving or seeking information. The English mood network allows for many possibilities, partly by means of the mood tags – though this discussion will also lead to mention of negative polar interrogatives and of modality.

6.3 Checking tag with falling tone

The speaker is not expressing any doubt about the proposition, nor about whether the addressee knows it to be true.

> **6** It's a lovely day, isn't it?
> **7** That's what I said, isn't it?
> **8** You don't like it, do you? (I can see by the look on your face; admit it!)

The possible motives for using tagged clauses of this kind in discourse are many, and it would not serve our present purpose to try to list them. Moreover, I am not trying to give an account of all the linguistic means a speaker has at his disposal for interacting with other people. What is being attempted here is a general, normalized statement of what the moods of the English clause contribute to the interpretation of discourse acts. Any particular discourse act will still have to be interpreted in the light of the situation – as I have indicated before (pages 4–7). The force of the checking tag with falling tone can, in this spirit, be stated as: speaker = knower, addressee = knower.

6.4 Checking tag with rising tone

The force of this is more difficult to generalize. The rising tone certainly contributes a note of uncertainty on the part of the speaker, but it seems that what he is uncertain about is not (at least in the first instance) the proposition he is stating. The speaker is 'knower' in the sense that he reserves the right to claim that status in the absence of any satisfactory denial or explanation for this mistake. If we consider example **9** we might say that it is the relation of the addressee to the proposition that is in doubt.

> **9** A: I'm going to buy a new coat.
> B: You haven't got any money, have you?

The speaker is treating him neither as knower nor as non-knower, but hesitantly. 'He may not know, though he ought

<table>
<tr><td colspan="2" rowspan="2">speaker treats</td><td colspan="3">addressee</td></tr>
<tr><td>as knower</td><td>as non-knower</td><td>with hesitation</td></tr>
<tr><td rowspan="3">self</td><td>as knower</td><td>declarative + tag falling

It's raining, isn't it?</td><td>declarative untagged

It's raining.</td><td>declarative + tag rising

It's raining, isn't it?</td></tr>
<tr><td>as non-knower</td><td>interrogative positive

Is it raining?</td><td>(modality)

It may be raining.</td><td></td></tr>
<tr><td>with hesitation</td><td>interrogative negative

Isn't it raining?</td><td></td><td></td></tr>
</table>

Figure 27 Table of meanings for indicatives

to' or 'He may know something I don't and thus be able to correct me, but in the absence of any such correction I shall stick to my belief'.

In Figure 27 I treat checking tags, both falling and rising, as declaratives, on the ground that speaker = knower in all of the declaratives.

6.5 Polar interrogatives, negative

Since in a polar interrogative the speaker is asking 'whether or not', it would seem that the contrast between positive and negative would be meaningless in this environment. But there is a meaningful difference between *Is it raining*? and *Isn't it raining*?. In the second of these the speaker suggests 'I would have thought it was but for something which has, after all, made me doubtful.'

The addressee is unhesitatingly credited with knowledge on the point, and the speaker does not indicate in which way he expects his doubts to be resolved. In a positive interrogative the speaker does not necessarily have any such conflict in his mind about whether he really knows or not. I interpret negative interrogatives, therefore, as meaning that the speaker is hesitant about which role to cast himself in.

6.6 Modality

It is possible for a speaker not to know, and to believe that the addressee does not know, and yet still want to talk about some proposition. In such cases we are dealing with possibility, indirect knowledge (inference), prediction, etc. This is where the modal auxiliaries come in (see pages 80–99).

6.7 Copy tags

In copy-tagged clauses the speaker is stating a 'message' derivable from the immediate situation. This may be a repetition of what someone has just said, or it may be an inference either from what someone has said or from some fact of the situation. The clause is sometimes offered as a challenge to withdraw a remark as in **10**:

> **10** I'm a self-styled liberal, am I?

Sometimes it is offered as a stimulus to further conversation as in **11**:

> **11** You've been with your colleagues a long time, have you?

or it may be simply a request for confirmation that a message has been safely passed as in **12**:

> **12** He's going to be late, is he?

If these are questions they are not questions about the polarity of the proposition, e.g. whether or not I am a self-styled liberal, but about whether that was the message or not. Copy tags should probably not appear in the same part of the mood network as ordinary indicatives, but go along with 'echoes', of which **13–20** are further types:

13	It's raining?	(Did you say / do I gather it is raining?)
14	Am I tired?	(Did you ask whether . . .?)
15	Where did I put it??	(Did you ask where . . .?)
16	You left it where?	(Where did you say . . .?)
17	Did who pay for the tickets??	(About whom did you ask whether he . . .?)
18	Where did I put what??	(About what did you ask where I had put it?)
19	Close the door?	(Did you ask me to close the door?)
20	Close what?	(What did you ask me to close?)

These are 'second order' questions; that is, questions not about their propositions but about whether the propositions were said, asked, or implied by somebody else. Note that the utterance echoed may be declarative, interrogative or imperative. (The double question mark means an echoed interrogative.) Unfortunately there will not be space to examine echo mood further in this book.

Exercise 6.3
The pronoun subject + P^{op} forms that we have been considering in this chapter also occur in some kinds of responses. Consider the following items as responses. Which of them are appropriate for responding to declaratives and which to interrogatives?

1 Is he? Don't they? Have I?
2 Yes, he is. No, they don't. Yes, I have.
3 So he is. So they don't. So I have.
4 So is he. Nor do they. So have I.

Exercise 6.4
How much do the items listed in exercise 6.3 have in common with mood tags? (Consider both their dependence on the form of the clause which is being responded to, and their internal structure.)

Exercise 6.5
A: They went to Spain for their holidays.
B: (i) Yes, they did *or*
(ii) Did they?

What difference does it make which way the responder answers? Can the intonation of the responses be varied between falling and rising? (It is assumed the reader has been studying English intonation in a parallel course. See also Appendix A.)

7 Imperatives

7.1 Principal types and their meanings

Moods are divided into two main branches, indicative and imperative. Whereas in indicative clauses the speaker is presenting a proposition as a question of knowledge, and the different types are distinguished according to how the role of knower is assigned, in imperatives the speaker is concerned with a proposition as some action to be carried out. The distinguishing role in the semantics of imperatives is that of *decider*, i.e. the person who opts for the action, who assumes the authority to decide that it should be carried out. This description of imperatives is, no doubt, rather broader than the sense in which the term has traditionally been used, including as it does some clause types that are usually known as *subjunctive*. It seems better to stretch the sense of the traditional term than to invent a new one to embrace both the traditional imperative and the subjunctive. The main types of imperative are illustrated in examples **1–4**:

1 Come here
2 Let's go to the pictures
3 Let him be more careful in future
4 The devil take the hindmost

Before we can analyse the meanings of these types we must bring into the picture another role, that of *performer*. In some indicative clauses a performer or actor appears as one of the elements in the proposition; usually this is the subject of the clause, as in **5**:

5 Bill went to the pictures

Bill is here the performer of the action; but this is an indicative clause and the performer is simply part of the proposition, in the same way as the process of going somewhere and the destination of the going. In imperatives, on the other hand, the question naturally arises of who, if anyone, in the situation of utterance is to carry out the action that has been decided upon. The performer is now usually one of the people involved as speaker or addressee as well as, at least by implication, a participant in the action named in the proposition. For instance in **1** the addressee is cast as performer, while in **2** both addressee and speaker are cast as performers. These contrast with **3**, where neither speaker nor addressee is performer. We will call the first two types *jussive imperative* and the third *optative imperative*. The fourth is the so-called 'subjunctive'. The meaning of these types is summarized in Figure 28.

<table>
<tr><td colspan="3" rowspan="3">speaker treats</td><td colspan="3">addressee</td></tr>
<tr><td colspan="2">as performer</td><td rowspan="2">as neither decider nor performer</td></tr>
<tr><td>not as decider</td><td>as decider</td></tr>
<tr><td rowspan="3">self</td><td rowspan="2">as decider</td><td>not as performer</td><td>Come here
jussive, exclusive</td><td>Come here, will you
jussive exclusive tagged</td><td>Let him be careful
optative</td></tr>
<tr><td>as performer</td><td>Let's go
jussive inclusive</td><td>Let's go, shall we
jussive inclusive tagged</td><td>Let me write it down
optative</td></tr>
<tr><td colspan="2">as neither decider nor performer</td><td></td><td></td><td>The devil take the hindmost
subjunctive</td></tr>
</table>

Figure 28

The difference between the two jussive types is that in the first the speaker is not included among the performers, while in the second he is. Apart from the differences in structure seen in examples **1** and **2** these two types are distinguished structurally by admitting of mood tags of different types as shown in **6** and **7**:

6 Come in, will you?
7 Let's go, shall we?

The meaning of the tag in each case is that the speaker defers to the decision of the addressee; in the untagged forms the speaker assigns to himself alone the role of decider, but in the tagged forms he is sharing the decision-making.

The first type of jussive is called *exclusive* (because the speaker is not included among the performers) and the second type is *inclusive*.

In optatives the speaker is still decider and the addressee is not, but the role of performer is separate from both of them. There may not be any very clearly specified performer (as in example **12**), or the performer may be some third party named in the proposition itself (as in **10**). Examples **8** to **13** are typical optatives:

8 Let him be careful
9 Let Bill be King Lear
10 Let the government put its own house in order
11 Let the messengers be brought to me
12 Let there be better and bigger Beethovens
13 Let there be no doubt about this

Possibly one should allow for the speaker to designate himself as performer in this type, as in **14**:

14 Let me write it down before I forget

But the addressee can certainly not be cast as performer. No tags are possible in the optative type.

The fourth type (given in example **4**) is the so-called subjunctive. Other examples are:

15 Peace be with you
16 God save the Queen
17 Long live the President

In general this is not a productive type of clause. Most examples are formulaic expressions and speakers do not feel free to coin new ones, because the language would seem too high-flown for any but the most exalted occasions, e.g. **Cheap be my lunch* or **The bus arrive early*. There are various subtypes of subjunctive. In addition to those illustrated in examples **15–17** there is a type that uses the auxiliary verb *may*:

18 May you be happy
19 May the Society flourish

From the semantic point of view these clauses are expressions merely of wish and not of decision. The speaker is not even treating himself as decider.

7.2 Jussive exclusives: vocative emphasis

There are two ways of expanding the nucleus of the jussive exclusive construction. One of these lays emphasis on the role of the addressee, as in **20**:

20 You come here

This is *vocative emphasis*. The vocative element need not be *you*; it could be *everybody*, *all of you*, *nobody*, *you boys at the back*. But even when the vocative element has what appears superficially to be third person reference, it is actually vocative, so that *everybody* is paraphrasable as 'all of you' and *nobody* as 'none of you'. The meaning of a clause with vocative emphasis is that the speaker is pointing the finger at the addressee, either to admonish him as in **21** or to make it clear who is being addressed as in **22** and **23**:

21 You find out for yourself
22 Nobody move
23 Everybody listen

The structural formula for a clause with vocative emphasis is Voc P.

24 All of you | go
Voc P

25 You | send | it | back
Voc P C^O C

Example **25**, in its written form, is ambiguous; *you send it back* could be interpreted as imperative, as above, or as declarative:

26 You | send | it | back (that's what happens)

S P C^{O} C

In spoken form there is no ambiguity as long as the placing of the tonic is normal, since the rhythm is different; in the imperative, the element Voc is a salient syllable while in the declarative it is non-salient.

27a *imperative:* // you / send it / back //
27b *declarative:* // ∧ you / send it / back //

However, the structural difference between these two clause types, which are so sharply distinguished semantically, is not quite so slender as this. In negative form the two are very different:

28a *imperative:* Don't you send it back
28b *declarative:* You don't send it back

It can be seen that in the imperative the predicator is split, giving a formula: P (Voc), where P = *don't . . . send.* In fact **28a** is quite clearly not declarative, but, in written form, it could be taken as interrogative: *Don't you send it back? Isn't that what happens*? However, the intonation is normally quite different: Tone 1 for the imperative and Tone 2 for the interrogative.

There is still another structural difference between the imperative clauses and both of the indicative types. This is connected with the concord that exists between subject and predicator in indicative clauses: *you / I / we / they send* v. *he / she / it / everybody / the boss* etc. *sends*. That is, for all person-number combinations except third person singular the indicative has the base form, e.g. *send*, while for the third person singular it has the *s*-form, e.g. *sends*. The imperative, on the other hand always and invariably has the base form. Now, when the element Voc is *you* and the verb is any verb but *be*, the fact that there is no concord in the imperative clause does not show up, because the verb would be in the base form in any case, e.g. *you send.* But if the Voc happens to be *somebody* the absence of concord is apparent:

29a *imperative:* Somebody come here
29b *declarative:* Somebody comes here

Again, if the verb happens to be *be*, which does not use the base form for concord with *you*, viz. *you are*, there is a sharp difference:

30a *imperative:* You be careful
30b *declarative:* You are careful

Similar differences appear in negative forms:

31a *imperative:* Don't anybody sit there
31b *interrogative:* Doesn't anybody sit there?

32a *imperative:* Don't you be silly
32b *interrogative:* Aren't you silly?

It will be seen that there are various reasons for not treating what in this book is called the element Voc as S. To summarize:

1 Subjects are obligatory elements, vocatives are not.
2 There is concord between subject and predicator; between vocative and predicator there is not.
3 Any combination of person and number is possible in subjects; in vocatives the reference is always second person (addressee), and this severely restricts the nominal groups that can appear in this function.

Whether Voc is a kind of subject or not (and of course it has things in common with subjects) is ultimately a matter of terminology and definition. In this book Voc and S are treated as distinct.

Before leaving the matter of vocative elements, it is desirable to draw attention to another kind of vocative that exists in English clauses. This is the vocative tag, symbol: Voc^t. Like Voc this element has the function of naming the addressee(s), but it has nothing to do with the mood of the clause, and is therefore not a mood tag. It can occur in clauses of any mood. Here are some examples, with Voc^t italicized; it will be noticed that some of them also have Voc in them.

Declarative

33a *George*, you look ill
33b You look ill, *George*
33c You, *George*, look ill
33d *All of you*, I'm going to jump

Interrogative

34a *You boys*, have you seen any policemen about?
34b Have you seen any policemen about, *you boys*?
34c *Children*, where's your father?
34d Where's your father, *children*?
34e *You*, what are you doing?
34f What's the time, *somebody*?

Imperative

35a *Ladies and gentlemen*, please don't panic
35b Please don't panic, *ladies and gentlemen*
35c You be careful, *Bill*.
35d *Bill*, you be careful
35e *Everybody*, listen
35f Listen, *everybody*

The vocative tag is not confined to a position at the beginning of the clause and it has its own intonational characteristics so that even when it is initial it is not confusable with a Voc:

36a *with* Voc^t // Everybody // listen //

36b *with* Voc // Everybody / listen //

The negative forms are also different:

37a	*with* Voc^t	Everybody, don't listen to him
37b	*with* Voc	Don't everybody listen to him
		or, more likely
37c		Don't anybody listen to him

Note that *nobody* can occur as Voc but makes no sense as Voc^t:

38a	*as* Voc^t	*Nobody, what time is it?
38b	*as* Voc	Nobody move (cf. Don't anybody move)

7.3 Jussive exclusives: polarity emphasis

A negative clause necessarily has emphasis on the choice between positive and negative simply by virtue of the fact that it is negative. The normal thing is to tell somebody to do something, not to tell him not to do something, unless you have reason to

		Without vocative emphasis	*With vocative emphasis*
Without polarity emphasis		Go	You go
With polarity emphasis	*negative*	Don't go	Don't you go
	positive	Do go	*Do you go

Figure 29

suppose he would otherwise do it. But an imperative that is not negative may be made quite emphatically not negative, as in **39**:

39 Do come here

So, for non-negative clauses there are two possibilities, given in **40**:

40a Come here
40b Do come here

For negative clauses there is no such distinction:

41 Don't come here

It will be noticed that the operator *do* occurs in both of the forms that have emphasis on the polarity.

When the system of polarity emphasis is combined with the system of vocative emphasis we find a gap in the paradigm, as Figure 29 shows. Items such as those in the bottom right-hand box of Figure 29 seem not to occur in contemporary English. It is interesting, however, that such forms are to be found in conversational passages in some nineteenth-century fiction.

7.4. Jussive exclusives: the verb *let*

There is an ordinary lexical verb *let*, historically closely connected with the imperative particles *let's* and *let* that occur in jussive inclusives and optatives, respectively. As an ordinary verb it can occur in clauses that have no connection with imperative mood as in **42**:

42a	*declarative*	He didn't let me drive
42b	*interrogative*	Have you let him speak yet?
42c	*rankshifted clause*	Letting them sit down (was unwise)

Like any other lexical verb, this one can occur as the predicator of a jussive exclusive:

43 Let me drive
44 Let him speak, please, will you?
45 Somebody let him sit down
46 Let us go out, will you?

Structurally these clauses are adequately accounted for under the heading *jussive exclusive*. However, the meaning of the verb *let* is such that they can be seen as yet another kind of imperative. This verb has the effect of passing the decision to the addressee, so that *let him speak* casts the addressee as the one who decides on his speaking. Semantically, therefore, it is possible to treat these clauses as a second kind of optative, distinguished from the first by whether it is the speaker or the addressee who is the decider. When the addressee is decider it makes sense to add the tag *will you*? But not when speaker is decider. For instance, example **12** is taken from a radio discussion about equality of opportunity, equality of status and inequality of talent; clearly this is speaker's decision and it would make no sense to add *will you*? Undoubtedly, however, some of the examples above are ambiguous, for instance **9** could be taken in either interpretation.

7.5 A note on *let's* and *let us*

There is a sharp distinction between the meanings of **47** and **48**:

47 Let us go out, shall we?
48 Let us go out, will you?

In the first of these *us* refers to the speaker and the addressee ('me and you'); in the second, *us* refers to the speaker and some third party, not the addressee ('me and somebody else, not you'). The first example is a rather formal way of saying *let's*, which would be the ordinary conversational form. In the second example *let's* is not a possible alternative. As the form of the tags shows, the first is jussive inclusive and the second is jussive exclusive – though of the type discussed in section 4 above. But it follows that without the tags *let us go out* is ambiguous.

The two senses of *us* are rarely distinguishable in the structure of English clauses. Normally, as in **49**, there is no indication which sense is intended except what can be gathered from the sense of the context:

49 They send us tickets

The same applies to the other first person plural items: *we*, *our*, *ours*.

Exercise 7.1

Attach the appropriate label, either *interrogative*, *declarative*, *jussive exclusive*, *jussive inclusive*, *optative* or *subjunctive*, to each of the following sentences. A few of the examples are ambiguous and require alternative labels. (N.B. Clauses of different mood may be used to perform very similar acts in discourse structure. Here we are focusing on grammatical mood and simply noting the discrepancies between the levels of grammar and discourse.)

1 Let's turn back to page 5.
2 Look at all the money there is in the country.
3 Now, help yourself, Mr Holohan.
4 No sound of strife disturb his sleep.
5 I suppose we'd better get started.
6 Let's get started.
7 There's been a suggestion that we get started.
8 Shall we get started?
9 I think you ought to come nearer.
10 Come nearer.
11 Let four captains
Bear Hamlet like a soldier to the stage,
12 For he was likely . . .
To have proved most royal;
13 and for his passage,
The soldier's music and the rite of war
Speak loudly for him:
14 Take up the bodies
15 – such a sight as this
Becomes the field,
16 but here shows much amiss.
17 Go,

18 Bid the soldiers shoot.
19 You push the button.
20 You like this music.
21 Let them eat cake.
22 Tell them to eat cake.
23 Tell me the answer.
24 What's the answer?
25 Pass the salt, please, will you?
26 I'd like the salt, please, if you don't mind.
27 Can I have the salt, please?
28 Let him alone.
29 Let him come on Thursday.
30 It would be a good thing if he came on Thursday.
31 Allow him to come on Thursday.
32 Don't think I'm complaining.
33 Let it be understood that I'm not complaining.

8 Modality

8.1 Modality: structure

Modality is the name of the system modal v. non-modal and is relevant to the grammar of clauses. A clause may be modal in various ways, as shown in **1** and **2**:

1 Possibly he is ill
2 He may be ill

In **1** the modality is realized by means of a modal adjunct and in **2** by means of a verbal group with a modal auxiliary as operator. We shall be concentrating on modality realized in the second of these ways. In the following examples the verbal groups are outside the parentheses and the modal auxiliaries are in italics:

3 (He) *will* appear (on Saturday)
4 (The programme) *may* have seemed (under-rehearsed)
5 *Can* (they) come (in)?
6 (A worry) *should* not be thought (about throughout the whole of the waking hours)
7 (It) *will* start to discharge (electrons) (Appendix BI, 1. 18)
8 (You) *ought* to be (aware of this)
9 (The recreational facilities) *must* have been provided (by the Council)

Modal auxiliaries are always initial in the verbal group and occur in finite verbal groups; in fact, they are always operators. When *be* and *have* occur as auxiliaries, they may be operators but are not necessarily so; for instance, they are not operators in the occurrences that are in italics in examples **10–12**:

10 (They) must *have been* provided (by the Council)
11 (He) is *being* cautioned (by the police)
12 (You) may *be* leaving (early)

Another word that occurs as auxiliary is *do*; this too, when it is an auxiliary, is always an operator, but it differs from the modal auxiliaries: *do* cannot be followed by another auxiliary, nor by *be* as main verb. In the following examples, *do* is contrasted with *may*, which is chosen as a typical modal.

13a He does speak quickly
13b *He does have spoken quickly
13c *He does be saving a lot of time
13d *He does be too proud

14a He may speak quickly
14b He may have spoken quickly
14c He may be saving a lot of time
14d He may be too proud

Modal auxiliaries are the only type of verb that does not vary in form for concord with the subject. This is illustrated in Figure 30.

Modal auxiliaries do not occur in imperative clauses. (The notion 'operator' is, in any case, applicable in only a rather restricted sense to the verbal groups that occur in imperative clauses.)

The items that occur as modal auxiliary are set out in three groups:

1 *Will, would, shall, should, can, could, may, might, must, ought*

These are the items that occur with greatest freedom in the modal auxiliary function. One of them, *ought*, differs slightly from the others in that the next verb is always preceded by *to* while the others are followed by the base form, e.g. *ought to go* but *may go*.

with modal verb	*with other verbs*	
he will come	he comes	he has come
they will come	they come	they have come
(*will* invariable)	(*comes* v. *come*)	(*has* v. *have*)

Figure 30

2 *Need, dare*

These occur as modal auxiliary, but with the restriction that they do not occur in positive declarative clauses:

15a Need I send one?
15b Needn't you go today?
15c They needn't try (need they?)
15d *They need try

16a Dare I send one?
16b Daren't you go today?
16c They daren't try (dare they?)
16d *They dare try

Need and *dare* do also occur as main verbs, and this function should be carefully distinguished from that of modal auxiliary.

17 They need more paper
18 He needs to find new digs
19 He dared to publish libellous material

Exercise 8.1
Confirm that *need* and *dare* in **17–19** are main verbs and not modal auxiliaries.

The modal *needn't* is easy to fit into the pattern of modal meaning, as we shall see. But, semantically, *dare(n't)* is somewhat marginal; no further notice will be taken of it in this chapter.

3 *Used*

This is another marginal item, exemplified in **20**:

20 He used to live in London

It fulfils most of the formal criteria for modal auxiliaries but usage is variable and many speakers do not treat it as an operator. In example **21** it is an operator, and in example **22** it is not:

21a Used he to live in London?
21b He usedn't (*or* used not) to live in London

22a Did he used to live in London?
22b He didn't used to live in London

This verb has little or nothing to do with modal meaning and will not be dealt with below.

8.2 Modality and tense

Many of the modal verbs go in pairs which, in their historical origin, were ordinary cases of present and past tense. These are *can/could, will/would, shall/should, may/might*. On the other hand *must* and *ought* do not belong to any such pairs. They are in origin past tense forms, but they do not straightforwardly function as such in the modern language. Even *could, should* and *might* do not always appear in contrast with the present forms *can, shall* and *may*. For example, although *could* contrasts with *can* in the two sentences of **23**, there is no such contrast in **24**.

23a He could speak Welsh (*meaning* He used to be able to speak Welsh)
23b He can speak Welsh (*meaning* He is able to speak Welsh)
24 He could have been delayed (*meaning* It is conceivable that he has been delayed)

In a similar way *should* frequently does not contrast with *shall*. In the following example it would be non-English to substitute *shall*:

25 He should be in the library (*meaning* It is virtually certain that he's in the library)

The facts of usage are evidently complex. However, the fact that the past tense forms of modal verbs sometimes have strange properties can partly be explained by reference to the kind of meaning that modality has. We shall now look at modal meaning in some detail, and return to the question of tense and time reference briefly later in this chapter (section 8.8) and at more length in Chapter 16.

8.3 Knowledge and influence

Modal expressions are ones in which the speaker is not dealing in straightforward assertions. There are two kinds of modality.

In *knowledge modality* the speaker is making an issue of what evidence there is for the truth of some factual proposition: he is predicting, or guessing, or inferring it, or stating a mere possibility. In *influence modality* he is talking about influences on the course of events, about the causes and conditions for things to come about. We will deal with each in turn.

Knowledge modality

In **26** are some examples of knowledge modality, each accompanied by a gloss which draws attention to the slant the speaker is taking on the proposition:

26a There may be some of that tea left (It is a possibility; I have no evidence to the contrary)

26b Bill could have posted the letter already (It is conceivable that he has done so; there is nothing to prevent my believing it)

26c He will be in the library (It is probable that he is there; there's reason to expect that he is; you're likely to find him there if you go and look)

26d You must be exhausted (I'm forced to this conclusion; I draw the conclusion from other knowledge I have)

Influence modality

The speaker may be pointing out the existence of conditions for things to come about, or he may even be trying to influence the course of events himself:

27a They may sit down (They are allowed to sit down; I give them permission. As far as my decision goes, there is no reason why they shouldn't sit down)

27b Harold can balance a spoon on his chin (Harold has this ability; he has it in him, so there's nothing to stop it happening)

27c Harold will help you carry that case (He has formed the intention; he has consented to do so; this makes the event probable)

27d You must send him a letter (You are morally obliged to do so; I insist upon it; there is pressure upon you to make the event come about)

The influences we are dealing with here either come from within the person who is to perform the action, or they originate in his environment. The ability and the intention of the performer are internal influences (see **27b** and **27c**). But permission and compulsion are external, it being a question of whether there is any moral pressure upon the performer.

It will by now have become evident that at least some of the modal verbs are capable of being used in both a knowledge and an influence sense. For instance *may* occurs in **26a** and in **27a**. In fact, it is possible to contrive examples which are ambiguous, and we can exploit this ambiguity to highlight the differences of meaning described above:

28 He should be here
(i) It is almost certain that he is here (knowledge)
(ii) He is under an obligation to be here (influence)

29 You must live near your work
(i) I infer that you live near your work (knowledge)
(ii) You are compelled to live near your work (influence)

30 They could have turned off the supply
(i) It is possible that they have turned off the supply (knowledge)
(ii) It was permissible for them to have turned off the supply (though they didn't do so) (influence) *or* They were able to turn off the supply (though they didn't) (influence)

Exercise 8.2

The following clauses are ambiguous between a knowledge and an influence interpretation. Provide glosses which will explain the two meanings.

1 Bill may work for the BBC.
2 Rosemary must paint in oils.
3 Jack ought to be asleep.
4 He should have wound up the clock.

Cutting across the knowledge–influence distinction there is another. Modal expressions may deal with a possibility on the one hand, or with a probability, a certainty or a necessity on the other.

Possibility (influence)

If Bill can touch the ceiling, it is possible for him to do so; there is no internal factor restraining him. And if he is permitted to come home late, this means there is no external factor restraining him.

Possibility (knowledge)

To say that Bill could be, or may be, in the garden is to say that there is no evidence to prevent us believing this to be so. As far as the evidence goes, it's a possibility.

We can generalize expressions of possibility as follows: there is no influence/evidence against . . . .

Probability/certainty/necessity (influence)

To say that Bill has consented to help with the work, or that he insists on helping, is to say that he has the intention, and this is an internal factor tending to promote the event taking place. To say that he must help is to say there is an external force tending to promote the event.

Probability/certainty/necessity (knowledge)

To say that Bill will be in the library, in a predicting sense, is to say there is evidence tending to lead to the belief that he is there. And if we say he must be in the library, we are saying the evidence is so strong that the conclusion is unavoidable.

These expressions of probability/certainty/necessity can be generalized as: there is influence/evidence in favour . . . .

(It is unfortunate that there is no word that will serve equally well for both certainty (which has more of a knowledge connotation) and necessity (which has more of an influence connotation).)

Figure 31 summarizes the types of modality described above and adds one or two further points of detail which will be commented on below.

8.4 Knowledge modality

1 Conjecture v. inference. The formal difference between the following pair corresponds to a slight difference of meaning:

	Knowledge		*Influence*	
Possibility	*conjecture:*	may	*permission:*	may can
	inference:	could	*ability:*	can
Probability/ certainty/ necessity	*conjecture:* *(prediction)*	will	*volition:*	will
	inference: *confident:* *tentative:*	 must should ought	*compulsion:* *confident:* *tentative:*	 must should ought

Figure 31

31a It may be in your pocket (conjecture)
31b It could be in your pocket (inference)

This is a meaning difference which speakers may not always feel a need to make use of, but the second puts more stress on the idea of reaching a rational conclusion. It is a difference between guesswork and brainwork. The same distinction applies in the lower half of Figure 31. The second sentence of **32** suggests a conclusion reached by means of thinking the matter out, and the first suggests an educated guess:

32a He will be in the library (conjecture)
32b He must be in the library (inference)

If the speaker added an expression like *I should think, I guess*, or *probably*, it would go more naturally with the first than with the second. The difference of meaning between what I have called conjecture and inference is more striking in the probability/certainty part of the paradigm than it is in the possibility part.

2 Confident v. tentative. Under the inference heading in the lower half of Figure 31 the speaker can be either confident or tentative. The tentative type allows for the possibility of having miscalculated:

33 He must be in the library (Doubtless)

34 He should/ought to be in the library (If I understand the matter aright)

3 Among the ways of recognizing a knowledge modality is the technique of using a two-part gloss of the following form:

35 It is possible that it is in your pocket
36 It is probable that he is in the library

The first part of the gloss isolates the type of modality by using such a word as *possible*, *probable*, *certain* etc., and the second part states the propositional content such as *that it is in your pocket*. In knowledge modalities the propositional part is a finite clause. This has some importance in the discussion of time reference in modal clauses. We can assess for its truth (or at least for its well-foundedness) a proposition located at any point in time, past, present or future: *I now judge it to be possibly the case that it was/is/will be in your pocket*. (See Sections 16.1 and 16.2.)

8.5 Influence modality

1 In the permission type *may* is more formal than *can* but in other respects they are interchangeable.

2 Volition can be weak or strong. It is a question of the conditions under which the performer forms the intention of performing. With weak volition he consents, or gives way to pressure, and with strong volition he insists, the intention being there without any urging. The difference can be seen in **37**:

37a She will bring her dog (We've asked her to and she has consented *or* She usually consents if you ask her)
37b She *will* bring her dog (There's no stopping her)

Many uses of *will* referring to future time are merely the predictive kind of knowledge modality. Thus *She will bring her dog* has another interpretation in which the speaker is predicting a future fact. In this case the volitional nature of the event is incidental; we assume she will bring it voluntarily since that is ordinarily how such a thing would happen. But in *The rain will be heavy* there is, of course, no possibility of reading a voluntary action into the clause.

3 We have spoken of ability and volition in connection with voluntary agents. These categories of modality could be extended to include also such expressions as those in **38** which are about the inherent properties of inert entities and situations (including animate beings when not acting voluntarily):

38a It can snow in January
38b This window can be tricky to open
38c This jug *will* keep falling over
38d Harold can be very obstinate
38e Harold *will* knock things over

Clearly the terms *ability* and *volition* would no longer be appropriate if our analysis were extended to cover these cases. But we may observe that these are only marginally modal in meaning. They have much in common with habitual aspect (see Chapter 16) and can be paraphrased with adjuncts like *always*, *usually* and *sometimes*:

39a It sometimes snows in January
39b This window is sometimes tricky to open
39c This jug is always falling over
39d Harold is sometimes very obstinate
39e Harold usually knocks things over

4 Like knowledge modalities, influence modalities can be glossed in a two-part expression. But this time the propositional part is expressed in a non-finite form:

40a You are permitted to have another piece of cake *or* It is permissible for you to have another piece of cake
40b Harold is able to touch the ceiling
40c Harold consents to be the first speaker
40d Harold is compelled to buy a new car *or* It is compulsory for Harold to buy a new car

The propositional part of the gloss gives the 'outcome' of the influence, e.g. having another piece of cake is the outcome of being permitted to have another piece of cake. The outcome cannot be located in time independently of the influence. Permission can only be permission to do something subsequently, and ability is a potential that can be realized only while the ability exists. So the time setting of the outcome is very different from the time setting of the proposition in a knowledge modality. (The point will again be taken up in Chapter 16.)

Exercise 8.3

Which of the following are knowledge and which influence modalities? Which could be taken in either way? Explain how.

1 He may be an MP.
2 Most of us can read.
3 Beethoven should be respected more.
4 These houses will actually fall down. (Appendix BII, ll. 61–2)
5 There must be some restriction.
6 That party might ultimately get in power.
7 It could only be construed as an incitement to disobey the law.
8 An Act passed for this purpose would contravene all constitutional precedent.
9 I wouldn't trust a murderer.
10 She needn't have hidden the key.
11 Thirteen letters in your name. That's very auspicious. You should be artistic.
12 I must have acted on your guidance.
13 It may end in your giving up the cannons for the sake of the Salvation Army.
14 I will even take part, if a trombone can be secured.
15 You needn't take orders from them.

8.6 Modality and negation

We have not yet looked at any modal clauses that are negative. Consider example **41**:

41 You must keep to the left

This can be negated in either of two ways, which are not equivalent. We can either say that it is not compulsory to keep to the left or that it is compulsory not to keep to the left:

42a You needn't keep to the left (It is not compulsory)
42b You mustn't keep to the left (It is compulsory not to)

Now it may be noticed that to say *It is not compulsory* is the same as saying *It is permissible not to*, and in fact that all expression of compulsion can be converted into expressions of permission by reversing the polarity of both the modality and the proposition. In Figures 32–35 we make use of the two-part glosses referred to above in sections 8.5(4) and 8.4(3). To take the sentence in Figure 33 as an example, *You needn't keep to the left* can be interpreted either as no compulsion to do

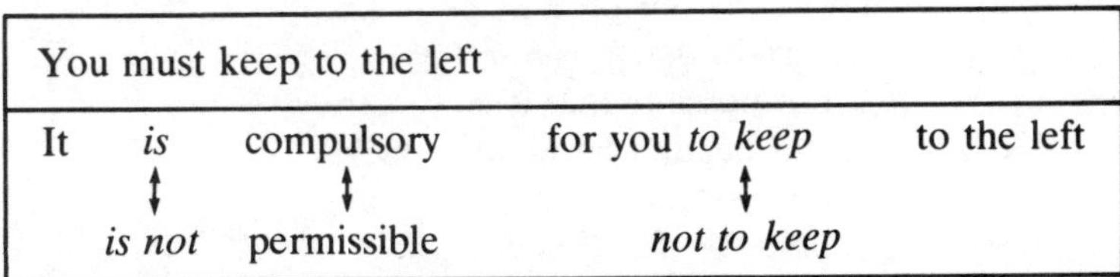

Figure 32

You needn't keep to the left				
It	*is not*	compulsory	for you *to keep*	to the left
	↕	↕	↕	
	is	permissible	*not to keep*	

Figure 33

You mustn't keep to the left				
It	*is*	compulsory	for you *not to keep*	to the left
	↕	↕	↕	
	is not	permissible	*to keep*	

Figure 34

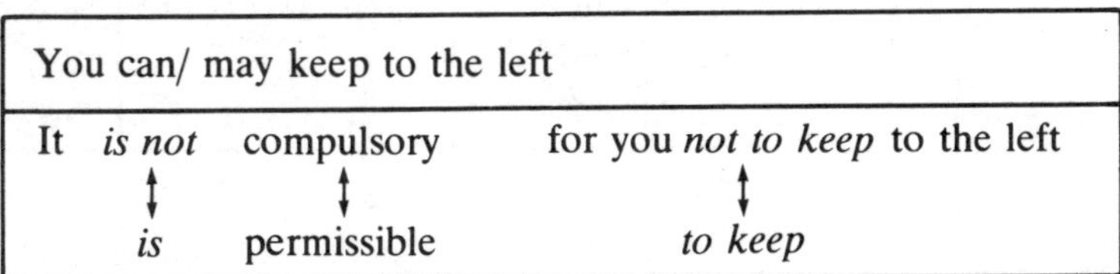

Figure 35

so or as permission not to do so, but this is not an ambiguity because these are two ways of saying the same thing.

There is a similar relation in the field of knowledge modality between expressions of possibility and expressions of certainty:

43a It must be in your pocket
It is certain that it is
It is not possible that it is not

43b It can't be in your pocket
It is certain that it is not
It is not possible that it is

43c It may not/needn't be in your pocket
It is not certain that it is
It is possible that it is not

43d It may/could be in your pocket
It is not certain that it isn't
It is possible that it is

Figure 36 shows the negative forms of modal verbs. It would have been possible to enter two negatives for many of the modal verbs, one for negating the proposition and one for negating the modality. However, since the same two forms would always appear elsewhere in the table, there would be an undesirable redundancy in doing this, so the table gives just the forms that negate the proposition. It may be noticed

	Knowledge		*Influence*	
Possibility	*conjecture:* may	may not	*permission:* may can	needn't
	inference: could	needn't	*ability:* can	can't
Probability/ certainty/ necessity	*conjecture:* will	won't	*volition:* will	won't
	inference: must	can't couldn't	*compulsion:* must	mustn't can't may not
	should ought	shouldn't oughtn't	should ought	shouldn't oughtn't

Figure 36 Negative modal verbs

that there is a certain amount of asymmetry in the patterns shown in Figure 36. First, *musn't* is not to be found in the knowledge column, but only in the influence column. (Some regional dialects do have a knowledge *mustn't*, e.g. Lancashire *We mustn't have come that way*.) A foreign learner of the language might well be puzzled why the negative of *We must be early* is sometimes *We mustn't be early* and sometimes *We can't be early*. Second, *can* does not appear anywhere in the knowledge column except in the negative *can't*. This is because people do not say *It can be in your pocket* meaning 'It is possible that it is in your pocket'. Finally, *may not* occupies different places in the two columns. *May* means either 'is possible' or 'is permitted to'. In knowledge modality *may not* means 'is possible that not'; but in influence modality *may not* does not mean 'is permitted not to' but 'is not permitted to'.

Exercise 8.4

1 *There could be a lot of expense involved* (meaning 'It is possible that there is a lot of expense involved'). This clause can be negated in either of two ways. One negates the modality and the other negates the proposition. What are these negative forms? What is the form that negates both the modality *and* the proposition?

2 Do the same with *They can walk on the grass* in the permission interpretation.

8.7 Subjective and objective modality

Modality is an important means of indicating what kind of communicative act is being performed in speaking. It shows particular kinds of involvement in the exchange with the addressee. It is for this reason that the topic has been brought in at this point in the book immediately after the chapters on mood. To the extent that a modal verb reflects the speaker's involvement in the act of communication we will say it is being used subjectively. But if it is being used only in order to make mention of some possibility, or certainty, or sanction, etc: to which the speaker himself is not necessarily committed, then it is being used objectively. The distinction is far more clear in influence than in knowledge modalities, so we will start with the influence type.

Many expressions of permission and compulsion are ordinarily intended as attempts on the part of the speaker to control people's behaviour:

44a Periodicals may not be removed from the reading room
44b Our industrial leaders should consult the workers
44c Bill must come home before midnight
44d The children can have some more cake

In **44a**, for instance, it is the library authorities who accept responsibility for the decision that removing periodicals is not allowed. This is clearly a subjective use of *may*. Similar remarks could be made about the other examples. When such a modality is interrogative, the addressee is being requested to make a decision:

45 Can the children have some more cakes? (Please make a decision on this point)

Influence modality of this kind has much in common in its communicative force with imperative mood. (See Chapter 7 on imperative mood and the role of decider.) However it is sometimes possible to take these modal verbs as denoting some necessity or sanction which is an objective fact quite independently of any decision made by the speaker himself, who is therefore not taking any responsibility for it, as in **46**:

46 In polar interrogatives the operator must be placed in front of the subject

I do not know in what proportion of occurrences modal verbs are used objectively, or to what extent non-modal verbs are used subjectively, but the following set of examples seems to show fairly clearly that where there is a straight contrast between modal verbs and non-modal verbs the modal ones are subjective and the non-modal objective:

47a The secretary must let me know the result tomorrow (I say so)
47b The secretary has to let me know the result tomorrow (It has been decided; not necessarily my decision)
47c You can go now (I say so)
47d You're allowed to go now (That is established; not my decision)

One way in which the modal verbs are certainly used objectively is when they are used in reported clauses, rather than in a free clause. (For a further explanation of this type of construction see section 16.1's discussion of example **17**, and sections 20.1–20.3.) It is quite clear that in **48** the speaker is not accepting responsibility for the decision:

48a It has been decided *that Bill may stay out late*
48b Mary said *that we must let her know where we were*

Turning now to modalities of volition and ability, we find that the primary use of modal verbs here is objective:

49a Bill won't answer the door (He has refused)
49b Bill can speak Japanese (He has that ability)

In **49** Bill's refusal and ability are objective facts; Bill may have made some decision, but there is no suggestion that the speaker has had anything to do with it. On the other hand, it is possible to convert this kind of expression to subjective use, especially when the subject is first or second person, or when the mood is interrogative as in **50**:

50a Can you open the window? (Not merely a matter of your ability; I'm hoping you will decide to do so)
50b I can hold the door for you. (Not just that I am able, but I'm actually offering)
50c Will you turn off the light, please? (Not just a question of whether you consent, but an attempt to get you to do so)

In knowledge modality, it seems that the primary use of modal verbs is subjective. The speaker is making some point about the probability of the truth of some proposition, and this is necessarily his own judgment. If he says *The train must be late*, we know he is not making a claim to direct knowledge, but has merely inferred it. Correspondingly, in interrogative mood it is the addressee that is being asked to assess the evidence:

51 Could the train be late? (Do you see a possibility?)

It is difficult to see how such utterances as these could be other than subjective. To state that a possibility or a certainty exists, is to commit oneself to a belief in it. But the modal verbs can certainly be used in reported clauses in an objective way, as in example **52**:

> **52** People are saying that the train may be late
> (*The speaker could add without contradiction*:
> But they are wrong: I know there is no such
> possibility)

Exercise 8.5

In which of the following is the modal verb used subjectively, and in which is it used objectively?

1 Mary is very clever. She can decorate a room in half a day.
2 Can you tell me the time please?
3 Don't lock the door. They might not have a key.
4 They needn't bother to let me know if they don't want to.
5 Mary won't tell her story; I've asked her.
6 It's possible it will rain tomorrow.
7 He told her she should save her money.
8 This place will be up for sale next month.
9 Jim ought to be grateful.
10 Answering a question the Prime Minister said the circumstances were unusual. Everybody must take care to avoid unncessary wastage.

8.8 Modality and past tense

An important factor in the distinction between subjective and objective modality is that it is only objective modalities that can be located in past time, or in fact in any time but the present. The speaker-involvement which subjectiveness is all about is involvement in the utterance that the speaker is making 'here and now'. Consequently when past tense forms occur in a subjective modality, they cannot be understood as having reference to past time. In these cases past tense has to be understood as meaning some other kind of remoteness than remoteness in time. The term *past* is misleading here. We would do well to remember that *present* also contrasts with *absent*, and that the Latinate term *preterite*, usually glossed as 'past tense', is derived from a spatial metaphor literally translated as 'gone by'. Past tense has to do with absence or remoteness or distance, either in time or in some more figurative sense. In subjective modality past tense imparts a kind of tentativeness:

53a The train might be late
(A more remote possibility than *may*)

53b That would be Bill's wife, I suppose
(A more tentative supposition than with *will*)

53c Might/could I open the window?
(A more deferential request than with *may* or *can*)

53d Could you move along a little please?
(This is a subjective, ability expression, more deferential than with *can*)

53e He could start coming earlier perhaps
(A tentative suggestion of subjective ability)

53f Would you turn off the light, please?
(A similarly tentative request)

However, there are some expressions of subjective modality where what are obviously past tense forms in their historical origin have nowadays no possible contrast with a present tense. Whether or not there is some sense of tentativeness in *could* and *should* in examples **24** and **25** (in the knowledge interpretation indicated), there is little justification for treating these as past tense forms.

The matter of time reference in modal clauses will be taken up again in Chapter 16, where, among other things, we shall deal with the past tense of objective modalities.

Exercise 8.6

Rewrite the following examples, preserving the sense as far as possible but using a modal verb. For instance *it is possible that the vicar is ill* can be rewritten as *the vicar may be ill*. Some of them may have more than one plausible rewriting. Decide whether the modality is of the knowledge or the influence type.

1 It is possible for democracy to be intolerant of minorities.
2 It is possible that democracy is intolerant of minorities.
3 (He said) he was going to be the happiest man in the world.
4 Presumably they weren't very pleased.
5 It's impossible for me to live for long without some kind of luxury.
6 (I suppose) it's not too late to change, is it?
7 It's obvious he'll agree.
8 He's obliged to agree.

9 You're not allowed to give them food.
10 It's almost certain there'll be some tickets available.
11 Surely the Second Coming is at hand.
12 No doubt it's Harold that fetches the crowds.
13 Harold has volunteered to mow the lawn.
14 It's possible he has been delayed.
15 It's possible he will have been delayed.
16 It's possible he was delayed.

Exercise 8.7
What do you make of the italicized part of: We*'d better* be careful?

The following data may suggest some lines of investigation:
1 *He has better put them away.
2 *He is having better put them away.
3 *We may have better be careful.
4 *They could have better go.
5 He'd better be standing there.
6 He'd better have gone by the time we arrive.
7 We'd better be careful, hadn't we?
8 You'd better not let them see you.
9 You hadn't better let them see you.
10 Had we better be careful?
11 *You'd bettern't be careless.
12 *We'd better be careful, bettern't we.
13 *Had better we be careful?

8.9 A note on *shall*

No attempt has yet been made to give a systematic account of the verb *shall*. Its place in the system is difficult to define, partly because there is considerable variation from one dialect to another, and partly because it is difficult to find parallels for it. The following remarks are therefore tentative.

Partly, *shall* is an optional first person alternative to *will* in the knowledge sense, used by some speakers:

54 I shall/will be in London this time next week

But it also has another sense illustrated in **55**:

55a He shall regret this

Influence	*volition*: will *determination*: shall *compulsion*: must

Figure 37

55b You shall have another piece of cake if you're good
55c Ireland shall have its freedom

In these uses *shall* expresses determination, either subjectively (the speaker's decision) as in **55a** and **55b**, or objectively as in a natural interpretation of **55c**. In the latter case the event is seen as ordained or predestined. This appears to be a kind of influence modality. Whether or not this is so, it belongs to a rather rhetorical style of language, especially in the objective sense. A usage which is certainly not rhetorical, however, but extremely colloquial is the interrogative with first person subject:

56a Shall I open the window?
56b Shall we go to the pictures?

This is a subjective use of *shall*. An appeal is being made to the addressee to determine whether the event shall take place. I tentatively suggest entering *shall* in the table of influence modalities as shown in Figure 37.

9 Adjuncts and prepositional groups

9.1 Adjuncts and complements

In Chapter 3 a broad distinction was drawn between adjuncts and complements. It was pointed out that the criteria there given for making the distinction were fairly crude, but that they were easily applied to such elements as those in italics in **1**:

1a Nationalism may not be *political* | *nevertheless*
1b We are repairing *the roof* | *at the moment*
1c They *slowly* lowered *the curtain*
1d They have awarded *Bill* | *a scholarship* | *for his excellent work*
1e He is *busy* | *tomorrow*

Exercise 9.1.
Assign the symbol C or A to each of the italicized items in **1**.

In Chapter 3 it was promised that the notion 'essential' v. 'inessential' element in a proposition would be analysed in more detail. We now undertake this analysis.

9.2 Linking adjuncts

The kind of element that is least essential to the proposition is the one that contributes no propositional content at all:

2a *Now* take the case of opera (Appendix BII, l. 45)
2b We *perhaps* need some more bread
2c *Frankly*, that film bored me to tears
2d The theatre is very healthy *on the whole* (Appendix BII, l. 47)
2e . . . and, *of course*, the whole thing'll be moving (Appendix BI, ll. 42–3)

Such elements as these are recognizable by their inability to receive the kind of focus of attention that is illustrated in **3**:

3a Are you repairing *the roof* at the moment, or is it the chimney?
3b Are you repairing the roof *at the moment*, or at some other time?
3c Are you *repairing* the roof at the moment, or are you doing something else to it?
3d We're only repairing *the roof* at the moment, not the chimney as well
3e We're only repairing the roof *at the moment*; we shan't still be doing it next week
3f We're only *repairing* the roof at the moment; we're not rebuilding it
3g We're not repairing *the roof* at the moment; we're repairing the chimney

In all of these some part of the proposition receives the focus of attention, and this part is italicized. When such clauses are spoken (or read aloud) the intonation makes it clear where the focus is. It does this by placing the tonic appropriately (see Appendix A). Any attempt to do this for the adjuncts in **2** will meet with failure, as the following ill-formed examples show:

4a *Do we need some more bread *perhaps*, or do we need it certainly?
4b *That film didn't bore me to tears *frankly*, it did so regrettably

The kind of meaning that these extra-propositional adjuncts have is suggested by the name 'linking adjunct'; they make no addition to the idea that is being communicated, but signal the way the speaker is presenting that idea. Either they express his own comment on it (comment adjunct), or they make it clear how the idea connects with other ideas already put across (connective adjunct). Items which commonly express the speaker's comment are *perhaps, possibly, certainly, really, frankly, hopefully, interestingly*, and some which express the type of coherence with the preceding discourse are *nevertheless, indeed, likewise, however*. More formal tests for distinguishing comment adjuncts from connective adjuncts, and for distinguishing various subtypes of each might be suggested, but here we must pass over this detail.

One thing that must be noticed is that many adverbial and prepositional groups can readily occur in different functions. (The point has been made before, and it will come up again and again, that it is important to distinguish between the grammatical class that an item belongs to and the function that it fulfils when it occurs as an element in a larger construction.) For instance, in **5–7** the **(a)** examples contain linking adjuncts and the **(b)** examples do not:

5a *Happily* there wasn't much mess (comment)
5b The children ran away *happily*
6a *On top of all that* she burnt the sauce (connective)
6b *On top of all that* she put the sauce
7a He *frankly* doesn't care (comment)
7b He *frankly* told us what he thought

Exercise 9.2

(a) Distinguish linking adjuncts from other adjuncts in sentences **1–14**:

1 Conceivably there won't be any trouble.
2 Did you find the way however?
3 He purposely crashed the car.
4 He spoke clearly.
5 They have arranged the furniture conveniently.
6 They have clearly arranged the furniture conveniently.
7 He conveniently didn't stop to talk.
8 They laid the table anyhow.
9 Anyhow, what do you think?
10 We shall have to be careful, though.
11 I break the eggs thus.
12 Thus the eggs were broken.
13 They divided the cake equally.
14 Equally, the loss will be very small.

(b) Which of the linking adjuncts in these sentences are comment adjuncts, and which are connective adjuncts?

(c) What difference in speech corresponds to the difference in punctuation between: *They laid the table anyhow* and *They laid the table, anyhow*. (See Appendix A on intonation for a discussion of this subject and a way of presenting your answer.)

9.3 Inherence in the process

In Chapter 3 it was offered as a test for adjuncts that they answer questions in *how? when? where?* and *why?* while complements answer questions in *who?* or *what?* We will call this the WH test. The reason why the WH test is satisfying in a large number of cases is that when we come to ask which ideas are essential to a process and which are merely detail we usually find that people and things are most inherently bound up in the process, while times, places, manners of action and reasons are only circumstances or conditions in which the process exists. For instance, the process of eating has to have a thing eaten and an eater, but where and when the eating takes place is a matter of detail.

8 The boy ate an apple yesterday in his bedroom

Thus **8** has two essential participants, *the boy* (which is the subject) and *an apple*, and two circumstantial elements, *yesterday* and *in his bedroom*. We conclude that *an apple* is C and that *yesterday* and *in his bedroom* are both A.

It has to be acknowledged, however, that the type of WH-interrogative is a separate matter from whether or not the element in question is inherent in the process. For some processes are essentially concerned with place or movement, and in these, therefore, items specifying place or direction cannot be considered mere detail. The italicized items in **9** supply information that could be asked for with *where?* but this information is an inherent part of the process, a fact that is not surprising when one considers the meanings of the verbs that are chosen. Insofar as these elements are inherent in the process, they are more like complements than adjuncts, and that is how I propose to treat them.

9a She went *to the cupboard*
9b He turned *off the path*
9c He has put the bread *on a plate*
9d They sent a report *to a newspaper*
9e He left his hat *in our hall*
9f His hat is *in our hall*
9g The voting takes place *in the lobbies*
9h Dickens lived *in London*

Some of these verbs that can take a place-complement can equally well take a time-complement, though they seem to be relatively few in number:

10a Dickens lived *in the nineteenth century*
10b The vote took place *last night*
10c The meeting is *on Tuesday*

Exercise 9.3

Pick out elements expressing ideas of time and place, i.e. questionable with *when* and *where*. Which of them are inherent in the process expressed by the clause, and which are merely circumstantial?

1 He kept his savings in an old sock.
2 His savings are in an old sock.
3 The thunderstorms approach in the evening.
4 The accident happened at five o'clock.
5 He kept the change last week.
6 The Attorney General remains in the Government.
7 The insects tend to react to each other. (BI, ll. 30–31)
8 He drove at a frightening speed.
9 The papers are delivered at 8 o'clock.
10 I wrote the postcard on the bus.
11 The bus veered to the right.
12 She fell over by the gate.

9.4 Prepositional groups

In Chapter 3 it was stated that the element 'adjunct' is often fulfilled by prepositional groups like *with kindness, as a joke, at the beginning of the century, by the door*, etc. It was also stated that nominal groups usually function as complements and not as adjuncts. But whether prepositional groups can function as complements was a question that was carefully avoided. Some grammarians take the criterion of componence as decisive: if it is a prepositional group it is not a complement but an adjunct. This has the merit of being a simple criterion to apply, but it goes against the principle that considerations of syntax and meaning should take priority over componence. In the present analysis of English clauses, I allow prepositional groups to be complements (when they pass the appropriate syntactic and semantic tests) but concede that there are important differences between complements that are prepositional and complements that are not.

There are two ways in which we may find a prepositional group to be a complement. One of these has already been presented; namely, where, although it can be questioned with *where?* or *when?* it is inherent in the process (see examples **9** and **10**). The other way is illustrated in **11**:

11a The Governors presented the chairman *with a medal*
11b He blamed the management *for the dispute*
11c He looked *at the directory*
11d We cannot cope *with the work*
11e They will consent *to any such arrangement*
11f I'm going to send a message *to the professor*
11g This law doesn't apply *to other people*

According to the WH test all of these are of the *who?/what?* type, but there is a complication since the preposition is not included in what is questioned but is left standing as shown in **12**:

12a What did the Governors present the chairman *with*?
12b *With* what did the Governors present the chairman?

The difference between these forms is merely one of formality, the second being the more formal in style. Similar results are obtained for the other examples in **11**. As far as this criterion goes, then, we might count these prepositional groups as complements. It is fairly clear that they are also inherent in the process; for instance we cannot say *They will consent* without taking an interest in what it is they will consent to. In this connection it may be pointed out that there are interesting correspondences between some of these examples and synonymous clauses using the same verb:

13a The Governors presented the chairman *with a medal*
13b The Governors presented a medal *to the chairman*

If *the chairman* is a complement in **13a** there is a strong case for counting *to the chairman* as a complement in **13b**; and the same goes for *a medal* and *with a medal*.

Exercise 9.4

Which of the italicized elements correspond to a prepositional *who/what* interrogative, and which to a *where/when/how/why* interrogative?

1 He always charged the customers *for/second/helpings of coffee.*
2 This letter is *for you.*
3 He attended *to the patients.*
4 He had to use force *on the door.*
5 I wrote a postcard *on the bus.*
6 He turned the power off *at the mains.*
7 He spoke *with discretion.*
8 He could read *at an early age.*
9 I wrote my name *on the envelope.*
10 They were not entrusted by the public *with such a task.*

9.5 Obligatory expression

The most frequently given characterization of the element adjunct is that it can be left out without detriment to the structure remaining. To put it another way, we ask whether the function which an item fulfils in a structure is obligatorily expressed. The answer is clear enough in some instances:

14a Bill read the newspaper *quickly*
14b *In the end*, we're bound to be successful
14c The UFO sightings have been written up *in detail* (Appendix BI, ll. 54–5)
14d I'm going to put salt *in the potatoes*

I take it that most English speakers would agree that **14a, b, c** have omissible elements and that **14d** does not.

There are, however, scores of cases where the criterion cannot so easily be applied. The reasons for our hesitation how to answer the test may be various. Sometimes it is not clear to what extent the omission of the item renders the clause dependent on its context for its interpretation. At other times it seems that an item may be omitted only provided that some other item is not, and it then becomes necessary to decide which of the two shall be given priority. In **15** I offer a list of examples in which there is, in my opinion, some cause for hesitation:

15a I blame the farmers *for this mess*
15b He turned *into a doorway*
15c The citizens cannot cope *with the new way of life*
15d Bill contributed fifty pence *to the fund*
15e They are generous *with their time*
15f He objected *to the suggestion*
15g He gave £10 *to Bill* | *for the ticket*
15h I'm going to put the books *away* | *in the cupboard*
15i He accused her *of insincerity*

The fact that the criterion of obligatory expression so often does not yield very definite results does not, of course, prevent us from reaching a decision on whether an element is an adjunct or not. We have seen that there are other criteria to fall back on. What we must do is decide which of the tests and how many of them an element must satisfy in order to count as a complement. The following section summarizes the criteria and reaches a decision on this point.

9.6 Summary of criteria

Five criteria have been discussed for distinguishing more essential from less essential elements within a clause. (It is assumed that S and P are essential, and these are not brought into the present discussion.)

1 Can the item be treated as exclusive focus of attention? (See examples in **3**.)
2 Is the item expressive of something inherent in the process referred to?
3 Can the item be questioned with *who/what*? (including prepositional *who/what* forms)?
4 Does the item have a function that is obligatorily expressed?
5 Is the item, in itself, nominal/adjectival or not?

Any item that fails test 1 is on that account excluded from further consideration and counted not simply as an adjunct, but as a linking adjunct – the most peripheral type of all.

Any item that satisfies test 2 or 3 or 4, or any combination of these, is a complement. If it fails all three tests it is an adjunct. This means that some complements, those that pass one or two but not all three of the tests, are on the way towards being adjuncts. There are, therefore, quite a few different kinds of complement; the differences will be discussed in the next chapter.

The fifth test is, in my analysis, relevant to distinguishing types of complement from each other rather than distinguishing complements from adjuncts; but it is mentioned here since some grammarians give it a higher status, such that items that fail test 5 are on that account ruled out of the complement category.

The application of these criteria is illustrated in Figure 38, which refers to examples **16–23**.

16 *Unfortunately*(a) they died *last year*(c)
17 He objected *to the proposals*(j) *with all his strength*(b)
18 The pound has risen *to its highest level for two years*(e)
19 The grass was cut *by the town council*(f)
20 Those pigeons are *on the cabbages*(g)
21 He gave *Bill*(l) *the ticket* (n) *as a bribe* (d)
22 The bottle stood *at the back of the shelf*(h)
23 He gave *£10*(m) *to Bill*(k) *for the ticket*(i)

Item		*Tests* 1	2	3	4	5	*Category*
unfortunately	(a)	–	–	–	–	–	A
with all his strength	(b)	+	–	–	–	–	A
last year	(c)	+	–	–	–	–	A
as a bribe	(d)	+	–	–	–	–	A
to its highest level for two years	(e)	+	+	?	?	–	C
by the town council	(f)	+	+	+	–	–	C
on the cabbages	(g)	+	+	–	+	–	C
at the back of the shelf	(h)	+	+	–	+	–	C
for the ticket	(i)	+	?	+	?	–	C
to the proposals	(j)	+	+	+	?	–	C
to Bill	(k)	+	+	+	?	–	C
Bill	(l)	+	+	+	+	+	C
£10	(m)	+	+	+	+	+	C
the ticket	(n)	+	+	+	+	+	C

Figure 38

Exercise 9.5
Analyse the following clauses using the following symbols:

S   subject
P   predicator
A^l linking adjunct
A   any other kind of adjunct
C^o object complement
C^i intensive complement
C   any other kind of complement (as yet undifferentiated) – mostly realized by prepositional groups

The first fifteen examples below are divided into constituents. In the remainder you are expected to make this division for yourself.

1 Their lack of understanding | was | apparent | in their behaviour.
2 He | neglected | his duties.
3 In truth | John | had been | that day | to Barnes Common.
4 The finest specimens | he | would bring | home.
5 The determination to possess objects that even surpassed these | tormented | the young man.
6 He | never | talked | to anyone | about his serious ambitions.
7 The groups | changed | more swiftly.
8 Now and then | a twig | snapped.
9 She | stood | in the yard | with her hands to her hair.
10 He | drove | the cart | over the cobbles.
11 He | passed | his hand | over the dog's back.
12 He | looked | at it | admiringly.
13 He | will (never) bother | you | with enquiries.
14 The man | peered | doubtfully | into the basket.
15 The only picture | was | an enlarged photograph.
16 I call him by his first name.
17 They arrived at the apartment door.
18 She had changed her costume some time before.
19 He regarded her intently with his head on one side.
20 She lowered her voice again.
21 You were crazy about him for a while.

22 The bottle of whisky was in constant demand.
23 It pulled me into my chair.
24 On Mondays eight servants toiled all day with mops.
25 A tinkling sound was made intermittently by the band.
26 They looked a little hungry.
27 They talked in earnest voices.
28 He was a German spy during the war.
29 It was making me uneasy that night.
30 As a matter of fact, they're absolutely real.
31 He smiled understandingly for an instant.
32 Then she answered me with a wan smile.
33 He drifted coolly out of nowhere.
34 She filled the pause with gasping, broken sobs.
35 One of the girls in yellow was playing the piano.
36 They harshly confined the prisoners to their cells.

9.7 Adjunct positions

Figure 39 shows four main positions that adjuncts may occupy in the sequence of clause elements. It also shows two minor positions, (x) and (y).

Position 1

The initial position is thematic, which means that it is occupied by what the speaker is announcing as his topic. For an adjunct to be placed first is usually rather emphatic as shown in **24**:

24a *Noisily*, they shut the gates
24b *At the last minute*, everybody was disappointed

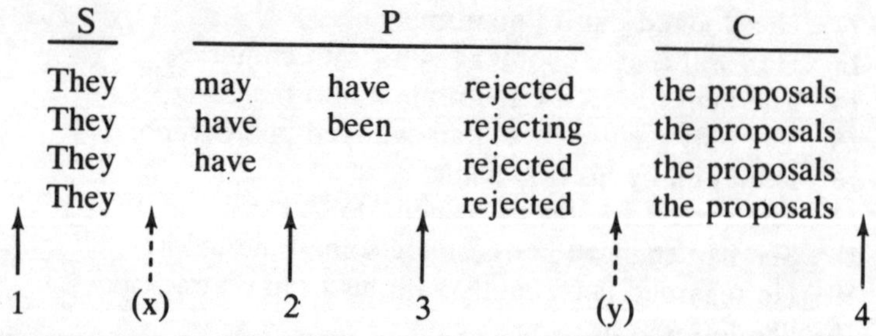

Figure 39

24c *Reluctantly*, we left him behind
24d *In London*, you liked walking

However, **25** shows that it is of much less special significance for a linking adjunct to be placed first:

25a *Naturally*, they may have rejected the proposals
25b *However*, she looked well

Position 2

The second position, shown in **26**, can be labelled *post-operator* since it comes immediately after the operator, when there is one. (For a definition of operator see section 5.3 above.)

26a They may *often* have rejected the proposals
26b They have *sometimes* been rejecting the proposals
26c We have *reluctantly* left him behind
26d He *simply* obeys his party conference

This second position includes the position after the main verb when this is an operator:

27a	She	is	*still*		unwell
27b	She	has	*often*	been	unwell
		(x)	2		

It would produce a rather unusual effect if the adjunct in **27** were placed in position (x), in front of the operator. But this is what happens if the operator is under focus and therefore receives the intonational tonic:

28a They sometimes <u>have</u> been rejecting the proposals
28b She still <u>is</u> unwell

(NB In these examples the underlining indicates the tonic syllable; see Appendix A.) Position 2 and position (x) cannot be distinguished from each other when there is no operator; in fact, position (x), it could be argued, depends upon there being an operator. Therefore, when there is no operator we will call this position 2, as in **26d**.

Position 3

There are some adjuncts for which position 3 is normal. These are among those which Quirk *et al*. 1972 (pp. 438–59) call *intensifiers*. This name is intended to describe their meaning, since these adjuncts express the intensity of the action (sometimes diminishing rather than increasing it). Examples of this position are given in **29**:

29a He *utterly* despises them
29b They have *completely* rejected the proposals
29c He'll be *bitterly* regretting his action
29d He may have *little* realized the trouble he was causing

It should be pointed out that position 3 often does not differ from position 2; there has to be more than one auxiliary verb for the difference to be realized. It is noteworthy that there is often a high degree of idiomatic bonding in such combinations as *bitterly regret, utterly despise*, and *little realize*.

Position 4

The fourth position could be described as *post-predicator*, as long as we understand that this also means after C^o or C^i when there is such a complement present:

30a He | has been speaking | *for two hours*
S P A

30b They | may have rejected | the proposals | *cheerfully*
S P C^o A

30c She | has been | unwell | *all this year*
S P C^i A

At this point the description of adjunct positions becomes rather detailed and tentative since there is a tendency for several adjuncts to come crowding into this final slot, and in that case there arises the question of what positions they take up relative to each other. The usual rule that is given is 'manner + place + time' as in **31**:

31a We laughed uproariously until midnight (manner + time)
31b He worked in the garden yesterday (place + time)
31c He worked hard in the garden (manner + place)

A complicating factor, however, is that adverbial groups tend to come before prepositional groups even when the latter are complements:

32a We laughed uproariously at our mistake
32b She went quickly to the cupboard
32c He blames the management very much for the dispute

This matter will not be investigated further here.

A final point about position 4 is that the normal sequence may be disturbed if C is a long and expanded constituent. It will then tend to get moved to final position at the expense of the adjunct as in **33**, where the C^{O} is *the proposals that the select committee put into their latest report*. In this case the adjunct *cheerfully* occupies position (y).

33 They may have rejected cheerfully the proposals that the select committee put into their latest report.

9.8 Manner adjuncts and action adjuncts

The term 'manner adjunct' has a wider and a narrower sense. The oldest tradition is to call manner adjuncts those which answer a question that contains *how?* plus an action verb, e.g. *How does he cure his patients? Surgically*. This would make all of the examples in **34** manner adjuncts. However, it is evident that strictly speaking only some of them are proper manner adjuncts and that the others are adjuncts of means or instrument:

34a He cures his patients *surgically* (*means*: by means of surgery)
34b Use the paint *sparingly* (*manner*: in a sparing manner)
34c You cook them *slowly* (*manner*)
34d You cook them *in salt water* (*means*)
34e They write *imaginatively* (*manner*)
34f They write *with ball-point pens* (*instrument*)
34g They got here *by bus* (*means*)

In **34** 'manner adjunct' is used in its narrower sense. It is to this sort of adjunct that the present section applies. Although the correspondence is not exact, manner adjuncts proper tend to be adverbial groups, while expressions of means and instrument are often prepositional.

Most adverbial groups that can occur in Position 4 as manner adjuncts can also occur in Position 2, but if they do so they may make a very different contribution to the meaning of the whole, as example **35** shows:

35a He filled the bucket *lazily*
35b He *lazily* filled the bucket
35c He *lazily* sat in an easy chair

In **35a** and **35b** *lazily* is easily interpreted as a manner adjunct, answering a *how*-question: 'he did it lazily, though he might have done it energetically'. In **35c** *lazily* does not differentiate the manner in which he sat in the chair, but rather describes the whole action as lazy: 'what he did was lazy; he sat in an easy chair' or 'his action was lazy; he sat in an easy chair' or even 'he was lazy; he sat in an easy chair'. We will call the adjunct in **35c** an action adjunct. This type of adjunct can be identified by means of the kind of paraphrase that has been given above.

Exercise 9.6
Distinguish manner adjuncts from action adjuncts in the following:

1 It had been raining *steadily* for hours.
2 He spoke *hesitantly*.
3 He *rudely* shouted in my ear.
4 They *resentfully* rejected the offer.
5 He *despondently* gazed out of the window.
6 He gazed *despondently* out of the window.
7 He broke the window *deliberately*.
8 He *deliberately* broke the window.
9 He met his enemies *bravely*.
10 He *bravely* met his enemies.
11 They *carefully* picked their way across the stream.

Judging from the kind of examples that are presented in exercise 9.6, there are two factors that influence the interpretation of the adjuncts in question: the first factor is the position of the adjunct and the second is the meaning of the adverb in relation to the rest of the proposition. For instance, *deliberately* is very unlikely to be intended as meaning 'in a deliberate manner' when it goes along with *break the window* (contrast with its meaning in *He spoke the words deliberately*, i.e.

'with a careful articulation'); it is more likely to mean 'intentionally, not accidentally'. So *deliberately* will be more likely to be taken as an action adjunct whether it comes in position 2 or position 4. On the other hand, the relation of *despondently* to *gaze out of the window* is less stable since we can either take *despondently* as a way of gazing out of the window (contrasting with *anxiously* or *absently*), or we can take gazing out of the window as a way of being despondent, a despondent act in itself. The way in which we understand *despondently* is therefore influenced by the position it occupies; in position 2 it is an action adjunct ('what he did was despondent: he gazed out of the window') and in position 4 it is a manner adjunct ('he gazed out of the window in a despondent manner rather than in some other way').

Action adjuncts fall into two types: those that can come under focus and those that cannot. Those in **36** can come under focus:

36a Did he *deliberately* break the window (or was it accidental)?

36b He didn't *voluntarily* send the money back (he had to be forced)

But in **37** *bravely* cannot come under focus without losing the status of action adjunct:

37 He *bravely* entered the burning house

As soon as we focus upon *bravely* it has to be taken as a manner adjunct:

38 He didn't *bravely* enter the burning house (it was in fear and trembling)

Many of the type that cannot come under focus come very close to being comment adjuncts, especially if they use some evaluative word like *bravely, foolishly* or *cleverly* rather than a word that is more objectively descriptive, e.g. *noisily, despondently* or *hesitantly*.

9.9 Summary

Example **39** gives the principal types of adjunct distinguished in the above discussion:

39 *linking*	(i) *comment*:	This would *no doubt* make it difficult
	(ii) *connective*:	This would *nevertheless* make it difficult
action:		They have *wisely* applied for a grant
		They have *accidently* dropped a crate
intensifying:		He is *absolutely* detesting it
manner:		They responded *courteously*
place:		He has spent all his money *abroad*
time:		He came home *last night*

Exercise 9.7

Using the above terminology, identify the types of adjunct italicized in the following examples:

1 There are too many unwanted dollars in circulation *outside America*.
2 They *openly* made attempts to influence the outcome of the trial.
3 *On tour*, the play didn't have much success.
4 *Perhaps* you wouldn't mind waiting for a few minutes.
5 She *very kindly* offered me a part in a play.
6 Once you have done that, you have *totally* undermined the constitutional rule of law.
7 Few people want to hold dollars *for long*.
8 Selling, *moreover*, has forced the price lower and lower.
9 I must *reluctantly* refuse to comply with your request.
10 I think that something happened to him *in the first war*.
11 He stole the goods *openly*.
12 She always spoke *kindly* to newcomers.

10 Complementation

10.1 Transitive and intensive clauses

In this chapter we shall see how clauses differ from each other in respect of the presence or absence of complements of various kinds. At this point it is necessary to remind the reader of the clause network that appears in Figure 8 above. The part of the network that deals with features that are realized by the presence of complements is given again in Figure 40.

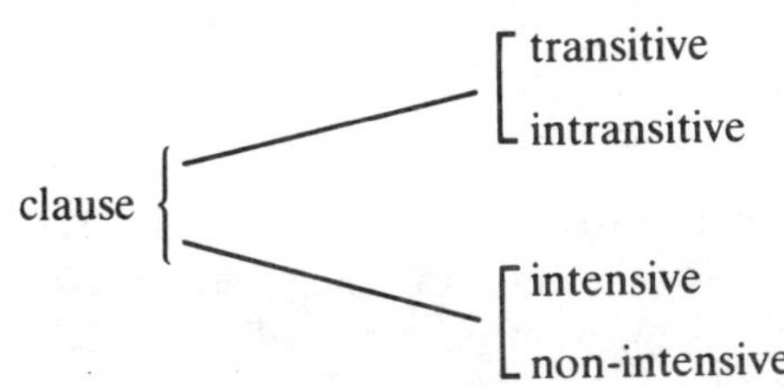

Figure 40

The four types of clause that are distinguished by means of this network are illustrated in **1**:

1a *intransitive non-intensive*: The car | has crashed
S P

1b *intransitive intensive*: The car | is | new
S P C^i

1c *transitive non-intensive*: The car | hit | a tree
S P C^o

1d *transitive intensive*: Harry | found | the car | useful
S P C^o C^i

Clauses that are intransitive and non-intensive need not detain us, since they contain no complement. The other three types are the subject matter of the next three sections.

10.2 Intensive clauses

Semantically the main characteristic of an intensive clause is that its proposition is concerned with the existence, identity or character of the subject. What is said about the subject is something that helps us to place it in our scheme of things.

Structurally considered, an intensive clause can exist without any lexical verb as predicator. In English the lexically empty verb *be* is used. The traditional name for this function of *be* is the *copula*. The copula performs a purely structural, linking function; all the lexical content resides in the subject and the complement, whether this is nominal, adjectival, prepositional or adverbial.

2 S P C^i

Bill | is | { **2a** tall
2b a policeman
2c the one in the raincoat
2d in the garden
2e away }

Some kinds of intensive clause have other verbs than *be*, and these verbs may have lexical meaning, but even so they only add something extra to what is essentially the intensive relation between S and C:

3a Bill grew tall
3b Bill became a policeman
3c Bill came into the garden

There are three basic types of intensive clause, which I shall call ascriptive, equative and locative:

4a *ascriptive*: That novel | is | very long
S P C^i

4b *equative*: Bill | is | the one in the raincoat
S P C^i

4c *locative*: Bill | is | in the garden
S P C^i

In the ascriptive type of intensive clause the complement is an attribute to the subject. Semantically it has the function of stating the significance or value of the subject by ascribing to it a property or function, or placing it in a certain class:

5a Bill is tall
5b Bill is a policeman
5c Bill is the head of the local force

(**5c** is to be taken in the sense that it describes Bill's occupation: 'that is what he does'. Contrast with **11d**.) In the majority of cases the C is an adjectival (**6**) or nominal (**7**) group:

6a 'The Times' is *quite expensive*
6b The following consideration is also *important*

7a 'The Times' is *a daily newspaper*
7b Old King Cole was *a merry old soul*

However, sometimes prepositional groups or members of even other classes occur at C. Example **8** gives sentences containing miscellaneous items at C:

8a Long skirts are *in fashion* again
8b Some of the pictures are *of great interest*
8c Bill is *in the police*
8d She is *in good health*
8e These strawberries are *for today's picnic*
8f The moral obligation of a minister is *to the crown*
8g The tap is *on*

Reversing the roles of subject and ascriptive complement is not possible; that is, even though the C may sometimes be brought into initial position, it remains a C. The subject cannot be the attribute:

9a Important | also | is | the following consideration
C^i A^1 P S

9b A merry old soul | was | he
C^i P S

There are various verbs besides *be* that can occur in ascriptive clauses. Some examples are given in **10**:

10a It appeared true
10b Beethoven seems a problem
10c This is becoming a serious matter

10d Albert got quite angry
10e The milk smells a bit sour

In the equative type of intensive clause, illustrated in **2c**, C is always a nominal group. Semantically, S and C are equated by identifying one in terms of the other. In general the pattern is reversible so that 'a is b' implies 'b is a' and vice versa, either item being the subject and the other the complement:

11a The problem is Beethoven
11b Beethoven is the problem
11c The head of the local force is Bill
11d Bill is the head of the local force
11e My favourite food is porridge
11f Bill is the one in the raincoat
11g I am the one at the back
11h The one at the back is me

The equative interpretation of **11d** should be contrasted with the ascriptive interpretation, **5c**. The equative clause can be paraphrased: 'Bill is identifiable as the head of the local force', while the ascriptive meaning is 'Bill functions as the head of the local force'. It happens that *the head of the local force* is an expression that makes sense in both interpretations, whereas *the one in the raincoat* is difficult to take in the functional sense.

Exercise 10.1
Which of the following are ascriptive clauses, which are equative and which are neither?

1 That bell sounds cracked.
2 That bell sounds the alarm.
3 This problem looks a tricky one.
4 The last one out was Arthur.
5 The last one out was frightened.
6 A swarm of flying insects is a very well-defined object. (Appendix BI, ll. 29–30)
7 They start becoming godlike. (Appendix BII, l. 18)
8 The most important one is the art form of country houses. (Appendix BII, ll. 36–37)
9 Joan tasted the stew.
10 The stew tasted salty.
11 Most of the members are in favour of the motion.

12 One of the difficulties is my broken leg.
13 Even more unnecessary was the withdrawal from participation in overseas trade.

The last type of intensive clause is the locative. It should be understood that this term is intended to suggest location in time as well as location in space, and even sometimes that very general spatial/temporal notion of 'being in existence'. Here again, we find the verb *be*, but, as the examples below show, other verbs also occur. Since the complements of place and time are especially frequent and important, it is useful to have a separate symbol for them. The symbol C^{loc} is used to stand for the locative complement:

12a The box | is | *under the bench*
S P C^{loc}
12b The strike | is | *tomorrow*
S P C^{loc}
12c The exam was *last Friday*
12d The exam occurred *last Friday*
12e The spoons are *here*
12f The spoons go *in this drawer*
12g Bill is *away*
12h Bill is *away on the continent*
12i Harold lives *out in East Anglia*

The items that perform the function of complement in this type of clause belong to various classes, among which the prepositional group, e.g. *under the bench*, is perhaps the most important. But adverb particles and combinations of adverb particles with prepositional groups are also very common, e.g. *away* and *away on the continent*. (See section 10.5 for adverb particles.) There is something to be said for treating clauses that contain a verb of motion plus a complement of place as a kind of intensive clause. The main argument for this analysis is based on the paradigm given in Figure 41. The forms that would fit into the blank in this table are given in **13**:

13 Bill went/came/got/etc. into the garden

If this analysis is accepted, other dynamic clauses with a C^{loc}

	stative	*dynamic*
ascriptive	Bill is a policeman	Bill became a policeman
locative	Bill is in the garden	?

Figure 41

are those in **14**:

14a The children are coming *back from the match*
14b The spoons have got *into the wrong drawer*
14c I have been *to the library*

(For the distinction between stative and dynamic clauses see sections 15.2 and 16.6.) There is a clear test for locative complements, namely that they are elements that can be questioned with *where?* (including *where . . . to?* and *where . . . from?*) and *when?* This is not to say that the distinction between C^{loc} and A is always sharp, but that that between C^{loc} and other C's is fairly easy to establish.

In the locative type of clause we frequently find the non-referential pronoun *there* (always unstressed) acting as subject. (See also pages 59, 62.) This is especially common with the verb *be* when the delayed subject is indefinite, e.g. *a box* instead of *the box*. Thus, instead of saying *A box is under the bench*, we usually prefer to say *There is a box under the bench*. The analysis of such examples is given in **15**:

15a There | is | a box | under the bench
S P S^x C^{loc}

15b There | are | some boxes | under the bench
S P S^x C^{loc}

15c There | is | a strike | tomorrow
S P S^x C^{loc}

The delayed subject S^x has an important property of ordinary subjects, namely, that it controls the number concord of the verb (*is* v. *are*) according to whether it is singular or plural. This is why it is treated here as a kind of subject, even though it does not invert with the operator in interrogatives:

16a There is a strike tomorrow
16b Is there a strike tomorrow?

10.3 Transitive clauses

In transitive clauses there is an object complement. We have already seen that the process referred to by the clause is one which carries over from one participant to another, and that, in fact, there may be yet another participant after that. I shall distinguish transitive clauses as being either single or double; single transitive clauses, shown in **17**, have one participant after the predicator and double transitive clauses, shown in **18**, have two. In these examples the object complements are nominal groups. When there are two objects these differ from each other in function; the one that comes first is the *indirect object* (C^{oi}) and denotes the recipient or beneficiary. The other is the *direct object* (C^{od}), the thing received.

17a Harold | made | a speech
S P C^{o}
17b I | hate | baked beans
S P C^{o}
17c The police | released | him | the next morning
S P C^{o} A

18a I | gave | him | some money
S P C^{oi} C^{od}
18b I | bought | him | a ticket
S P C^{oi} C^{od}
18c The agency | found | me | a new job
18d Let's read | them | the notice
18e I | asked | you | a question
18f I | 'm going to tell | them | the facts
18g I | tipped | the driver | 50p

The remaining types of transitive clause have a prepositional group as complement. Again, they may be single or double transitive. I shall distinguish prepositional complements with the symbol C^{ob}, standing for oblique object. We will consider in turn four types of examples involving a C^{ob}; the first two types, illustrated in **19** and **21**, are single transitive:

Type 1

19a They | objected | to the plan
S P C^{ob}

19b I | didn't believe | in their pretensions
S P C^{ob}

19c He | can't cope | with the new way of life

19d He | resorted | to unfair methods

19e He | is going to enlarge | on the topic

19f They | have asked | about the sales effort

With all of these there is a passive equivalent in which the preposition is left standing at the end of the clause:

20a The plan was objected to

20b The new way of life can't be coped with

The verb usually has a particular preposition dependent on it: *cope* calls for *with*, *resort* calls for *to*, etc.

Type 2

21a This land | belongs | to the crown
S P C^{ob}

21b Harold | doesn't care | for parsnips

21c The ghost | appeared | to Scrooge

21d The programme | consisted | of three symphonies

This type is like Type 1 with the exception that there is no passive equivalent: **The crown is belonged to by this land*, etc.

Type 3

22a He | blamed | the dispute | on the management

S P C^{o} C^{ob}

22b He | searched | the room | for the papers
22c They | are fighting | the bosses | for better conditions
22d They | have asked | the manager | about the sales effort
22e I | bought | a ticket | for him

Here there are two transitive complements, but only the first corresponds to the subject of a passive equivalent. Thus, we can have *The manager was asked about the sales effort* but not **The sales effort was asked the manager about*. Some of these examples correspond to a double transitive clause with an indirect object. Compare the clauses in **23**:

23a I | bought | him | a ticket

C^{oi} C^{od}

23b I | bought | a ticket | for him

C^{o} C^{ob}

(The term 'indirect object' is here used only for the sort of object that is exemplified by *him* in **23a** not for the sort that has a preposition in **23b**.) Others correspond to a clause containing the same verb but with a different arrangement of the complements, e.g. corresponding to **22a** there is *He blamed the management for the dispute*. (It is not claimed that all clauses of the type exemplified in **22** correspond to one of these other types of clause.)

Type 4

24a They | took | pains | with the negotiations

S P C^{o} C^{ob}

24b He | made | reference | to the context
24c They | are paying | attention | to the time scale
24d We | must put | a stop | to these practices

There is a close idiomatic link between the verb and the C^{o}: *take pains, make reference, pay attention, put a stop*. There is a comparatively small number of such expressions. What characterizes this clause pattern is that each complement corresponds to the subject of a different passive equivalent:

25a (i) Pains were taken with the negotiations
(ii) The negotiations were taken pains with
25b (i) Reference was made to the context
(ii) The context was made reference to
25c (i) Attention is being paid to the time scale
(ii) The time scale is being paid attention to
25d (i) A stop must be put to these practices
(ii) These practices must be put a stop to

Some speakers of English intuitively favour a different analysis of examples like **19a** from that which is given here. In this alternative analysis *objected to* is taken as a constituent:

26 He | objected to | the plan.
S P C^{O}

The arguments in favour of the analysis are that, first, the preposition is highly dependent on the verb: you can't have *object* without *to*, and in some cases there is an even stronger bond between verb and preposition, as in *He doesn't care for porridge*; and, second, that *the plan* in some ways functions like an ordinary C^{O}.

I argue, however, that there is stronger evidence in favour of the analysis I have given. First, the point of interruption comes between *objected* and *to*, not between *to* and *the plan*:

27a He objected strongly to the plan
27b He doesn't care much for porridge
27c He asked enthusiastically about the sales effort
27d He asked the manager about the sales effort

Second, when such interruption occurs, there is no longer a correspondence of the complement with the S of a passive equivalent:

28a *The plan was objected strongly to
28b *The sales effort was asked enthusiastically about
28c *The sales effort was asked the manager about

In short, in an example like **27d** there is little justification for

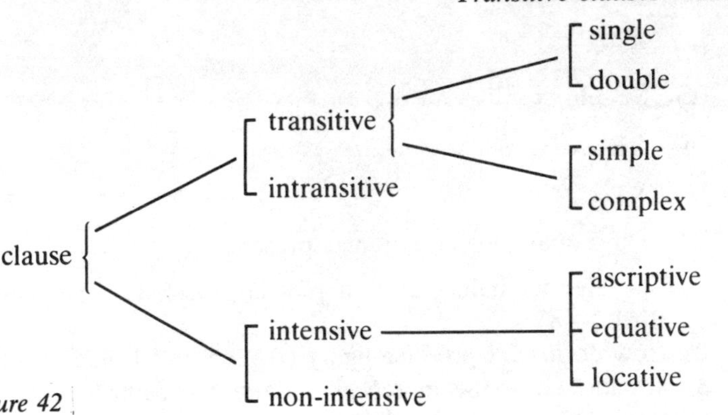

Figure 42

taking *asked about* as a constituent; and yet the relation between *asked* and *about* is the same in **27d** as it is in: *He asked about the sales effort*. The idiomatic dependence between *object* and *to*, and *care* and *for*, etc. is to be noticed, but there is no need to assume that such dependence determines the constituency of grammatical structures.

The distinctions within the transitive type of clause that have been presented in this section can be captured as in Figure 42 (I also take this opportunity of adding the new features that are dependent on the feature 'intensive'). These distinctions are realized as described in **29** and **30**:

29 *single*: there is one transitive complement
double: there are two transitive complements

simple: each transitive complement is a C^{o}

complex: the last transitive complement is a C^{ob}; any other is a C^{o}

30 *single simple*: Harold made a speech
single complex: Harold objected to the plan
double simple: I gave him some money
double complex: He blamed the dispute on the management

Exercise 10.2
Sort the following examples (mostly drawn from Appendix B) into the patterns (a) to (e).

(a) SP

(b) SPC^{o}

(c) SP C^{oi} C^{od}

(d) SP C^{o} C^{ob}

(e) SP C^{ob}

(NB There may also be adjuncts present.)

1 The electric field causes a glowing discharge. (Appendix BI, ll. 7–8)
2 How do insects produce light? (Appendix BI, ll. 12–13)
3 We looked at the insects in a darkened room. (Appendix BI, l. 25)
4 They confused the light with an unidentified flying object. (Appendix BI, ll. 27–28)
5 The insects tend to react to each other. (Appendix BI, ll. 30–31)
6 The shape changes all the time. (Appendix BI, l. 33)
7 They migrated in swarms.
8 Nobody took a swipe at one of these UFO's with a butterfly net. (Appendix BI, ll. 63–65)
9 The law attaches a penalty to a breach of trust.
10 The Government has given these men a promise.
11 These three different types of equality do overlap. (Appendix BII, l. 22)
12 Civilization depends on some degree of inequality. (Appendix BII, ll. 24–25)

It cannot be claimed that the analysis of transitivity presented in this section captures all of the detail that is relevant in this area of English grammar. It must be looked upon as an interim statement. It would be very much beyond the scope of this book to survey all that has been discovered about this topic in the last decade. In **31** I add some notes on a miscellaneous collection of cases that are left over:

31a He broke the window *with his elbow*
31b He broke the window *with a brick*
31c The car was provided *by his firm*
31d Bill sold John the carpet *for £50*
31e I am going to sing a song *for you*
31f I am going to clean the windows *for you*

The italicized elements in these examples hover on the border between adjuncts and complements.

In **31a** and **31b**, if the question is *How did he break the window?* the answer might be *accidentally, through carelessness, by turning too quickly* or *with his elbow*. All of these therefore seem to be adjuncts. But if we are asking about a deliberately used instrument, we can ask either *How did he break the window?* (answer: *with a brick*) or *What did he break the window with?* (answer: *a brick*). So the arguments for and against treating expressions of instrument as adjuncts are fairly evenly weighted. In **31c** there is no such doubt about the WH-interrogative. It has to be *Who was the car provided by? By his firm* is the element that indicates the agent, our example being the passive equivalent to *His firm provided the car*. Since the agent is an inherent part of the process, it is perhaps best to count *by his firm* as a complement, even though it is quite regular for such an agentive element to be left out (witness the many passive examples that have been used above which have no agentive element in them). In **31d** it is a question of the verb *sell*. There are a few processes which seem to have more than the usual number of inherent roles. Selling is one of these, since it has a seller, a purchaser, a thing sold, and a price for which the thing is exchanged. The price is thus an inherent part of the process, and though it is not usually obligatory to state what it is, it is nevertheless not quite what we would normally mean by a circumstance. In **31e** and **31f** the element introduced by the preposition *for*, expressing a person who benefits, sometimes corresponds to an indirect object as in **32**:

32 I am going to sing you a song

But this does no appply to **31f**: **I am going to clean you the windows*. It is possible to use the indirect object construction when the process is one in which the direct object is something that is produced, obtained or presented. Thus *Buy a ticket* means 'obtain a ticket by purchase', *Dig a trench* means 'produce a trench by means of digging', *Sing a song* means 'present' or even 'produce a song'. So we can have *Buy him a ticket, Dig him a trench* and *Sing him a song*. But *Clean the windows* does not mean that the windows are obtained or produced; they are there all along. So **Clean him the windows* sounds very odd and difficult to interpret. Similarly, **Paint him* *the wall* is odd, but *Paint him a picture* is perfectly natural. There seems to be little difficulty in accepting as complements of the oblique type the *for*-constituents that correspond to an indirect object. The case for those that do not so correspond may be weaker. Even so, the WH-test indicates complement status (*Who for?* not *Why?*):

33 Who are you going to clean the windows for?

10.4 Transitive-intensive clauses

A clause such as that in **34** is both transitive and intensive:

34 He called us liberals

S P C^o C^i

The relation between the subject and *us* is transitive, while that between *us* and *liberals* is intensive, corresponding as it does to the intransitive *We are liberals*. Similarly the intransitive locative in **35a** is paralleled by that in **35b**:

35a The car is in the garage
35b He | put | the car | in the garage

S P C^o C^{loc}

36 and **37** are further examples of transitive intensive clauses. The clauses in **36** have an ascriptive relation between C^o and C^i:

36a He found them difficult
36b This made him angry
36c He left the window open
36d I received the parcel damaged
36e They will probably make him chairman

The clauses in **37** have a locative relation between C^o and C^{loc}. The verbs in this pattern have a sense of causing something to be in a certain place.

37a He | left | the spoon | in his cup

S P C^o C^{loc}

37b I | have taken | the books | back to the library
S P C^{o} C^{loc}

37c She threw the flowers downstairs
37d He packed the children off to school
37e She keeps the money in an old teapot
37f He should put those guns away
37g The silly child got his head between the railings

Exercise 10.3

Some of the following clauses are transitive intensive, (C^{o} C^{i} or C^{o} C^{loc}) and others are double transitive (C^{oi} C^{od} or C^{o} C^{ob}). One is ambiguous. Which is which?

1 I allowed them their expenses.
2 He left the school all his books.
3 You've made this box very strong.
4 She's probably going to leave the window open.
5 It'll save you a lot of trouble.
6 I've caught you some trout.
7 I think him of sound mind.
8 They have covered the floor with matting.
9 She turned the pudding onto a plate.
10 I've told you all there is to tell.
11 I found her a very good secretary.
12 You ought to share that cake with James.

10.5 Adverb particles

An important functional element for which we have not yet accounted is the one that goes under the traditional name of *adverb particle*. This name is noncommittal on the question whether it is a complement or an adjunct. Here it will be treated as a kind of complement, since, as the examples in **38** show, they are usually essential elements:

38a They washed *up*
38b They washed the plates *up*
38c They washed *up* the plates
38d He's showing *off*
38e He never looks *up*

38f They put the boxes *down*
38g They put *down* the boxes

When there is a C^{o} present, the particle may come before it or after it (see **38b** and **38c**, and **38f** and **38g**). What these particles do is define or restrict the process by adding to the meaning of the verb; sometimes they contribute a place or direction specification, in which case they may be considered to be instances of C^{loc}, as in **38f**, **38g**, but quite often do not have such a locative function. For want of a better label I shall call this function *particle complement* (C^{part}). Many combinations of verb and particle are highly idiomatic. Some extreme examples are given in **39**:

39a He held out for three hours
39b They have turned down my application
39c They will give off light (Appendix BI, ll. 59–60)

These are idiomatic in that there is no predicting from a knowledge of the meaning of *hold* and *out* that *hold out* would mean 'continue resistance'; similarly, there is no predicting the meaning 'reject' for *turn down*. These combinations of verb and particle are traditionally known as *phrasal verbs*. The degree of idiomatic bonding is variable, and so is the kind of verb–particle combination, as a consideration of the clauses in **40** will suggest:

40a We had to turn them away
40b He turned back
40c He turned off the light
40d He turned on the light
40e He turned out a liar
(*a liar* = C^{i}, cf. *He was a liar*)
40f He turned out a liar
(*a liar* = C^{o}, cf. *He turned a liar out*)
40g He turned up in the end
40h He turned in some good work

The more highly idiomatic phrasal verbs provide classic illustrations of the fact that lexical items are not necessarily words. The examples in **41** show the structure of clauses containing the element C^{part}:

41a He | is showing | off
S P C^{part}

41b They | have turned | down | my application
S P C^{part} C^{o}

41c They | have turned | my application | down
S P C^{o} C^{part}

Particles functioning as C^{loc} can be distinguished from these by the fact that they are expandable with a prepositional group:

42a He | went | off (to the station)
S P C^{loc}

42b He | turned | back (towards the shore)
S P C^{loc}

The items that can fulfil the function of particle complement are words like *back, down, out, away, off, on, up, over*, etc. Most of these can also function as prepositions. Care should therefore be taken not to confuse two kinds of structure:

43a He | turned | off the road
S P C

43b He | turned | off | the light
S P C^{part} C^{o}

In **43b**, the sequence of C^{part} and C^{o} is reversible. If we reverse it, this gives: *He turned the light off*. In fact, had the object been a pronoun, the separation of the verb from the particle would have been virtually obligatory: *He turned it off*, not **He turned off it*. This is not the case with the prepositional group in **43a**. Here the sequence is not reversible and if a pronoun occurs it has to come at the end: **He turned the road off* is ill formed, but *He turned off it* is all right.

Exercise 10.4
Which of the following contain adverb particles, and which prepositional groups?

1 I shall wake up the children.
2 I shall make up the fire.

3 I shall look up the chimney.
4 I shall look up the meaning.
5 He turned down the next alleyway.
6 He turned down the next applicant.
7 He ran through the recording.
8 He ran through the town.
9 He enlarged on the topic.
10 I wouldn't part with this copy
11 I don't care for that picture.

There is still one minor detail that needs mention. Certain kinds of clause structure have a prepositional remnant:

44a That matter | was referred | to
S P ?

(*cf. the active counterpart*: Somebody referred to that matter)

44b What | did (they) refer | to?
?C^o P (S) ?

(*cf. the polar*: Did they refer to something?)

44c Those paintings | we | shall (certainly) bid | for
?C^o S P (A) ?

(*cf. the neutral theme*: We shall certainly bid for those paintings)

It has often been observed that prepositions are difficult to pin down. From one point of view they belong with a following nominal group, and yet they can acquire a kind of independence in certain structures, or even show dependence on a verb. Without wishing to claim any finality for the decision, I propose assigning the function C^{part} to the prepositional remnants illustrated in **44**, and C^o to the prepositional objects that have been separated from their prepositions:

45 What | did (they) refer | to?
C^o P (S) C^{part}

Exercise 10.5

Analyse the following clauses, first by distinguishing broadly only S, P, C and A, and then more delicately as follows:

S		A^{l}	– linking adjunct, connective or comment
S^{x}	– delayed subject	A^{time}	
P		A^{place}	
C^{i}	– intensive complement, ascriptive or equative	A^{man}	– including manner, means and instrument
C^{loc}	– intensive complement of the locative kind	A^{int}	– intensifying
C^{o}	– direct or indirect	A^{act}	– action adjunct
C^{ob}	– oblique object	A^{x}	– other or borderline types
C^{part}			
C^{x}	– other or borderline types		

1 The other Ford plants will go along with us.
2 That will be our recommendation at Monday's meeting.
3 The Midland section of the car industry has been having its ups and downs today.
4 Four thousand other Landley men have walked out on strike.
5 On a brighter note, the long-running carburettor strike in Birmingham is over.
6 The Goldhill men voted for further talks.
7 In view of the developments during the day, that may be a wise move.
8 The Druid Lane Plant shutdown will eventually lead to lay-offs at Goldhill.
9 No pay policy in the past has run into trouble of this magnitude at this stage of the cycle.
10 Nobody has come up with a plausible alternative.
11 They bargained within the prescribed limits.
12 They bargained within what their employers could economically stand.

13 Their employers could economically stand such terms.
14 They will sort out the Landley situation.
15 What they get is going to be more than 5 per cent.
16 The breaking of 5 per cent is going to be the primary target.
17 Mr Clanger may well be defeated in that division.
18 He was forced into a November election.
19 That defeat forced him into a November election.
20 That prospect seemed remote indeed.
21 That election has changed the whole atmosphere in which the government is functioning.
22 They didn't vote for that.
23 It went through without a division.
24 He is going to make a pretty full statement.
25 He has just returned from a visit to Mozambique.
26 It is the largest open-air school in the world.
27 They have divided the camp into two parts.
28 (There is a part for the girls and a part for the boys.) In the boys' case, they are almost entirely under canvas.
29 There are also young mothers with babies there as well.
30 Most of them participate in the liberation struggle in one way or another.
31 Potentially these young people could be the fighters of next year or the year after.
32 There were white curtains at the side.
33 We did a rather ambitious programme.
34 We had a little reunion in Olderham a couple of years ago.
35 They sent for me.
36 The cat got onto the stage.
37 I threw it into the audience.
38 I learned a great deal from it.
39 They moved us to another theatre.

11 Phase

11.1 Predicators in phase

In the last two chapters we have been concerned with the verbal patterns that encode what a speaker wants to say about the world. These are the patterns that fulfil what has been called the ideational (or referential) function of language. Propositions are essentially ideational, and complements are essential to the integrity of propositions. So Chapter 10 was entirely concerned with patterns that have an ideational purpose. Adjuncts at most give circumstantial detail and so are peripheral to the structure of propositions, and they may, in fact, be more concerned with other functions of language, with the way a speaker is interacting with his audience, or with the links he is making between what is being said now and what has been said before. Chapter 9, therefore, was partly concerned with ideational meaning and partly with other kinds of meaning. In this chapter we deal with another aspect of clause grammar that has an ideational function. We could think of these new patterns as extended propositions, in that there is more than one predicator together with whatever complements and adjuncts the extra predicators bring with them. This is a complex area of English structure and it is not intended to do more than introduce it.

The name by which I shall call the occurrence of one predicator appearing dependently on another is *phase*. (Another term that has been used is *catenation*, referring to the 'chaining' of predicators.) Here is an example:

1 I | wanted | to give | them | a present

S P P C^O C^O

Here there are two verbal groups, one with the main verb *want* and the other with *give*. The second verbal group is necessarily non-finite, i.e. it has no possibility of being modal or tensed. Non-finite verbal groups begin with *to*, or *n*-form or *ing*-form or base-form, e.g. *to give, given, giving* or *give*. All of these occur in phase, but those occurring most commonly are *to*-form and *ing*-form. Further examples are given in **2**:

2a I | remember | giving | them | presents
S P P C^o C^o

2b He | is hoping | to be | a member of parliament
S P P C^i

2c I | 'll help | to wash | the dishes
S P P C^o

In all of the above examples the S is subject of both predicators; for instance, in **2a** 'I' does the remembering and also the giving. But a second predicator brings with it the possibility of a second subject, distinct from the first:

3a I | wanted | you | to give | them | a present
S P ? P C C

3b I | remember | you | giving | them | a present
S P ? P C C

In both of these clauses *you* functions both as object of the first predicator and subject of the second. The symbol for this dual function is C^o/S.

The occurrence of a second predicator in phase with the first depends on the selection of a main verb that permits it. For instance, *remember* allows a phase construction but *walk* does not. If a phase verb is also selected for the second predicator a third predicator can be introduced, and so on. There is no limit to the number of predicators there may be. In **4** there are clauses with four predicators each. Only the last P in each example does not have another P dependent on it:

4a I *want* you *to ask* him *to watch* them *play*
4b I *remember* you *telling* me *to help* her *wash* up

Phase is thus a recursive pattern; it can be repeated indefinitely.

The C^o/S element has the properties of an object in varying degrees. For instance, it is always an object in so far as a pronoun will appear in the objective case: *me* not *I, him* not *he*, etc. Further, it is often possible to find contrasts of active v. passive voice in association with either the first or second predicator. In **5a** the first P is passive. The active clause corresponding to this is **5b**, in which the item *him* is an object in respect of the predicator *taught*:

5a He | was taught | by me | to play | the piano
S P C P C^{O}

5b I | taught | him | to play | the piano
S P C^{O}/S P C^{O}

By contrast with this **6a** does not correspond to a passive **6b**:

6a I wanted him to play the piano
6b *He was wanted to play the piano

(However, **6b** is well formed in another interpretation; see the discussion of **17**, below.) The nominal item following *want* also lacks object status in another respect. It can be displaced by the object of the second predicator when this is passive:

7a I | wanted | you | to give | them | a present
S P C^{O}/S P C^{O} C^{O}

7b I | wanted | them | to be given | a present | by you
S P C^{O}/S P C^{O} C

In other words the object of *want*, in a phase structure, is not inalienably tied to this function. But with some other phase-verbs the case is different. The object of *persuade* or *ask*, for instance, is inalienable. In the following examples the second one in each pair is not synonymous with the first:

8a I persuaded him to buy some shares
8b *I persuaded some shares to be bought by him
9a I persuaded him to be interviewed by the Press
9b I persuaded the Press to interview him

Phase structures can be divided into various types by means of the following criteria. First whether or not there is a C^{O}/S, and second whether the dependent predicator is *to*-form, *ing*-form, *n*-form or base-form. Phase verbs can then be classified according to whether they occur in the various phase structures or not. Some verbs occur in a wider range of structures than others; for example, *pretend* must have a *to*-form following it, and cannot take a C^o/S:

10 He pretended to faint

On the other hand *want* occurs in a number of different patterns:

11a I want to go
11b I want you to go
11c I want you sitting quietly

Exercise 11.1
Consider the following verbs from the point of view of the variety of phase structures they fit into: *decide, remember, escape, see, manage, continue, postpone, hear, deny.*

It is not only verbs that allow a second predicator in phase. Some adjectives also allow it. When there is a new subject for the second predicator the preposition *for* is introduced:

12a	He	is	ready	to lock	the door	
	S	P	C^i	P	C^o	
12b	We	are	sorry	to be	late	
	S	P	C^i	P	C^i	
12c	I	am	prepared	for you	to be	late
	S	P	C^i	C/S	P	C^i

11.2 *Want* and *need*

There is a point of special interest with the verbs *want* and *need*. Both of these occur in phase constructions of various types. From the point of view of voice, there is nothing very remarkable about some of the patterns, but in some places in the following paradigms *ing*-form phase can be substituted for a passive *to*-form or an *n*-form:

13a These shoes need somebody to repair their soles
13b These shoes need their soles ?**to be repaired*/*repairing*
13c These shoes need their soles *repaired*/*repairing*
13d These shoes need *to be repaired*/*repairing*

14a I need somebody to repair these shoes
14b I need these shoes ?**to be repaired/repairing*
14c I need these shoes *repaired/repairing*

15a I want somebody to repair these shoes
15b I want these shoes *to be repaired/repairing*
15c I want these shoes *repaired/repairing*

It is evident that after *need* and *want* the *ing*-form of the next verb acquires a different syntactic value from that which it normally has. *Want* has a further peculiarity in that *these shoes* can be the subject of *want* only if the next verb has the *ing*-form:

16a *These shoes want to be repaired
16b These shoes want repairing

11.3 An alternative view

In many descriptions of English, phase structures are treated as cases of embedding, or rankshift (see section 4.1 and Chapter 23). This would mean assigning to example **4a** a structure like that in Figure 43. It is not my intention to discuss this alternative, except very briefly to say that I think there is little justification for regarding *him to watch them play* or *you to ask him to watch them play* as constituents in **4a**, which is what this alternative entails;

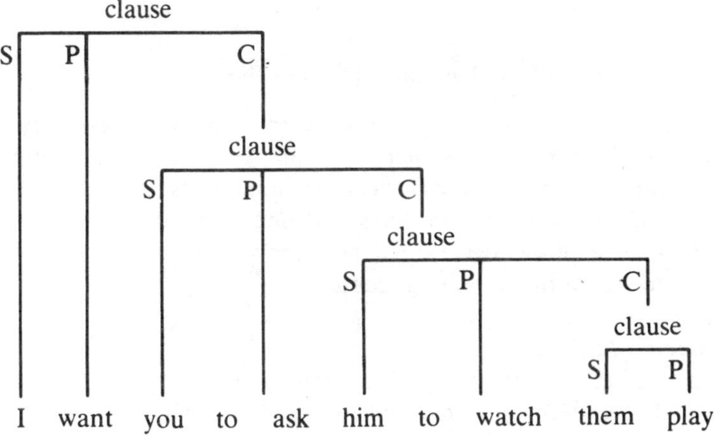

Figure 43

and also that the alternative does not adequately represent the status of the C^o/S element, which is not only the subject of the second predicator but the object of the first. Hereafter I assume, for the sake of the argument, that the phase interpretation rather than the embedding one is correct. There is in this area of English grammar a great deal of purely arbitrary complexity. That is, it is difficult to find more than fragmentary connections between meaning and form. Neither the phase nor the embedding view of the phenomena provides a satisfying explanation of the complexity.

11.4 Non-finite clauses of purpose

Care should be taken not to confuse phase structures with the structure exemplified in **17**:

17	He |	went |	there ||	to learn |	the language
	S	P	C^{loc}	P	C^o

This is a structure consisting of two clauses, the second one being bound to the first, which is therefore the dominant clause. There are two tests for this structure. First, the bound clause could be paraphrased with *in order to* as in **18**:

18 He went there in order to learn the language

Second, it is possible to reverse the sequence of the clauses as in **19**:

19 To learn the language, he went there

Phase structures fail both these tests. Phase is the dependency of one predicator on another; certain verbs permit another predicator in phase and others do not. It is clear that the bound-clause construction illustrated in **17–19** has nothing to do with such a phase structure dependency since almost any verb could occur in the dominant clause.

Exercise 11.2
Which of the following are phase structures?

1 I intended you to read up to page 100.
2 I saw him waiting for the bus.
3 Waiting for the bus, I saw him.

4 I read it to be prepared.
5 He is prepared to find her waiting for him.
6 I don't like that painting of London Bridge.
7 You can see this glow fanning out in all directions. (Appendix BI, ll. 25–26)

Exercise 11.3

In what ways, if any, can the following be reorganized with passive predicators? (e.g. *He intends you to send the change: He intends the change to be sent (by you); The change is intended to be sent by you; You are intended to send the change.*)

1 The leader tried to play the piece by himself.
2 I heard them opening the door.
3 The captain commanded the guards to bring in the prisoners.
4 I caught them stealing apples.
5 They kept me waiting.
6 She keeps sending telegrams.
7 I want you to be on your guard.

Exercise 11.4

There are two instances of phase in Appendix BI, ll. 54–65. Find them and examine them in some detail. (One of them is adjectival, e.g. the examples in **12**, above.)

12 Theme

12.1 Textual organization

At several places above, reference has been made to different kinds of meaning that grammatical systems may have. In sections 3.1 and 5.1 a distinction was drawn between the propositional organization of a clause and the interactional organization. In the first the speaker is encoding some idea about the world outside, making reference to some subject matter that he wants to talk about. In the other he is signalling to the addressee what kind of communicative act he is performing, so that the addressee knows how he is supposed to react. Mood and modality belong to the interactional kind of organization and the systems of complementation and phase belong to the propositional kind. In sections 5.4 and 11.1 a third kind of organizing principle was introduced. Here the speaker is giving to what he says a verbal texture, arranging the parts of his message in sequence, placing emphases to show that 'at this point this idea is paramount in such and such a connection', and showing how what he is saying now coheres with what has been said earlier. Section 5.4 introduced the idea of a theme. The theme is the part of a clause that the speaker has chosen to present as 'what I am talking about at this point in the developing discourse'; the rheme is 'what I have to say about it'. Section 11.1 pointed out that connective adjuncts show how what is being said now is connected with what went before: *however* means 'in spite of what has been said', *therefore* means 'as a consequence of what has been said', *for instance* means 'as an example of what has been said' and so on.

Somewhat controversially it has been suggested that all language is exhaustively analysable in terms of three largely independent functional components:

1 *Ideational*, i.e. the propositional or referential
2 *Interpersonal*, i.e. the interactional or attitudinal

3 *Textual*, i.e. the component that organizes an utterance as a continuous verbal structure proceeding from what comes earlier to what comes later

The suggestion is that the majority of utterances are simultaneously organized on each of these three planes, like three strands intertwined in a single three-ply cord.

Without entering into the controversies as to whether these three components are sufficient, or just how independent they are of each other, I shall adopt them as a useful set of concepts for talking about the grammar of English and the meanings that the various grammatical systems have. In this chapter I shall give a rather brief account of the main principles of textual organization in the clause. The general name for this grammatical area is *theme*, a term which also has the narrower sense in which it was used in 5.4. In the broader sense theme means 'thematic organization', the organization of a clause with respect to selection of topic.

Here is a paradigm of thematic organizations. The first clause is neutral, or unmarked, with respect to each of six kinds of marked organization. In this connection *unmarked* means that the clause is organized so as to be as independent as possible of its verbal context for its interpretation. All of the marked forms in one way or another require a verbal context to explain the motive for choosing 'this way of putting it'.

1 The fitter sent these documents to the office

2a These documents the fitter sent to the office
2b To the office the fitter sent these documents

3a It was the fitter that sent these documents to the office
3b It was these documents that the fitter sent to the office
3c It was to the office that the fitter sent these documents
3d It was the office that the fitter sent these documents to

4a The fitter, he sent these documents to the office
4b These documents, the fitter sent them to the office

5a He sent these documents to the office, the fitter
5b He sent these documents to the office, the fitter did
5c The fitter sent them to the office, these documents

6a The one who sent these documents to the office was the fitter
6b What the fitter sent to the office was these documents

6c Where the fitter sent these documents was (to) the office

6d What the fitter sent these documents to was the office

6e What the fitter did to these documents was (to) send them to the office

6f What the fitter did was (to) send these documents to the office

7a // the fitter sent these documents to the office //

7b // the fitter sent these documents to the office //

7c // the fitter did send these documents to the office //

7d // the fitter sent these documents to the office //

For the intonational notation in **7** see Appendix A. The unmarked version, **1**, has the tonic falling on the first syllable of *office*. The examples grouped under **2–7** in this paradigm differ from each other in respect of which element in the original unmarked version has been selected for thematic emphasis. The unmarked clause has the structure S P C^{o} C^{loc}. Example **2a** selects the C^{o} *these documents* as theme, while **2b** selects C^{loc} *to the office* as theme. The range of different elements that can be selected differs from one kind of thematic organization to another. Examples **2–7** represent the different kinds of structural reorganization of the unmarked form. I shall use the following names for them: **2** thematization; **3** *it*-theme; **4** preposed theme; **5** postposed theme; **6** identification; **7** information.

From the length of the paradigm, which could certainly be extended, the reader may judge the amount of space that would be needed for a detailed examination of these structures and their meanings. My treatment will be brief: I shall take each structure in turn, and rather than spell out its formal characteristics, I shall give a diagrammatic display of the difference between the unmarked and the marked version.

12.2 Thematization

1 Not all kinds of clause element can be selected with equal freedom for front position. The effect is more striking with C^{o} than with C^{loc}, and the least marked of all is a time or place

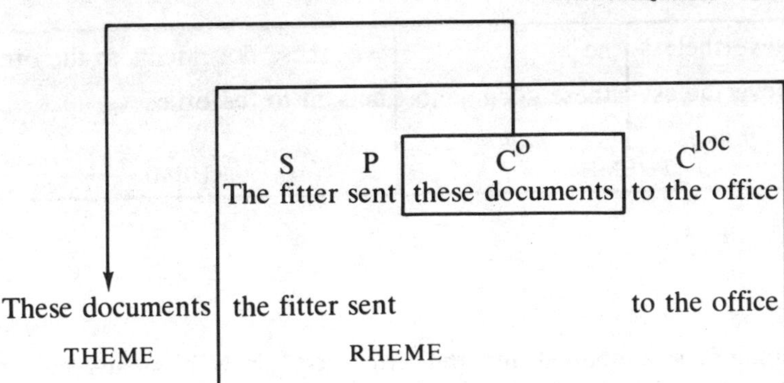

Figure 44

adjunct. P cannot be fronted at all except in a rather different kind of structure which involves fronting not just P but also its complements, and, moreover, adjusting the form of the verbal group so that it can be split:

8 (The fitter said he would send these documents to the office and) send them there he did
P C^{o} C^{loc} S P^{op}

2 In the unmarked structure (given in **1** and shown in Figure 44) the theme is the mood-indicating part of the clause. This point is explained at more length in section 5.4.

3 Elements that are not part of the propositional content of the clause can be placed first without prejudice to the selection also of a propositional element:

9a Nevertheless, he sent these documents to the office
9b Nevertheless, these documents he sent to the office

The connective adjunct in **9** is indeed a theme, but a minor or subsidiary theme, and we must recognize a major theme in addition to it. The theme structure of these clauses is given in Figure 45.

4 A marked major theme is often something that has been mentioned before, or something prominent in the situation of utterance. In our example the demonstrative *these* assists us in

Nevertheless	he	sent these documents to the office
Nevertheless	these documents	he sent to the office
minor	*major*	
THEME		RHEME

Figure 45

imagining a context for the utterance, since it means either 'mentioned before'. or that the speaker is indicating them in some way such as holding them in his hand.

12.3 *It*-theme (see Figure 46)

1 With *it*-theme one of the marked options is to select the S for special attention (see **3a**). This is not possible in thematization, since there the S is the unmarked choice. As with thematization P cannot be selected.

2 The most ordinary intonation for a clause with marked *it*-theme organization is Tone 13: // it was the fitter that sent these documents to the office //

3 A clause like *It was the chair that broke* is ambiguous between the interpretations given in **10a**, **10b**:

10a (The table didn't break)
It was the chair | that broke
it-THEME | RHEME

10b (What was that thing in the corner of the garage?)
It | was | the chair that broke
S P C^i

10a is a marked version of *The chair broke*. **10b** is not. The normal intonation for **10b** would be different from that for **10a**, but in writing the ambiguity would remain.

4 The meaning of *it*-theme can be brought out by noting the effect of putting it into interrogative mood:

11 Was it these documents that the fitter sent to the office?

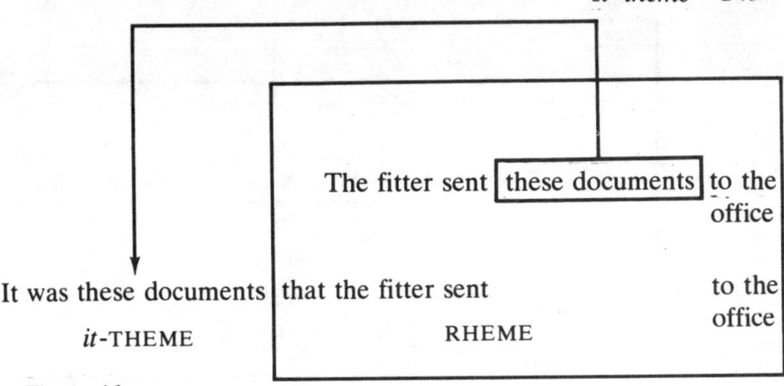

Figure 46

It-theme states or asks explicitly what the theme of the clause is: 'This is what I am talking about', or 'Is this what you are, or I should be talking about?

5 Sometimes the first half of an *it*-theme structure occurs by itself. This happens when the substance of the rheme is derivable from the context or the situation:

12a (*The fitter sent something to the office*)
It was these documents
(*Meaning* it was these documents that he sent to the office)

12b (*A knock is heard at the door*)
It's probably Bill
(*Meaning* It's probably Bill that has just knocked at the door)

Exercise 12.1
Write out the unmarked version of the following *it*-theme clauses. Which element in the unmarked version is selected for *it*-theme treatment? Which are ambiguous like **10** above?

1 It's fish that we're having for dinner.
2 It's for dinner that we're having fish.
3 It's us that are having fish for dinner.
4 It was by train that we travelled.
5 It's the typist that does all the work.
6 It's the typist that does all the work that sits at that desk.
7 It's on the radio that they announce the results.
8 It's Bill that makes the mistakes.
9 It's the food that I can't stand.

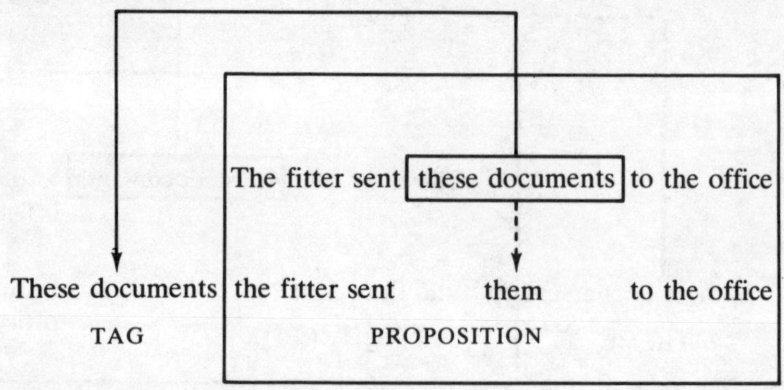

Figure 47

12.4 **Proposed theme** (see Figure 47)

The tag is not a mood tag such as we studied in Chapter 6. It is what Sinclair 1972 (pp. 83–4) calls a gloss tag, because it provides a gloss on, or explanation of, the pronoun that is to follow, in this case the pronoun *them*. In this structure the tag has the status of a theme that is separated from the clause-structure proper; it is a bald announcement of theme given without being integrated fully into the clause. This structure occurs in rather informal varieties of English, and would almost certainly be rejected in a formal prose style. Nevertheless it occurs systematically in those varieties where it does occur. (See an example of it in Appendix BII, 1.21.) The next structure, the postposed theme, which is also informal in style, is almost a mirror image of the preposed theme.

12.5 **Postposed theme** (see Figure 48)

1 When it is the S that is glossed and the clause is declarative, there is the further option of adding the operator to it, so that the postposed theme is not just the S but also the declarativeness of the clause (see **5b**).

2 In both preposed and postposed theme the proposition has, in a sense, an ordinary theme of its own, but the likelihood of its being a marked structure is very severely diminished. The thematic aspect of the total structure is as in **13**:

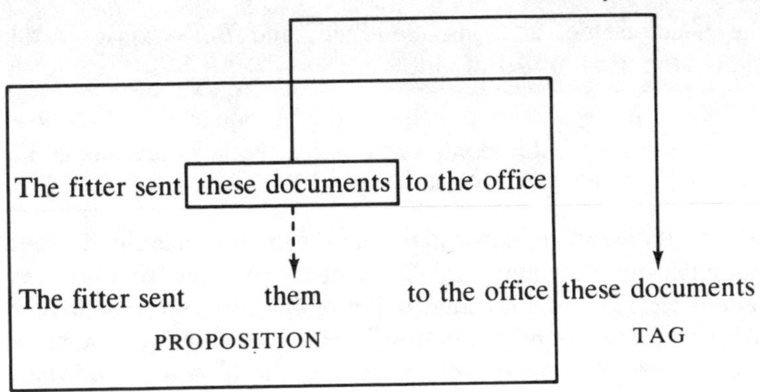

Figure 48

13 The fitter | sent them to the office, | these documents
THEME | RHEME | POSTPOSED THEME

12.6 Identification (see Figure 49)

1 The overall structure is an equative clause (see section 10.2, especially the discussion of example **11** in that section). The structure could be reversed to give: *These documents were what the fitter sent to the office.* Any equative clause presents one of the equated elements as the identifier of the other. For instance, in *The headquarters is Bill's house*, the speaker may be speaking as if in answer to the question *Which is the headquarters?* If so,

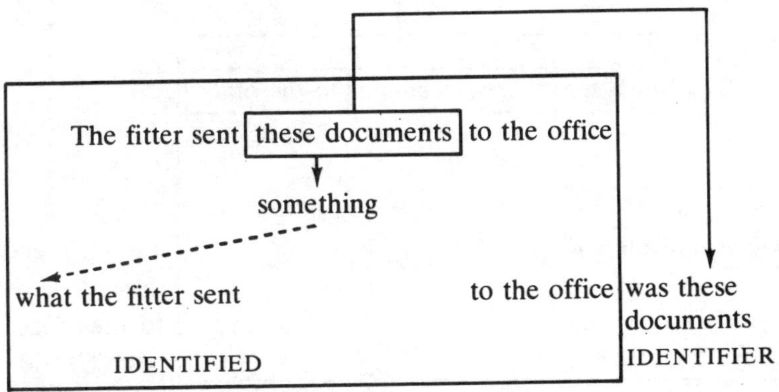

Figure 49

the headquarters is being identified, and *Bill's house* is the expression used to identify it:

> **14** I'll meet you tomorrow at the headquarters. (And since you probably don't know which the headquarters is, I'll tell you.) The headquarters is Bill's house

2 In thematic identification the element identified is a nominalization involving a WH-item; for example *what the fitter sent to the office* is a nominalization of *the fitter sent something to the office.* The nominalization is so called because it is a nominal group derivable from a clause structure. (In the case of **6a**, where it is a person that is referred to by the WH-item, we cannot just say: *who sent these documents to the office*; it has to be *the one who . . .*, or *the person who . . .*, etc. Similarly, *what he sent* could be replaced by *the thing that he sent.* The word *what*, in this context, is functioning as headword of a nominal group as well as a WH-item introducing the rankshifted clause.)

So the meaning of **6b** is 'I am identifying the things that the fitter sent to the office as *these documents*'. It is, of course presupposed that the fitter sent something to the office.

3 In thematic identification, the identifier may be more than a single clause element; it may be P together with certain C and A elements. This possibility is illustrated in Figure 50 which shows a fairly complex structural difference, involving the occurrence of

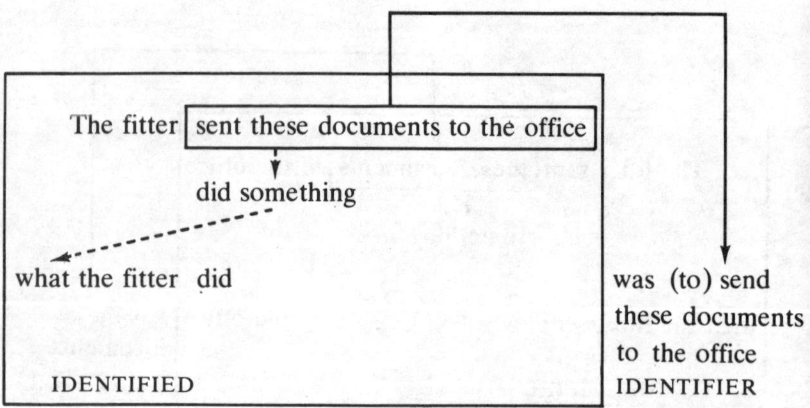

Figure 50

did something in place of P C^{o} C^{loc}, and then the use of *what* in place of *something.*

4 Nominalizations with a WH-word can occur anywhere where a nominal group can occur. In **15** they are occurring in structures that have nothing to do with identification, but one of them is acting as a postposed theme:

15a What he said | was | brief
S P C^{i}

15b I | referred | to what he said
S P C^{ob}

15c It | was | brief, | what he said
S P C^{i} | POSTPOSED THEME

15d What he said | shocked | us
S P C^{o}

Exercise 12.2

Some of the following are examples of *it*-theme, some are examples of postposed theme, some are of identification, and some are none of these. Say which is which. For those that are examples of marked thematic organization give the corresponding unmarked version:

1 It was a forgery, what he bought.
2 It was a watercolour that he bought.
3 What he bought was rather expensive.
4 What he bought was the Mona Lisa.
5 (Who said 'I came, I saw, I conquered.'?) It was Julius Caesar.
6 It took them two days to reach Margate.
7 It's television aerials that you have to look out for.
8 It is with inexpressible concern that I now find myself under the necessity of adding to the above description.
9 Where they're going for their holidays this year is Tenby.
10 A loaf of bread is what we chiefly need.
11 The one who rang for the waiter was Tom.

12 She's terribly late, that social worker.
13 They sent it by post, what was written at the last session.
14 The one who fell down the steps broke his neck.

Exercise 12.3

(a) In Appendix B I, ll. 1–10 there are three occurrences of the word *it*. Two of them are involved in *it*-theme structures and one is not. Which are?

(b) Sort out the structures into their unmarked versions.

(c) In the same passage, lines 55–65, there is an instance of identification. Sort it out. (It is rather heavily disguised and will take some disentangling.)

Exercise 12.4

Appendix B II, ll. 15–17 has an instance of identification. Sort it out and also notice and comment on the form of the mood tag *aren't you?*

12.7 **Information** (see Figure 51)

1 Information structure is not on quite the same footing as the other five types of organization; the domain in which it operates is, properly speaking, not the clause but the tone group. (See

// the fitter	sent	these documents	to the office NEW	//
// the fitter	sent	these documents NEW	to the office GIVEN	//
// the fitter	sent NEW	these documents GIVEN	to the office	//
// the fitter NEW	sent	these documents GIVEN	to the office	//

Figure 51

Appendix A.) Each tone group is one unit of information; it is what the speaker has chosen to present as a new piece of message. As such it may be something less or more than a clause. For instance a broadcast news item is likely to be packed with pieces of new material which the listener could not be expected to have already in mind. Example **16** is one clause, but four information units:

> **16** // a forty per cent // pay claim for // council manual workers has been // put to the employers //

2 Each information unit has to have some new material in it, otherwise there would be no point in creating the information unit in the first place. It may also contain given material, material which the speaker is treating as recoverable from the context, either literally or by implication, and which is mentioned only as a point of reference for the new material. The new material is shown to be new by receiving the intonational tonic, which falls on the last accented syllable of the constituent under focus. In our examples above, *off* is the last accented syllable of *to the office*, and *doc* is the last accented syllable of *these documents*.

3 Material that comes after the constituent under focus in the same information unit is explicitly given:

> **17** (. . . and so when a thunderstorm approaches)
> // or a series | of thunderstorms //
> NEW | GIVEN
>
> (Appendix B I, l. 4)

In **17** *of thunderstorms* is recoverable from the immediately preceding context; what is new is the idea of a series rather than a single one. A further example is given in **18**:

> **18** (Is it possible that a mass of insects like this and of the size you've described would show up on a radar screen?)
> . . . // locusts | are known to show up on radar screens //
> NEW | GIVEN
>
> (Appendix B I, l. 48)

Some items are in their very nature inherently given. The word *there*, when it means 'the place just mentioned' (rather than 'the place I am pointing to'), is inherently given. Thus in **19** the explicitly given material is also inherently given:

19 A: (Have you been to the office this morning?
B: Yes,) // the fitter sent | these documents | there
| NEW | GIVEN

4 Material that precedes the constituent under focus is ordinarily unspecified and can be taken as either given or new according to what makes the best sense. In example **20** it is sometimes actually given, and sometimes, in part, actually new:

20 (MW: You were talking about opera)
BC: // I was talking | about economics //
UNSPECIFIED | NEW

MW: // I'm talking | about houses //
UNSPECIFIED | NEW

(which are nothing to do with art, . . .)

// they are to do with | the way people live //
UNSPECIFIED | NEW

(Appendix B II, ll. 54–8)

(NB It is also possible to make this unspecified material explicitly given by using a special intonation of the pretonic, detail for which there is unfortunately no space here; or it could be made explicitly new by creating a separate tone group for it, e.g. // I'm talking about // houses //)

5 By definition, unmarked information structure is the placing of the focus so that none of the material need be taken as given except what is inherently given. This is the structure that makes least appeal to the context for its interpretation. What this means is that unmarked information structure has its focus on the last constituent that is not inherently given. If the focus falls elsewhere it is a marked structure, as in **17** and **18** above, or in **21**:

21a // the fitter sent these documents | there //
UNSPECIFIED | NEW

21b // the fitter sent | these | documents to the office //
UNSPECIFIED | NEW | GIVEN

Marked information structure is necessarily contrastive in

meaning. It occurs in a context where something contrary to what is now being said has been said, or suggested, or in some way mentioned or hinted at. When we say that some item is inherently given but new, we mean that the contrast is new; in **21a** *there* means that place rather than anywhere else where it has been suggested he might have sent them.

Exercise 12.5

Turn to Appendix B I, ll. 11–26, and find four cases of explicitly given material. (The tone group boundaries are not indicated, but it is sufficiently clear where they would fall.)

13 Voice

13.1 Voice in clause grammar

The system of voice is the contrast between active and passive. Voice is, in the first instance, a system in clause grammar, since it affects first, the relation between the subject and the rest of the proposition and second, the presence or absence of an object and an agentive complement:

1a	*active*:	The window |	broke	
		S	P	
1b	*passive*:	The window |	was broken |	(by somebody)
		S	P	(C^{ag})
2a	*active*:	Bill |	broke |	the window
		S	P	C^{o}
2b	*passive*:	The window |	was broken |	(by Bill)
		S	P	(C^{ag})
3a	*active*:	Bill |	pushed	
		S	P	
3b	*passive*:	Bill |	was pushed	
		S	P	

13.2 Voice in the verbal group

This kind of clause organization is reflected in the structure of the verbal group as well as in the various configurations of S, P and C. The verbal group that realizes P in a passive clause is a passive verbal group, and conversely for active (see Figure 52). What makes passive verbal groups passive is the presence of a form of *be* (auxiliary) followed by a particular form of the main verb. This is the *n*-form and is shown in Figure 53. (The *n*-form is the same as that which occurs after auxiliary *have*, e.g. in *has broken*, . . . *has paid.* Many verbs do not make the distinction between *n*-form and *d*-form. The *d*-form is the form that realizes past

	active verbal group	*passive verbal group*
	broke	was broken
	sings	is sung
	has painted	has been painted
	is trying	is being tried
Figure 52	to pay	to be paid

	be		*main verb*		
	be		break	=	broken
	being		sing	=	sung
	been	*n*-form of	paint	=	painted
	was		try	=	tried
	were		pay	=	paid
	is		etc.		etc.
	are				
Figure 53	am				

tense, as in *he broke, sang, painted, tried, paid*, etc. The name *n*-form does not, therefore, mean that there is necessarily an *n* in the spelling or /n/ in the pronunciation. It is the form which occurs after *be*, when *be* has passive function, and after *have*, when *have* has perfect function.) What makes active verbal groups active is the absence of any indication that they are passive; i.e. passive is positively realized, but active is neutrally realized. (The terms passive and non-passive would be more apt.) So to convert a passive verbal group into an active one is to take something away. This is shown in Figure 54. The passive forms, written down the side of the diagrams (*is being eaten*, etc.), include the encircled items *be* and *en*. The active forms, which are written along the bottom, omit them.

Exercise 13.1

Identify the verbal groups in the following clauses. State whether they are active or passive and convert each into the opposite: e.g. *is encouraging* (active), *is being encouraged* (passive).

1 Otherwise art wouldn't be encouraged.
2 Hc should be paid more.
3 Our whole civilization has been built on it.
4 She is not going to allow him to write a symphony.

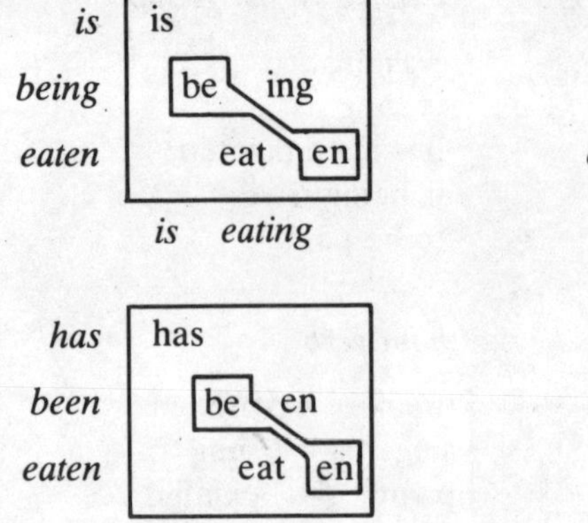

Figure 54

5 This fact is ruining opera.
6 Harold is now being offered an opportunity.
7 I have given them a promise.
8 One could only construe it as an incitement to disregard the law.
9 They were entrusted with the task by the public.

13.3 The meaning of voice

The examples given in section 13.1, above, suggest that we can take two perspectives on voice contrasts. One is illustrated in **4**:

4a Bill pushed
4b Bill was pushed

Here the relation between S and the rest of the proposition is focused upon. The subject is the same in each example, but, in the second *Bill* is on the receiving end of the process, and in the other he is not.

However, it is also true that in **4a** it is possible to introduce a C^{O}, (*somebody*), while in **4b** it is not. Again, in **4b** we can supply an agentive complement (*by somebody*), while in the first we cannot. So the second perspective focuses on this difference:

5 Somebody pushed Bill v. Bill was pushed by somebody
6 Bill pushed somebody v. Somebody was pushed by Bill

In **5** and **6**, reading across the page, the C^{o} of the active is identical with the S of the passive, and the S of the active is identical with the C^{ag} of the passive.

The two perspectives are complementary to each other and not in competition. There are large numbers of English verbs that can occur in transitive active, intransitive passive and intransitive active clauses:

7a	Bill broke the window	*transitive active*
7b	The window broke	*intransitive active*
7c	The window was broken (by Bill)	*intransitive passive*

The contrast between **7a** and **7c** is the second perspective. That between **7b** and **7c** is the first.

13.4 Agency

We will look first at the active/passive contrast as it affects the relation of the S to the rest of the proposition. Like the verb *break* are *move* and *open*:

8a The branches moved
8b The branches were moved

9a The door opened
9b The door was opened

In the active clause there is no suggestion of any agency. The process is presented as just happening spontaneously. But in the passive, first, an agent is implied (even if not specified) and second, the agent is to be understood as something distinct from the subject.

Very large numbers of verbs (unlike *break*, *move* and *open*) have an inherent sense of agency, e.g. *throw*, *eat*, *wash*. Such verbs normally appear in S P C^{o} active structures:

10a Bill threw the ball
10b We ate the apples last month
10c They washed the curtains yesterday

These clauses can readily be converted into passives of the type *The ball was thrown by Bill.* The verbs in these clauses do, however, have another active voice function:

11a This ball throws nicely

11b These apples eat rather dry
11c The curtains have washed well

The occurrence of such clauses in discourse is rather restricted; the first of the above examples suggests a context of 'games discourse', the second, 'culinary discourse' and the third 'housekeeping'. Although the verb implies that agency is necessarily involved, it is the quality or capacity of the subject that is stressed rather than the fact that it is being subjected to a process by an agent. Indeed, no agentive complement is possible: **This ball throws nicely by the players.*

12a The curtains have washed well
12b The curtains have been washed well

So the contrast between **12a** and **12b** again shows that active voice is non-committal on agency, while passive voice draws attention to the action of an agent but makes the agent distinct from the subject (NB These remarks apply to 'action' clauses, but not, for example, to *The story wasn't believed.* No agent can be involved in a process of believing, since believing is not an action.)

A few verbs fit the series of patterns given in **13**:

13a He raced the horses (at Goodwood)
13b The horses raced (at Goodwood)
13c The horses were raced (at Goodwood)

The horses are clearly a sort of actor in all these clauses, but in the first and the last there is a superior agent, i.e. the horses are not free agents, but acting under compulsion. Again, we can summarize the meaning of the passive by saying that it implies the existence of an agent separate from the subject. Active voice is in this respect, inexplicit.

Exercise 13.2

Try out the verbs given below by fitting them, if possible, into these three patterns:

$S' P^{act}$ . . . e.g. The car is moving.

$S' P^{pass}$ . . . e.g. The car is being moved.

$S P^{act} C^{o,}$ . . . e.g. I am moving the car.

where S′ and $C^{O\prime}$ are the same nominal group and are involved in the process referred to in the same way.

sit, rattle, store, waken, spend, fill, march, mend, play, stand, stretch, drop, shine, announce, perceive, hate, see, grow, work.

13.5 Thematic organization

So far we have looked at voice as it affects the interpretation of the proposition, especially the relation of the subject to the proposition as a whole. We now turn to the second perspective on voice, and see it as a means of organizing the sequence of elements in the clause.

14a Paul | explained | the mistake
S P^{act} C^{o}

14b The mistake | was explained | by Paul
S P^{pass} C^{ag}

The effect of choosing the active voice is to put *Paul* first and *the mistake* last. Normally the first item in a clause is the speaker's topic (or theme, see sections 5.4 and 12.2), and the last is what the speaker judges to be most informative to the addressee (new information, see section 12.7 and Appendix A, section 2). The structure for **14a** is given in **15**:

15 THEME | RHEME
// Paul explained the mis<u>take</u> //
— | NEW

(The symbol — indicates unspecified for given or new.)
Let us suppose the speaker wants to choose different items from *Paul* and *the mistake* as theme and new. If we keep the voice active, there are the following possibilities, all of which produce some effect of special emphasis:

16 THEME | RHEME
// the mis<u>take</u> // Paul ex<u>plained</u> //
NEW | — | NEW

In **16** the implication is almost inescapable: 'But there was something he didn't explain'. If we wanted *explained* as new without any special implication, this structure would not do.

17 THEME | RHEME
// Paul explained the mistake //
NEW | GIVEN

Example **17** makes *Paul* new information, but at the expense of treating the remainder as given, as though answering an implied question *Who was it that explained the mistake?* Moreover, supposing we wanted *the mistake* as theme, this would not do.

18 THEME | RHEME
// the mistake // Paul explained //
NEW | NEW | GIVEN

In **18** we have *the mistake* as theme, and *Paul* as new, but still at the expense of treating *explained* as given and implying a contrast for *the mistake:* 'As for the mistake in particular, who was it that explained it?'

The passive voice enables the speaker to choose *the mistake* as theme without any implied contrast, and it enables him to put the agent last as new information without implying any given information:

19 THEME | RHEME
// the mistake was explained by Paul //
— | NEW

Alternatively, it enables him to omit any mention of the agent, and thus bring the predicator into final position:

20 THEME | RHEME
// the mistake was explained //
— | NEW

It is important not to underrate the effect of choice of theme as an explanation for the occurrence of passive voice. The theme will usually be something that emerges from the preceding discourse, and so will be either given or unspecified; quite often it is inherently given (e.g. *the mistake*, where *the* implies that we know what mistake is being referred to, or *this*, meaning 'what I have just referred to'). Thus the passive voice may occur as a natural consequence of needing to choose a particular referent as theme. This point can be illustrated by reference to the first clause in the passage in Appendix B I. The theme is *they*, the moths whose migrating habits have already been mentioned. The new and most informative idea is the thundery conditions in which the migration tends to occur. The verb selected is *encourage*, and this means that if *they* is to come first and *very thundery close conditions* is to come last, the clause naturally settles into a passive mould. It would be inept to phrase it as *Very thundery close conditions encourage them in their migration*.

13.6 S P C^i structures

We have seen that *be* + *n*-form appears in a passive verbal group. However, *n*-forms have another function; like adjectives they can occur as head of an adjectival group, and hence function as complements of the ascriptive kind:

21 This window | appears | broken
S P C^i

Here *broken* is not part of the verbal group at P, which is simply *appears*. But we know that *be* can occur as main verb and be followed by a C^i, as in *The window is dirty*. It follows that **22** is ambiguous between S P C^i and S P:

22 The window was broken

23a	The window	appeared	broken
23b		seemed	
23c		looked	
23d		was	
	S	P	C^i

24 The window | was broken
S P

The clauses in **23** describe a state of affairs. No agentive complement can be added, and no manner adjunct can be added:

25 *The window looked broken carelessly (by the boys)

On the other hand, **24** describes an event — it is dynamic rather than stative. An agentive complement and a manner adjunct can be added:

26 The window was broken carelessly (by the boys)

Here are further ambiguous examples:

27a The spectators were moved
27b The house was insured
27c The new proposals were advanced
27d His hands were bandaged

The distinction between S P and S P C^i is sharp enough when the verb has a potentially dynamic sense. However, it is not in the last resort clear-cut, since it depends upon several independent criteria. So there are, alongside cases of ambiguity, also cases of indeterminacy:

28a The story was not believed
28b His action was justified by his need for employment

Exercise 13.3

Identify all the cases of *be* + *n*-form in the first passage in Appendix B. Which of these are clearly passive predicators? Which have the *n*-form as a C^i? Which are difficult to handle in these terms?

14 The verbal group 1

14.1 Full verbal groups

We shall be mostly concerned with verbal groups of the 'full' kind, that is, with those which have a main verb in them, and not with the kind which are dependent on a context for their interpretation, such as those in *Have they?* or *But I can't*. Example **1** gives some illustrations of full verbal groups:

1a	sits	**1b**	to have produced
	has been wearing		finding
	is carved		being found
	couldn't be faulted		having come
	can apply		worn
	is giving		to be asking

Those in **1a** are finite and those in **1b** non-finite.

14.2 Main verb and auxiliary

Full verbal groups consist of one or more words and have a main verb in final position. Any words that come before the main verb are auxiliaries. We can assign functional symbols to these elements of structure: v for main verb and a for auxiliary. For example:

2a couldn't be faulted
a a v

2b having come
a v

2c sits
v

2d finding
v

Some words can occur either as auxiliaries or as main verbs; in **3** *do* is sometimes one and sometimes the other:

3a She does the potatoes with this knife
v

3b I've done my essay
a v

3c I didn't rest
a v

3d We do do the tango
a v

3e What did you do?
a v

In Chapter 5 we pointed out that *have* and *be* also occur in both functions. As main verbs these have peculiarities and we shall postpone treatment of them until the section on polarity in the verbal group in the next chapter. The verbs *need* and *dare* also occur variously as main verb and modal auxiliary (see Chapter 8, examples **15–19**.

Exercise 14.1
Identify the verbal groups that occur in this passage:

A: Ah well, they have been given the promise that, I suppose, the Labour Party will foot the bill on money, but they've had removed from them the penalty which the law attaches to a breach of trust on the part of a councillor, a deliberate breach of trust, which is that they should be disqualified from acting as councillors again, and thus they are given a privilegium in the strictest sense, that is to say a privilege, a special law for them which doesn't apply to other people who deliberately break the law in similar circumstances.

B: Of course, the Labour Party Conference did call on the next Labour government (because it took place before Labour came to power) to indemnify these men; so morally do you think that Mr Crosland is justified in his action?

14.3 Verb morphology

Most verbs have a variety of inflected forms. For all verbs but one, namely the verb *be*, the maximum number of forms is six (this is counting the infinitive particle *to* as part of one of the forms:

1	*base form*	take	do	walk	(symbol: ø)
2	*to-form*	to take	to do	to walk	(symbol: t)
3	*ing-form*	taking	doing	walking	(symbol: ŋ)
4	*n-form*	taken	done	walked	(symbol: n)
5	*d-form*	took	did	walked	(symbol: d)
6	*s-form*	takes	does	walks	(symbol: s)

The majority of verbs do not make any distinction between *n*-form and *d*-form. For instance, the verbs *walk*, *wait*, *hope*, *own* occur in the same inflected form in both *I have walked*, *waited*, etc. and *I walked*, *waited*, etc. But a sufficiently large number of verbs do make the distinction for it to be simpler to assume the existence of homonymous *n*- and *d*-forms for verbs like *walk*. The verb *be* has nine forms. In Figure 55 the functionally equivalent forms of other verbs are given on the right.

base form	be		take	ø
to-form	to be		to take	t
ing-form	being		taking	ŋ
n-form	been		taken	n
d-form, singular	was	d^1 }	took	d
d-form, plural	were	d^2 }		
s-form	is		takes	s
am-form	am	am }	take	ø
are-form	are	are }		

Figure 55

Exercise 14.2
Consider the morphological peculiarities of the following verbs: *put*, *split*, *beat*, *come*, *win*, *lose*, *tread*, *sell*.

14.4 Structure in the verbal group

We have already seen that the verbal group has a structure consisting of a main verb standing alone or preceded by one or more auxiliaries: (a . . .) v. Simultaneously with this there is another structural organization. Finite verbal groups differ from non-finite groups in the first word. The first word, therefore, is the element that has the function of marking the finiteness of the whole group. We will use the symbols f, for *marker of finiteness*, and b for *marker of non-finiteness* (the choice of letter is suggested by the contrast between 'free' and 'bound'.) These are illustrated in **4**:

4a	*finite*	is taking; takes
		fa v fv
4b	*non-finite*	being taken; to take
		ba v bv

For the majority of verbs there are three forms that occur in initial position in finite groups. These are the forms that occur at f:

5a	*base form*	*take*	They take their time
		have	They have taken their time
5b	*s-form*	*takes*	He takes his time
		has	He has taken his time
5c	*d-form*	*took*	He took his time
		had	He had taken his time

There are four forms that occur at b; these are given in **6**:

6a	*base form*	*take*	I saw him take it
		have	I saw him have it
6b	*to-form*	*to take*	I want you to take it
		to have	I want you to have taken it
6c	*ing-form*	*taking*	I saw him taking it
		having	I saw him having it
6d	*n-form*	*taken*	I want it taken
		had	?

The base-form occurs at both f and b. This, however, does not apply to the verb *be*, which is the only verb whose base form does not occur at f. Other verbs use the base-form in the first and second persons:

7a I take it
7b You take it

However *am* and *are* occur in place of *be* in these persons:

8a I am here
8b You are here

Exercise 14.3
Using the symbols f, b, a and v, write out the structure of the verbal groups identified in exercise 14.1. Write the symbol for the form of the verb above the word thus:

s	ŋ	t
is	taking	to take
fa	v	bv

14.5 Some verbal systems

Verbal groups are either finite or non-finite. For the time being we will concentrate on the finite type, which means that we shall be focusing on what happens in initial position however many words there happen to be in the group as a whole.

Finite groups are tensed. That is to say, they select either past or present. They are also either modal or non-modal. This is illustrated in Figure 56. (Although it will serve present purposes, this network is a simplification of the facts. The relation between tense and modality is not so straightforward as it suggests. The reader is referred to sections 8.2, 16.1 and 16.3 for a discussion of some of the difficulties.)

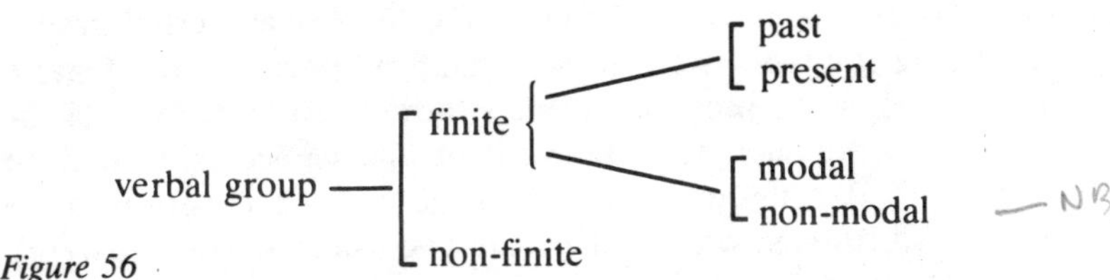

Figure 56

Modal groups have a modal auxiliary at f; such groups must therefore have at least two words in them, a modal auxiliary and a main verb. Let m stand for the element *modal auxiliary*. At this point we may economize in our structural notation by omitting the symbol a. All auxiliary elements are either some particular kind of auxiliary (such as the modal kind) or else are simultaneously the element that marks finiteness, or both. For present purposes the symbol a can be treated as redundant; any element that is not v can be taken to be a. The gaps in the following examples will shortly be filled in.

9a may study
fm v

9b may have studied
fm v

9c ought to assume
fm v

9d ought to have been adding
fm v

The form of the verb that occurs immediately after the modal auxiliary is determined by the subclass of modal verb that occurs. Most modal verbs require the base-form of the next verb, but *ought* and *used* require the *to*-form.

The tense features, past and present, are not realized by the presence of an auxiliary but by the form of the first word in the group, whatever this happens to be, and however many words there are in the group. It should be appreciated that the difference between *They take it* (present) and *They took it* (past) is the same contrast as that between *They are taking it* (present) and *They were taking it* (past), or *They have taken it* (present) and *They had taken it* (past). One sometimes meets with reference to *They have taken it* as a past tense, because it is talking about a past event. But this is to ignore the fact that *have* contrasts with *had*. *Have taken* is present perfect, and *had taken* is past perfect. (For further discussion of the perfect see sections 14.7 and 16.2.) Figure 57 distinguishes verbal groups according to tense. It can be seen that the present tense feature is realized by the presence of the *s*-form or the base-form of the first word (though with the verb *be* the choice is *s*-, *am*- or *are*-form). Past tense is realized by the use of the *d*-form of the first word (though with *be* there are two *d*-forms, *was* and *were*).

present	*past*
They export them	They exported them
He gives it away	He gave it away
You have forgotten them	You had forgotten them
She has brought some	She had brought some
We are sending it	We were sending it
He is trying them	He was trying them
They have been eating it	They had been eating it
He has been eating it	He had been eating it

Figure 57

any verb but be		
subject	*finite element*	*examples*
third person singular	*s*-form	He *takes* it It *has* vanished The one over there *looks* dry
any other person and number	base-form	I *take* it They *have* vanished The ones over there *look* dry

Figure 58

be		
subject	*finite element*	*examples*
first person singular	*am*-form	I *am* taking it I *am* here
third person singular	*s*-form	He *is* taking it The one over there *is* dry
any other person and number	*are*-form	They *are* vanishing The ones over there *are* dry

Figure 59

subject	*finite element*	*examples*
first or third person singular	d^1	I/He *was* there The one over there *was* dry
any other	d^2	You/We/They *were* being told The ones over there *were* dry

Figure 60

14.6 Subject concord

In present tense, variation between *s*- and base-form, or *s*-, *am*- and *are*-form, is determined from outside the verbal group by the properties of the subject. This is illustrated in Figures 58 and 59. In the past tense only the verb *be* varies for subject concord, as shown in Figure 60.

14.7 More systems

Finiteness, modality and tense are all realized in the first position in the verbal group. But first position may also be last, next to last, next but one to last, and so on. The architectural principle is suggested by Figure 61. The question that arises is what determines the number of places and the selection of verbs to fill them. Apart from modality there are three further systems that are realized by the presence of an auxiliary. These are voice, continuous aspect and perfect secondary tense. I shall deal with each of these in turn.

```
            fv
          f v
        f . v
      f . . v
    f . . . v
```

Figure 61

1 Voice: active v. passive

Passive voice is realized by the presence of the verb *be* as an auxiliary followed by the *n*-form of the next word. This is illustrated in Figure 62.

		. . .	*be*	*n-form*
			was	taken
		has	been	taken
		is	being	taken
Figure 62	may	have	been	taken

In the analysed groups in **10** the symbol p represents the element passive auxiliary:

10a was taken
fp v

10b has been taken
f p v

10c may have been taken
fm p v

Active voice has no realization other than the absence of what realizes the passive.

	. . .	*be*	*ing-form*	. . .
		is	taking	
	may	be	taking	
may	have	been	taking	
		is	being	taken
	may	be	being	taken

Figure 63

2 *Continuous aspect: continuous v. non-continuous*

This is often called progressive aspect (as well as progressive tense and continuous tense. I have chosen the term continuous so that we do not have another term beginning with the letter *p*). The feature 'continuous' is realized by the presence of *be* followed by the *ing*-form of the next word (which need not be the main verb). This is illustrated in Figure 63. We must of course distinguish between the verb *be* and the element of structure which it is fulfilling. In its passive function it is symbolized by p, and in its continuous function by c:

11a is taking
fc v

11b is being taken
fc p v

11c may be being taken
fm c p v

We must particularly note that it is the form of *be* that comes *before* the *ing*-form that is the continuous auxiliary.

The feature 'non-continuous' has no realization other than the absence of *be* followed by an *ing*-form.

	...	*have*	*n-form*	...	
		has	taken		
	may	have	taken		
		has	been	taking	
	may	have	been	taking	
Figure 64	may	have	been	being	taken

3 Perfect secondary tense: perfect v. non-perfect

(This is sometimes called perfect aspect. For an explanation of the notion 'secondary' tense see Chapter 16.) The feature 'perfect' is realized by the presence of the verb *have* followed by the *n*-form of the next verb, as shown in Figure 64. In the structural notation in **12** I use h to represent the element *perfect auxiliary* since the letter p is pre-empted:

12a may have taken
fm h v

12b has taken
fh v

12c may have been being taken
fm h c p v

Non-perfect is realized only by the absence of any realization for the perfect. The last item in **12** shows the sequence of auxiliaries, supposing that more than one occurs. It can be regarded as a sort of total formula: m h c p v. It is unlikely that all will occur together, but if two or more do occur this formula gives the sequence. The sequence is thus predetermined, and since no other sequence is possible the sequence is, in itself, of no significance. This is not the full story, however, since we have still to describe the auxiliary *do* and also the structure of complex verbal groups containing forms such as *be going*, *be able*, for instance, *He is going to fall*, and *They may be able to help*.

14.8 Non-finite groups

Although we are still concentrating mainly on finite verbal groups, it is worth pointing out here that the passive, continuous and perfect occur in both finite and non-finite groups. Some examples of non-finite groups are given in **13**:

13a to be taken (*passive*)
13b to have been taken (*perfect passive*)
13c having taken (*perfect*)
13d to be taking (*continuous*)
13e having been taking (*perfect continuous*)
13f to have been being taken (*perfect continuous passive*)
13g to be being taken (*continuous passive*)

The system network in Figure 65 shows four simultaneous systems.

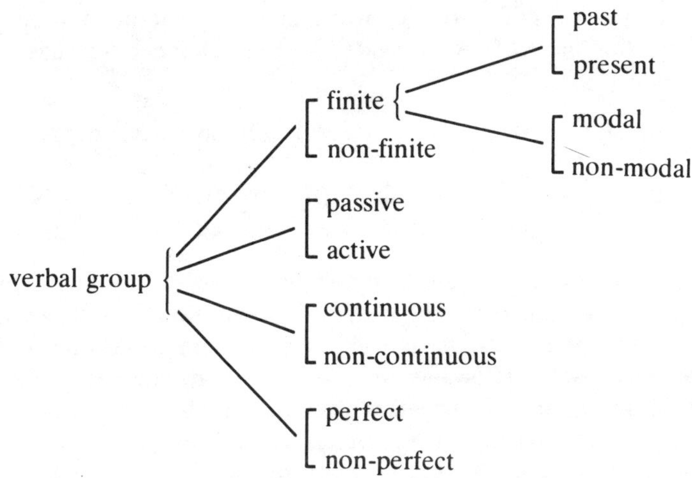

Figure 65

Exercise 14.4
Identify and analyse the verbal groups in the following sentences. For each one that is finite but not modal note whether it is present or past.

1 He has been with us often.
2 This matter is exciting politicians at the moment.
3 She could have been arguing in favour of inequality.
4 I take the line that we should try to think in terms of what looks neatest.
5 To have seen that, he must have had good eyesight.
6 Were you saying that?
7 It was published the following year, I think, and had been translated into French before a year had passed.

15 The verbal group 2

15.1 Polarity in the verbal group

In Chapter 5 we saw that the negative particle follows, or is attached as a suffix to, the word in first position in a finite group; this means it is associated with an element that has the function f, as in **1**:

1a (i) is beginning (ii) will have been begun
fc v fm h p v
1b (i) isn't beginning (ii) won't have been begun
fc neg v fm neg h p v

But there is a rule against combining neg with any main verb except *be* (or sometimes *have*), i.e. there are no forms **beginsn't* or **broken't*. *Be* and *have* will be dealt with in section 15.2. Making separate allowance for these, we can say that a finite verbal group that is negative, but not modal, or perfect, or continuous or passive, nevertheless must contain an auxiliary. This accounts for the presence of the auxiliary *do*, which is always initial and finite and hence the marker of tense and concord, as in **2**:

2a (i) begins (ii) broke
fv fv
2b (i) doesn't begin; (ii) didn't break
f neg v f neg v

The auxiliary *do* also occurs, if there is no other auxiliary present, when the mood of the clause requires a split predicator, as in **3**:

3a (i) It is beginning (ii) It begins
fc v fv
3b (i) Is (it) beginning (ii) does (it) begin.
fc v f v

Negation and interrogation of the polar kind have something in common. In both of them, though in different ways, polarity is made prominent; negation explicitly says 'no', and interrogation asks 'whether or not?' In an ordinary positive declarative such as **4** the polarity has no special prominence:

4 I'm going to Canada

The expected polarity of a statement is positive; ordinarily one does not say that something is not the case unless there is reason to believe that somebody might think otherwise.

It is nevertheless possible for a positive declarative to be used in explicit contrast to a negative, i.e. for the fact that the clause is not negative to be highlighted, as though the speaker wanted to say *I'm not not going to Canada*. The usual way of expressing this meaning in English is to give the finite auxiliary a special rhythmical prominence:

5 // ^ I / am / going to / Canada //
6 // ^ it / is / raining //
7 // ^ he / has / sent his a/pologies //

When the verbal group has no auxiliary for any other purpose, *do* must again be supplied to act as salient syllable as in **8**:

8 // ^ he / did / go to / Canada //

The forms that contrast with examples **5–8** in this systematic way are those in **9**:

9a I'm going to Canada
9b It's raining
9c He's sent his apologies
9d He went to Canada

The verbal groups which must have an auxiliary, even if it is only *do*, are those in which the polarity is a point of special significance. We will assign to these groups the feature 'polar emphasis'. Other verbal groups are necessarily positive, not pointedly so, but by default, since they have no polar emphasis. This is illustrated in Figure 66. It is the verbal groups with polar emphasis that occur when a split predicator is required.

Polar emphasis, then, is realized not necessarily by inserting an auxiliary verb, but by raising into rhythmical prominence an f which is separate from v. An f which is not also either m, or

no polar emphasis	/ wəz / going /əd / gone	went
polar emphasis negative	/ wɒznt / going / hædnt / gone	/ dɪdnt / go
positive	/ wɒz / going /hæd / gone	/ dɪd / go

Figure 66

fm	is realized by	*will*, *may* . . .
fh	is realized by	*have*, *has*, *had*
fc fp	are realized by }	*am*, *is*, *are*, *was*, *were*
fv	is realized by	*bring*, *brings*, *brought*; *cook* . . .
f	is realized by	*do*, *does*, *did*

Figure 67

h, or c, or p, or v is realized by *do*; this is shown in Figure 67. (See examples **1–3** for illustrations.)

15.2 *Be* and *have*

We noted in Chapter 5 that *be* can function as main verb, as in **10**:

10a He's late
10b He was my cousin
10c Harold has been treasurer for two years

All cases of main verb *be* behave like auxiliaries in respect of polar emphasis; it is not required to introduce *do*, which would give ungrammatical forms like **He does be late*; **He doesn't be late* and **Does he be late?*

It is therefore necessary to distinguish between the function v and the function of main verb *be*, which we will call copula (cop).

11a He is late
f cop

11b He is being awkward
fc cop

In Chapter 5 the element in a verbal group which is of special significance in the realization of mood was called the operator. The operator is definable as an element in a verbal group which is f and not v.

Exercise 15.1

Identify and analyse the verbal groups in the following examples. For each one write out the features of the group as well as the structural formula, for instance:

I'm thinking in these terms

am ŋ
'm thinking
fc v
Finite, no polar emphasis, non-modal, present, non-perfect, continuous, active.

1 It seemed quite natural that they should again be seated at the table where they had discussed so many subjects of public importance.
2 They oughtn't to be taken by surprise, because they *have* been warned and they do bring these troubles on their own heads.

Exercise 15.2

(a) Which of the verbal groups dealt with in exercise 14.1 and 14.3 have the feature polar emphasis? There is one that is emphatically positive. Explain why it occurs.
(b) There is also a case of an emphatically positive verbal group in Appendix BII, ll. 21–3. Explain this.

Have also occurs both as main verb and auxiliary. As main verb it has sometimes a dynamic sense and sometimes a stative one:

12a *dynamic*: They had a ride on a donkey
12b *stative*: They had a very big garden

In rather formal varieties of British English the main verb *have* is treated as an operator when it is stative:

13a Had they a big garden? (cf. Had they got . . .?
Did they have . . .?)
13b I haven't any time (cf. I haven't got . . .)

Usage is variable, however; the use of *do* for declarative, positive polar emphasis is perhaps not uncommon:

14 He does have a new car (cf. He has got a new car)

Have has other things in common with copula *be*. Consider the following pairs of examples, where the meaning and structure are very similar, but one has *be* and the other *have*:

15a There is a picture on the wall
15b The wall has a picture on it

16a Your letter is in his pocket
16b He has your letter in his pocket

When main verb *have* is an operator we will give it the function cop; in this way both *be* and *have* are differentiated from other main verbs, which have the function v:

17a Has he your letter in his pocket?
fcop
17b Has he got your letter in his pocket?
fh v
17c Does he have your letter in his pocket?
f v

15.3 Complex verbal groups

In the verbal groups we have examined so far there is a close association between the elements, giving a unity to the structure of the whole group. On the other hand, in phase structures the verbal elements fall into two parts with a more remote connection between them: first, a second lexical verb has to be selected; and also there is often a nominal item intervening. For this reason the clause in **18** is said to contain two predicators:

18 I *want* them *to have finished* soon

However, it is not true that there are no connections at all from one predicator to the next; the choice of forms in the second verbal group is usually limited by the choice of lexical verb in the first as shown in **19**:

19a *I tried to have turned the key
19b *I wanted turning the key
19c *I deny to have said that.

Since we have, on the one hand, verbal groups, forming a tightly constructed unit, and, on the other, phase structures involving two such units which are not, however, totally unconnected with each other, it is worth asking whether there are not intermediate cases where what might appear to be candidates for analysis as phase structures are better treated as single verbal groups, though of a more complex kind than any we have looked at so far. Some examples of what is meant are given in **20**. The items in parentheses are the items whose status is in question:

20a They *are going to appoint* somebody next week (be going)
They *may be able to send* it (be able)
He *is liable to break* the windows (be liable)
It *happened to fall* over (happen)
20b He *is bound to come* tomorrow (be bound)
He *was to be accused* of treason (be)
20c They *may have to be going* soon (have)
He *has tended to write* novels mainly (tend)
She *turned out to have* died (turn out)
20d He *came to see* what they meant (come)
We *got to know* them quite well (get)
The birds *have begun to eat* the crumbs (begin)
20e He *keeps finding* rabbits in the garden (keep)
They *have started introducing* new rules (start)

The groups **20a–20e** are suggested by a tentative classification of the structures, which I shall refer to briefly later. More important for present purposes is to find some syntactic argument for treating the verbal items italicized in **20** as either one predicator or two.

In true phase structures each predicator is assessed separately for voice. For instance, **21** has two active predicators, which are underlined:

21 I *heard* them *opening* the door

P^{act} P^{act}

The second one can be made passive provided the position of *the door* is adjusted:

22 I *heard* the door *being opened*

P^{act} P^{pass}

Alternatively, *them* in **21** could be moved to subject position:

23 They *were heard opening* the door

P^{pass} P^{act}

Again, **22** could have *the door* brought into subject position, giving two passive predicators:

24 The door *was heard being opened*

P^{pass} P^{pass}

By contrast with these, the examples in **20** which have an object, can be made passive by passing the object across the whole of the underlined item into subject position at one go:

25a The birds *have begun to eat* the crumbs

P^{act}

25b The crumbs *have begun to be eaten*

P^{pass}

26a They *have started introducing* new rules

P^{act}

26b New rules *have started being introduced*

P^{pass}

Exercise 15.3

Convert the following into passive clauses. Omit the agentive complement.

1 They may be able to send it next week.
2 People are liable to break these cups.
3 The police are likely to have seen them.
4 They would by now have been beginning to build it.
5 They tended to disregard our feelings.

The form of the passive clauses that are the answers to exercise 15.3 suggests that items like *may be able to send* can be considered as single predicators. *Be able*, *be going* etc., have some of the properties of auxiliaries; the name *semi-auxiliary* has been suggested for them by Quirk *et al*. (1972, pp. 67–9). The above paragraphs do not mention all of them.

It is interesting to examine the meanings of the verbs and adjectives that occur in the semi-auxiliaries. Some of them have meanings similar to what in some languages are 'aspects' of the verb. Here is a description of this kind of meaning from Hockett (1958, p. 237):

> Aspects have to do, not with the location of an event in time, but with its temporal distribution or contour. They show contrasts of meaning of the following sorts: 'He is singing,' 'He has been singing,' 'He sings habitually,' 'He sings repeatedly,' 'He is beginning to sing,' 'He is bringing his song to a close.' English has no inflectional aspects, but it shows two two-way aspectual contrasts by the structure of the verb phrase:
>
> *he sings* : *he is singing*
>
> .. ..
>
> *he has sung* : *he has been singing*

Some of the semi-auxiliaries like those given in **27–29** have meanings of this aspectual type:

27 He *kept* breaking the record (i.e. repeatedly)
28 He *got* to know them quite well (i.e. inception of a state)
29 They have *stopped* enforcing this law (i.e. cessation of action)

Others contribute a modal meaning. In **30** there is an element of knowledge modality, and in **31** of influence modality:

30a He *is bound* to be convicted
30b He *seems* to worship her
30c They *are going* to be disappointed

31a Imprisonment *is able* to break their spirit
31b We *had* to advise them to withdraw
31c He *is liable* to annoy his opponents

The distinction between aspect and influence modality is perhaps rather blurred in some cases, e.g. *tend*, *happen* and *turn out*.

The chief point to notice about these meanings is that the language seems to have converted some of its lexical items to quasi-grammatical uses. A look through various grammars of English will show that grammarians tend to treat this set of items as a plundering ground for new modalities, tenses and aspects. One picks on *keep* as a frequentative aspect; another finds an extra contrast of aspect in the passive voice (e.g. *It was broken* v. *It got broken*); another brings in *be going* as a secondary future tense (see section 16.2); still another fills in gaps in his paradigm of modal auxiliaries by means of *have (to)* and *be (to)*.

Let x represent the semi-auxiliary in these complex groups: then the maximum pattern of auxiliaries occurring before and after x is as follows: (m) (h) (c) x (h) (c) (p) v. It is unlikely that all of these options would be realized at once, but if they were the result would be:

32 (He) may have been tending to have
m h c x h
been being treated (badly)
c p v

The tentative classification of the structure referred to above, in relation to example **20**, is as follows:

Type (a) does not have c before x.
Type (b) allows nothing before x.
Type (c) allows the full range.
Type (d) does not allow h or c after x.
Type (e) does not allow h or c after x and allows (in some cases requires) *ing*-form after x (e.g. *keep singing*), while all the others require the *to*-form (e.g. *be able to sing*).

Exercise 15.4

Which of the following contain phase structures, and which contain complex verbal groups with semi-auxiliaries?

1 She is sure to serve the dinner soon.
2 I am keen to read that book.
3 We agreed to hear their complaints.
4 We started ringing the bell.
5 We remembered ringing the bell.
6 The manager is trying to dismiss him.
7 They appear to have filled the bucket.
8 We may fail to find the solution.
9 They are likely to do the tango.
10 They are happy to invite you.
11 It will start to discharge electrons. (Appendix BI, l. 18)

15.4 Non-finite verbal groups

Example **33** gives some typical non-finite groups occurring in bound clauses. Some are passive, some are continuous and some are perfect, while others are none of these, and some have combinations of passive and perfect, etc. Note that the form of the first word varies between *ing*-form and *to*-form.

33a *To find* out, we must look it up
33b *To have been found* out, he must have been very careless
33c *To have lost* his way, he must have been very careless
33d He must be rich, *to be thinking* of buying that
33e For Bill *to get* here early, he will have to start before six
33f For Bill *to have got* here early, he must have started before six
33g *Finding* out the real state of affairs, I decided to go home
33h *Having been found* out, he went away
33i *Having lost* his way, he asked a policeman
33j Without *looking* round, he went off
33k Without *having looked* round, he went off
33l With the sitting room *being decorated*, we are having to live in the kitchen

Non-finite groups where the first word is in base form also occur, but much more restrictedly:

34 Rather than just *sit* here, let's play patience

Some non-finite groups begin with an *n*-form, and these never have any auxiliaries:

35a *Painted* last year, the house still looks smart
35b *Painted* every year, the house always looks smart

These are probably best treated as alternative forms of passive *ing*-form groups such as *having been painted*, and *being painted*.

It is by no means a simple matter to describe the range of structures available in non-finite groups since different ranges are available in different contexts. We have already seen that besides occurring in bound clauses, they occur as second predicator in phase. They also occur in rankshifted clauses; here are some examples where a clause is functioning as subject of a clause. In **36** the whole rankshifted clause is italicized:

36a *Building houses* is expensive
36b *To have been questioned by the police for two hours* is no joke
(cf. It is no joke *to have been questioned by the police for two hours*)
36c *Having sent for the doctor* was a mistake
36d *Your having sent for the doctor* was a mistake

We shall not here attempt a description of the distribution of non-finite groups, but simply note that where an option is available between *ing*-form and *to*-form groups, there is often a clear distinction of meaning:

37a To hear the difference, listen carefully
37b Hearing the difference, listen carefully

In the first of these the hearing follows the listening as a result. In the second, the hearing does not follow the listening, but precedes it or overlaps with it.

38a For Bill to get here early, we must ring up his wife
38b With Bill getting here early, we must ring up his wife

A similar contrast of meaning is apparent here. In **38a** ringing up his wife is undertaken with the prospect of getting Bill here

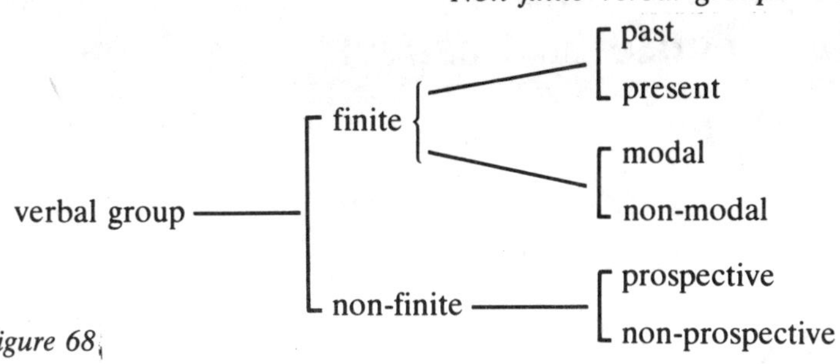

Figure 68

early. In **38b**, first Bill gets here early, or at least it becomes known that he will do so, and then the ringing up occurs. This system has been named 'prospective v. non-prospective' (see Sinclair 1972, pp. 186–7). Prospective is realized by the *to*-form of the first word and non-prospective by the *ing*-form.

To some extent these meanings can be found also in phase structures:

39a I tried to close the window
39b I tried closing the window

In **39a** the closing of the window is the goal aimed at. In **39b** the closing of the window and the trying are equivalent, e.g. the closing of the window was an attempt to get the room warm: 'I tried closing the window, but the room was still cold'.

Figure 68 summarizes the systems that affect the first place in verbal group structure.

Exercise 15.5

Consider the meaning contrasts, if any, between the following:

1(a) I remembered to post your letter.
(b) I remembered posting your letter.
2(a) I prefer to write with a pencil.
(b) I prefer writing with a pencil.
3(a) I intended to get here early.
(b) I intended getting here early.

16 Tense and aspect

16.1 Tense

In this book the term 'tense', used without qualification, means primary tense, the system whose terms are *past* and *present*. The systems of tense and modality together provide the features of finite verbal groups. We have already dealt with modal meaning at some length in Chapter 8, where it was shown that modality either expresses the speaker's assessment of the factuality of a proposition of which he has no direct knowledge, or expresses some condition on the fulfilment of the proposition: permission, compulsion, capacity or willingness. Tense is usually described as referring to time, but it does not refer to time in the way that items like *tomorrow*, *the week after next*, *last year* and *in 1976* do. It is not the same thing as specifying a particular time. In the following examples **1** contains an explicit time reference and **2** does not:

1 He comes tomorrow
2 He reads the *Guardian*

It might be better to say that tense makes the proposition compatible with reference to certain periods of time, rather than that it refers to time itself.

Further, it is indeed the case that, without any indication to the contrary, a past tense form like *he came* is incompatible with reference to present or future time; so that **3** does not make sense:

3 *He came tomorrow

But it is certainly possible for past tense not to have a past-time value:

4 In the original plan he came tomorrow
5 I thought he came tomorrow
6 If he came tomorrow, what would you do?

The effect of past tense here is to make the proposition unreal or hypothetical. The proposition is distanced from the present situation in which the speaker is operating, but not in a temporal sense. Another instance of non-temporal distancing can be imagined for **7**:

7 I only wanted a cup of tea

This might not have any past time reference at all, but might rather mean 'I want a cup of tea but am too polite to say so outright'. Use of the past tense is less challenging to the addressee. A similar explanation could be given for *thought* in **5**: 'I actually think so, but you seem to think the opposite, so I am toning down my way of putting it in deference to you'. The meaning of past tense seems to be a distancing of the proposition in some way (often temporal) from the situation of utterance.

Present tense has no such distancing effect; the proposition is presented as fully real and actual in the present situation. Present tense is frequently used when reference is made to future time:

8 The new students arrive next week
9 Harold is voting Conservative tomorrow
10 They are going to send us some food

In all of these examples there is a present actuality about the future event; the present situation has the seeds of the future within it.

When past tense is accompanied by past time-reference, the addressee is being told 'I am not referring to the present situation'. But past tense in itself gives no information on what past situation is being referred to. It is necessary that somewhere in the context there should be a specification of what situation is meant; this might be in an adjunct, as in **11**:

11 He wasn't listening at the lecture yesterday

Or it could be in a separate clause as in **12** and **13**:

12 While they were talking, Jack wasn't listening
13 They were talking, but Jack wasn't listening

In these the situation in which Jack wasn't listening is referred to in the other clause; that other clause itself contains a past tense and so we must look to a wider context to identify the situation in which they were talking. In conclusion, present tense needs no contextualization to identify the situation referred to but past tense does.

In Chapter 8 (sections 8.2 and 8.8) there was a brief discussion of tense and modality. It was pointed out that subjective modalities cannot be located in past time since the very meaning of subjectiveness is that the speaker is indicating how he intends his utterance to be taken. Therefore in subjective modality, past tense, when it is possible at all, has to have a non-temporal interpretation.

14 The train might be late

For instance, **14** does not mean 'It was possible that the train was late' but 'It is remotely possible that the train is, or will be, late'.

The case is different with objective modality. This can be located in the past. We will illustrate this point first by reference to influence modalities (ability, volition, permission and compulsion) and then in connection with 'past reports'. Modal expressions of ability and volition are primarily objective. With some restrictions, they can be put into the past tense with a past time-reference:

15a Bill could touch his toes in those days
(he was able to)
15b Bill *would* sit in Fred's chair last night
(He insisted)
15c He wouldn't come in
(He refused)

Permission and compulsion modalities are primarily subjective and have to be reinterpreted objectively when they refer to the past. Moreover there are severe restrictions on what modal verbs can be used in this way. Only *could* and *might* can be used, not *must*, *needn't*, *should* or *ought*:

16a He could/might go out whenever he wanted to
(he was allowed to)
16b *He must catch the early train

(The meaning of **16b** cannot be 'He was obliged to catch the early train'. This meaning is expressed by means other than a modal verb: *He had to catch the early train*; *He was obliged to catch the early train*.)

The idea of a past report can best be introduced by means of the examples in **17**, some of them with a modal verb in the reported part of the construction and some without:

17a They say there is trouble in the docks
17b They say there will be trouble in the docks
17c They said there was trouble in the docks
17d They said there would be trouble in the docks
17e She thinks Harold is an MP
17f She thinks Harold may be an MP
17g She thought Harold was an MP
17h She thought Harold might be an MP

Each of the examples in **17** consists of two clauses, first a reporting clause containing a reporting verb such as *say* or *think*, and then a reported clause. For a detailed description of reported clauses and related matters, see Chapters 19–22. For the present we need only note that the modalities that occur in the reported clauses are necessarily objective. For instance, in *She thinks Harold may be an MP, but I know for a fact that he isn't* the verb *may* reflects her doubt, not the speaker's. Second, when the reporting clause has a verb in the past tense, as in **17c**, **17d**, **17g** and **17h**, we have a *past report*, i.e. the speaker is reporting somebody's words or thoughts from a past occasion. In such a case it is usual for the reported clause also to be in the past tense. It would not be true to say that the tenses of the verbs in the two clauses may not vary independently of each other, e.g. *She thinks Harold was an MP*; *She told me Harold is an MP*. But I am at present concerned only with the case where there is a concord of tenses between the two clauses. The chief point in the present discussion is that in past reports the modal verbs occur in the forms given in Figure 69, which are therefore best regarded as past tense forms. The present tense equivalents are also given. It will be seen that in some cases the past form of the modal verb does not differ from the present form, and also that *must* (a verb that is sometimes said to have no past tense form or function) functions as a past tense in past reports. (For a discussion of *could* and *should* in the present tense paradigm see section 8.2, examples **24** and **25**.)

The examples of past reports given in Figure 69 are all of

	past		
She thought that the tank	might	might not	be empty
	could	needn't	
	would	wouldn't	
	must	couldn't	
	should	shouldn't	
	ought	oughtn't to	
	present		
She thinks that the tank	may	may not	be empty
	could	needn't	
	will	won't	
	must	can't	
	should	shouldn't	
	ought	oughtn't to	

Figure 69

knowledge modalities. The same observations are valid for influence modalities. For example:

18a She told him he must catch the early train
18b She told him he might leave early

16.2 Secondary tense

I shall be dealing with two secondary tenses, the perfect and the future:

19a *perfect*: He has taken my coat
19b *future*: He is going to take my coat

Primary tense takes the situation of utterance as its point of reference. Secondary tense can only be interpreted by reference to primary tense somewhere in the context. We will start by concentrating on perfect secondary tense. The perfect is not confined to occurrence in finite verbal groups, as **20c** shows:

20a He has broken his promise
20b He had broken his promise
20c Having broken his promise . . .

In **20a** there is present (primary) tense in the same verbal group as the perfect. In **20b**, which is also finite, the primary tense is past. The perfect refers to a time prior to the time indicated by the primary tense; in **20a** he broke his promise sometime before the moment of speaking and in **20b** he had broken his promise sometime before the past moment referred to by *had*, which has to be identified by reference to the context. Example **20c** is not finite, so we must refer to the primary tense of the following clause:

21a Having broken his promise, he sent his apologies
21b Having broken his promise, he sends his apologies

In **21a** he broke his promise sometime before an occasion in the past; in **21b** he broke his promise sometime before the moment of speaking. The non-finite clauses could be paraphrased as follows:

22a Since he had broken his promise . . .
22b Since he has broken his promise . . .

The significance of the combination of primary tense with perfect tense can be illustrated by contrasting the present perfect with the past non-perfect:

23a He has painted the house
23b He painted the house

Both these examples refer to a past event of painting the house, but **23a** places the event in a period of time that includes the moment of utterance; time adjuncts in this clause could include *today*, *this year*, *this century* (periods which include the moment of utterance) but not *two hours ago*, *yesterday*, *last year*, because these are periods which came to an end before the moment of utterance. The significance of the present perfect is that the painting of the house is a feature of the present situation: for instance, the results of the painting are still to be seen; the house looks smart. Once the paint has faded the painting of the house may no longer seem such a present fact. It would then be more appropriate to use the past non-perfect, **23b**.

The relevance of a past event to a present situation is a matter of the speaker's point of view. Even if the paint has become shabby, the painting of the house may still be considered to have present relevance for some other reason. For instance, the speaker may be thinking of the experience of painting that he gained. The relevance that the speaker sees in the past event might be summarized in a clause beginning *so* . . . :

24a He has painted the house, so it looks smart
24b He has painted the house, so I know he can do such things
24c He has painted the house, so now he is free to do other jobs

The past non-perfect does not mean that there is no such relevance to the present situation, but simply that, if there is any, the speaker is not drawing attention to it.

It should be noted that present perfect does not necessarily refer to an event of recent occurrence; nor does the past non-perfect necessarily refer to an event in the remote past:

25a This country has been invaded several times, but not since the eleventh century
25b I dropped the teapot two minutes ago

A good many past events do not retain their relevance to later history for very long; new paint does not last for ever. So it is usual for the present perfect to refer to the recent past, but this is not part of its meaning.

The term 'perfect' may tend to suggest that the past event is necessarily complete. This would certainly be the favoured interpretation of **26**:

26 I have written to them

However, the present perfect is compatible with continuous aspect:

27 I have been writing to them

Here, the writing may, but need not, be finished. Moreover, the perfect can be used with processes that are not events but states:

28 He has been a teacher for twenty years

There is no suggestion that he is going to stop being a teacher from now on. So whatever *perfect* might mean in the description of other languages, it does not mean 'completed process' in English.

Exercise 16.1
Refer to the passage given in exercise 19.4 (page 249). Identify

past non-perfect verbal groups and present perfect verbal groups. Explain the different meanings of these choices in relation to this context.

16.3 The modal perfect

The perfect tense has a special significance in combination with modal verbs, and the significance is somewhat different with knowledge modality from what it is with influence modality. We will look first at the knowledge type. The reader will remember that modal verbs in the knowledge interpretation are used primarily in a subjective sense. This means that the modality itself cannot be located in past time. Nevertheless, the speaker may be making a present assessment of the evidence for a past, a present or a future event or state. (See section 8.4.) One of the uses of the perfect tense is to make reference to a past time in combination with a present assessment of truth:

29a The train may have been delayed
(It is possible that the train was delayed, *or*
It is possible that the train has been delayed, *or*
It is possible that the train will have been delayed)

29b He will have posted the letter yesterday
(It is probable that he posted the letter yesterday)

29c He will have posted the letter by now
(It is probable that he has posted the letter by now)

29d He will have posted the letter by this time tomorrow
(It is probable that he will have posted the letter by this time tomorrow)

In the glosses to all these examples the modality is expressed in the present tense: 'it *is* possible/probable . . .'.

In influence modality the case is different. Here it is possible for the modality to be objective, which means that a past-tense modal verb can be used with reference to past time. In this case the perfect tense has a specially interesting effect, a 'contrary-to-the-facts' implication, which is brought out in the glosses in **30**:

30a Bill could have gone to the party
(It was permissible for him to go to the party; but he didn't)

30b He should have sent his apologies
(It was obligatory for him to send his apologies; but he didn't)

30c He needn't have been so apologetic
(It wasn't obligatory for him to be so apologetic, but he was)

30d He could have swum to the shore
(He was able to swim to the shore, but he didn't)

30e He would have helped me
(He intended to help me, but he didn't)

In this paradigm, the verb *must* lives up to its reputation and fails to appear, so that **31** cannot possibly be a past-tense influence modality meaning 'He was obliged to go to the party, but didn't'. It can only have a knowledge interpretation ('It is certain that he went/has gone/will have gone to the party') or, less likely, be taken as a present-tense influence modal, as described in the next paragraph.

31 He must have gone to the party

It is possible for influence modalities to occur in the present perfect, in which case the modality may but need not be subjective. In this case reference is being made to future time:

32a He must have dug the garden (by the time we move into the new house)
(It is compulsory for him to have done so before that future occasion)

32b Bill can have left early
(It is permissible for Bill to have left early on that future occasion)

32c I can have got the dinner ready by then
(I am able to have got the dinner ready by then)

The existence of a volitional type to complete the examples of **32** is doubtful.

Figure 70 may help the reader to sort out the rather complicated facts about time reference in clauses containing modal verbs.

NB A major point that has not been covered for lack of space is the occurrence of modal verbs in conditions:

33a If you speak louder, I'll hear you better

33b If you spoke louder, I would hear you better

knowledge non-perfect (a) no past time reference even with past tense modals (b) except when occurring in past reports	(a) It might be in your pocket (It's *remotely possible*) (b) He thought it might be in his pocket (. . . *that it was possible that it was* . . .)
knowledge perfect modality is present; proposition is past, present or future time	They may have been delayed (*It is possible that they were, have been or will have been delayed*)
influence non-perfect (a) past tense refers to past time (but *must*, *should*, *ought* and *needn't* do not occur) (b) also in past reports (*must*, *should*, etc. do occur)	(a) He could touch his toes in those days (*He was able to*) (b) She told him he must leave early (. . . *that he was obliged to leave early*)
influence perfect (a) past tense refers to past time (contrary to the facts); *must* does not occur (b) present tense refers to future time	(a) He should have sent his apologies (*He was obliged to but he didn't*) (b) He must have gone to bed by the time we get home (*It is compulsory for him to do so*)

Figure 70

Exercise 16.2

Rewrite the following examples, preserving the sense as far as possible but using a modal verb. Some of them may have more than one plausible rewriting. Decide whether the modality is of the knowledge or the influence type.

1 He's supposed to have told her by tomorrow.
2 It wasn't necessary for him to tell a lie (though he did).

3 It's not inevitably true that he told a lie.
4 It's conceivable that he didn't tell a lie.
5 He had a chance to change his job (but he didn't).
6 It's possible that he changed his job.
7 It's possible that he has changed his job.
8 It was obligatory for the door to be locked (but it wasn't).
9 It is obligatory for the door to have been locked (by some time in the future).
10 It's certain they were asked to avoid a confrontation.

Exercise 16.3
Explain the possible senses of

1 The road should have been repaired.
2 He could have been killed.

Exercise 16.4
Why are the following not capable of an influence interpretation?

1 They must have moved to another house last year.
2 She can't have taken mine yesterday.

16.4 Future secondary tense

The future secondary tense is realized by the semi-auxiliary *be going*. (See Chapter 12, pp. 182–7.) Other semi-auxiliaries also have future implications:

34a He *is liable* to be late
34b He *is bound* to object
34c He *is about* to try

The justification for picking out *be going* for special treatment is that it has a more purely 'future' significance than the others. It is secondary future significance, however. Reference is made to a time subsequent to the time indicated by a primary tense:

35a He was going to vote Conservative
35b He is going to vote Conservative

Example **35a** places the voting in a period subsequent to the time indicated by *was*:

36 When I saw him yesterday he was going to vote Conservative

It can be seen that the time for voting might be any time after I saw him, including yesterday, today or tomorrow.

The future secondary tense is often said to suggest intention on the part of the performer. Example **35** suggests that it was/is his intention to vote Conservative. This is merely the favoured interpretation when the verb, e.g. *vote*, denotes a voluntary action and is active. In **37** there is no suggestion of intention:

37a He is going to die
37b He is going to sneeze
37c He is going to be punished

The meaning of the future secondary tense is that the future is imminent in the situation being talked about; the signs are there already. This meaning is somewhat different from that of the predictive modal auxiliary:

38a He will die
38b He will be punished

Here the death and the punishment seem less immediately threatening.

The semi-auxiliary *be going* is usually easily distinguished from the lexical verb *go*. In fact they can occur together:

39 He's going to go tomorrow

There are however occasional cases of ambiguity, as in **40**:

40 He's going to help us

(a) two clauses: In order to help us, he's going (somewhere). Here, *going* is the lexical verb

(b) With future secondary tense: SPC^{O}

To incorporate the future tense into the notation for verbal groups we need a symbol for the *be* and a symbol for the *going*: g^1 and g^2. The analysis of *is going to help* is given in **41**:

41 s ŋ t
•is going to help

fg^1 g^2 v

16.5 Continuous and habitual aspect

In addition to the continuous, English has a habitual aspect, but there is this important difference between them, that the continuous is always overtly realized (by the *be+ing* structure) while the habitual is optionally realized; that is, the meaning may be habitual even when there is no difference in structure from the non-habitual:

42a *non-habitual*: Bill went to town on the bus (*referring to one occasion*)
42b *habitual*: Bill went to town on the bus (*referring to repeated occasions*)
or: Bill used to go to town on the bus
or: Bill usually went to town on the bus
or: Bill often used to go to town on the bus

It can be seen from these examples that when the habitual aspect is overtly realized, this is done by using either the quasi-modal *used (to)* or a frequentative adjunct like *usually*, *normally*, *often*, *always*, *sometimes*, *never*, *seldom*, or both. However, *used (to)* is only available for reference to past time.

What is important for our present purposes is the ambiguity of *Bill went to town on the bus* since which way we interpret this influences the way we understand the continuous aspect, when this is added:

43a Bill was going to town on the bus (on that one occasion)
43b Bill was going to town on the bus (in those days)

In the present tense the ambiguity is less striking, but it is still there:

44 Bill goes to town on the bus

In most contexts we would interpret this as having habitual meaning: 'Bill normally goes to town on the bus'. But in some special contexts, such as in the synopsis of a plot or in a running commentary, the non-habitual interpretation would be normal:

45a She leaps from the battlements to her death
45b Now Smith runs up and bowls and Jones gives it a careful prod and there are no runs

Similarly, the present continuous is ambiguous:

46a He is going to town on the bus (this morning) (*non-habitual*)
46b He is going to town on the bus (every day this week) (*habitual*)

A process, whether or not it is seen as habitual, may consist of constituent events. Thus **47** can be seen as one event – a double shout. Hence in **48** it is the double shout that is repeated.

47 He shouted twice
48 He used to shout twice

So the meaning of habitual aspect is more than the mere repetition of a process. It means that the repetition (or perhaps, rather, the frequency) of the process is characteristic of the situations that are being talked about (see Comrie 1976, pp. 26–32). General or universal truths are in habitual aspect, in the present tense:

49 Oil floats on water

This also goes for less universal truths that nevertheless characteristically hold of something or somebody:

50a Millstone talks nonsense
50b This material washes nicely

16.6 Stative and dynamic processes

Before looking in more detail at the meaning of the continuous aspect and the ways in which it combines with the habitual, it will be convenient to make the distinction between stative and dynamic processes. This has to do with the way processes are distributed in time. Stative processes are those which do not develop with the passage of time, but merely continue:

51a Harold is an MP
51b He thinks the country is going to the dogs
51c I hope not
51d The station is by the river
51e That seems a pity

51f He doesn't know why
51g I love you

Such processes as these have the quality of continuity without change. This does not mean that Harold may not cease to be an MP, but that to be an MP does not involve any change of state.

On the other hand, there are dynamic processes, which involve change and development and which therefore have a more complex distribution in time than mere continuity. These processes have a 'beginning/middle/end' structure. They include: *eat a meal*, *sneeze*, *write essays*, *jump over a ditch*, *tell a story*, *get to know French*, *become an MP*, *get taller and taller*, *cease to love*, *go mad*, *stop being an MP*, *die*, etc.

In section 16.4, above, all the illustrations of habitual aspect were of the dynamic type, but habitual aspect is also possible with stative processes. The same state of affairs can be manifested on different occasions or in different instances:

52a He was in the garden (every time I went by)
52b He was always in the garden
52c The post office is usually near the station (in various towns).

16.7 Continuous aspect

The meaning of continuous aspect has always proved difficult to pin down. One explanation of the meaning is that it presents a dynamic process, or series of processes, as being of temporary duration:

53a *non-habitual*: She was singing at Covent Garden (The performance was destined to come to an end, but had not yet done so)
53b *habitual*: She was singing at Covent Garden (a series of performances, part-way through, but a temporary arrangement)

These meanings are highlighted by comparing them with the non-continuous *She sang at Covent Garden*, which means either that the process is being seen as single and entire (non-habitual) or that she sang repeatedly as a permanent arrangement (habitual: *She used to sing at Covent Garden*).

Temporary duration cannot be the whole explanation,

however, since **54** has no suggestion that the process is going to come to an end:

54 The moon is going round the earth

Here the meaning seems to be that one process is seen as simultaneous with another; for instance, 'While the earth is going round the sun, the moon is going round the earth; so every now and then we get an eclipse . . .'. The simultaneity explanation also holds good in the following, where the continuous suggests an overlapping of the processes in time, while the non-continuous suggests that one event follows another:

55a They were having dinner when I arrived
55b They had dinner when I arrived

Example **55a** speaks of the having dinner as a background or framework for my arrival. However, the simultaneity explanation does not work so convincingly for **56**:

56 (Where's George?) He's sitting in my office

It does not seem necessary to understand a reference to some other simultaneous process here.

It seems that what is needed is a common principle that underlies both simultaneity and temporary duration. One possibility is that continuous aspect views the process as contingent, or incidental to some other focus of interest. Whether a process is simultaneous or temporary or both, it may be contingent:*

57 A: What on earth are you doing?
B: I'm trying to find a paperclip that's fallen behind my desk.

Trying to find a paperclip explains why the speaker is kneeling on the floor. The opposite of a contingent process can be seen in sports commentaries. The key events in a cricket match are not seen as incidental, or explanatory of other events, or as providing a background against which they take place; they are focused upon their own sake, each making its own contribution

*This term, as applied to the English aspect usually called progressive or continuous, is suggested in Comrie (1976).

to the developing match (see example **45b**). In more everyday situations we do not give running commentaries on what is 'happening now'; it is not customary to talk about on-going events except for the sake of their relevance to something else.

Whether or not we have now succeeded in summing up the meaning of continuous aspect satisfactorily, it seems that continuous aspect is not compatible with stative processes. This may be because an enduring, unchanging state cannot aptly be seen as a contingent one. So the following are not possible:

58a *That is seeming a pity
58b *I'm loving you
58c *He isn't knowing the way
58d *The station is being near the post office

A process which superficially seems to be stative but which has the continuous aspect, usually has to be interpreted as dynamic:

59a I'm loving you more and more every day (i.e. 'getting to love you . . .')
59b You're being careless (i.e. 'behaving carelessly')

It is true, however, that some verbs denote processes which are not very clearly either stative rather than dynamic or vice versa. Thus it would not be easy for a foreign learner of English to predict whether the following examples would be acceptable:

60a He is living in Wales
60b I'm hoping to see them soon
60c ?* He's not believing us

Some dynamic processes are of such short duration that it is not often necessary or appropriate to view them as contingent: they cannot easily be seen as the background against which some other event is taking place, nor can they easily be presented as part way through and soon to be over. An example would be **61**:

61 The balloon burst

Consequently, when such a process appears in the continuous, it seems to be stretched in time, suggesting, perhaps, a slow-motion film:

62 The balloon is bursting

On the other hand, long-lasting processes may become shrunk by the continuous aspect; **59b** shrinks the enduring characteristic of carelessness into a piece of careless behaviour.

16.8 Habitual and continuous in combination

We saw above (section 16.4) that habitual and continuous aspects can combine, so that *He was going to work on the bus* may have a habitual interpretation. The characteristic repetition of the process is of short duration: 'He was going to work on the bus repeatedly for the time being.' We could symbolize the structure as in Figure 71.

continuous (*habitual* (he went to town on the bus))

Figure 71

In such a case as this it is not possible to include *used (to)* as an overt mark of habitual aspect; the use of this would produce a different meaning:

63 He used to be going to town on the bus

Example **63** suggests a context like 'whenever I saw him . . .'. This is indeed a combination of habitual with continuous aspect, but in a different order: not the contingency of the habit, but the habituality of the contingency. This is schematized in Figure 72.

habitual (*continuous* (he went to town on the bus))

Figure 72

Thus there are three interpretations of *He was going to town on the bus* according to what it is that is seen as contingent (i.e. on-going, temporary, simultaneous), and these are given in Figures 73–75.

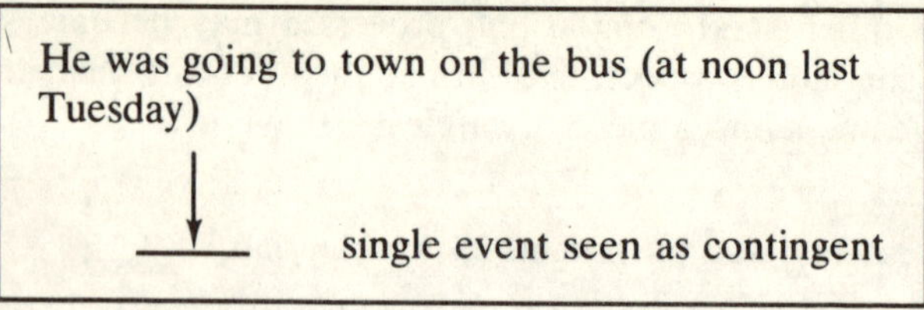

Figure 73

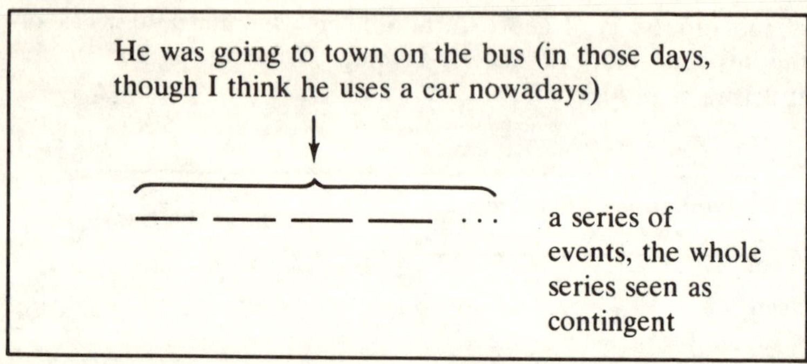

Figure 74

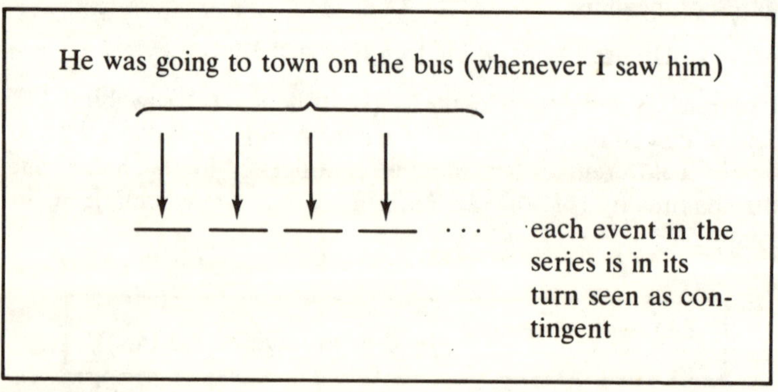

Figure 75

The use of frequentative adjuncts in combination with continuous aspect usually suggests the interpretation given in Figure 75:

64a He was often peeling potatoes (when I arrived)
64b She is usually getting the car out (when they pass)

However, it does seem possible to find frequentative adjuncts (though not *used to*) in the type shown in Figure 74, even though they probably occur only rarely:

65a In those days I was often cooking the dinner (The temporary arrangement was that I often cooked the dinner)

65b He was usually sending on any letters (For the time being it was customary with him to send on whatever letters there were to send)

65c You are rarely writing for the *Guardian* these days (The present state of affairs is that you rarely write for the *Guardian*)

Exercise 16.5

Refer to Appendix BI, ll. 29–44. Is the aspect of the clauses in this passage predominantly habitual or non-habitual? In connection with this question, note the use of the modal verbs *will* and *can*. Identify any continuous verbal groups and suggest why the continuous feature occurs rather than the non-continuous.

Exercise 16.6

Refer to Appendix BII, ll. 42–9. Explain why the continuous verbal groups occur.

17 Clause complexes 1

17.1 Free and bound clauses

We are now to look at the ways in which clauses can be combined with each other to form clause complexes. The question of the relation between clause complexes and sentences will be taken up later (page 224); for the present the term *sentence* will be used rather loosely and more or less synonymously with 'clause complex'. Example **1** contains sentences consisting of either one or two clauses; the clause boundary, if any, is indicated with a bar line:

1a I'll go on Friday, || which is his birthday
1b It hasn't clicked
1c Live || as long as you can
1d I suspect || they are stealing apples
1e Not being allowed visitors, || he gets bored
1f Think || before you speak

For the sake of simplicity we shall confine our attention at first to complexes consisting of two clauses.

Clauses enter into the construction of sentences in one of two ways: they are either *free* or *bound*. The distinguishing characteristic of free clauses is the fact that within them the grammar provides mood options which signal the way in which the speaker is involving himself and his addressee in an act of communication. (See Chapters 5–7.) It is not always necessary for a speaker, or writer, to signal this kind of information. The circumstances in which language is being used may be such that it would be superfluous. For instance, it is not necessary to print on the cover of *The Concise Oxford Dictionary*: 'This book is called *The Concise Oxford Dictionary*'. It will be understood that the sentence *Concise Oxford Dictionary* is being used in an informative spirit. Thus the grammar of the free clause allows the speaker to opt out of the mood system and produce a moodless free clause. Moodless clauses are *minor* clauses, which means that they have no predicator; and since subject is a function defined by relation to a predicator, they have no subject either. Moodless clauses are tied very closely to the situation in which they are uttered. (The word 'uttered', should be understood as applying to both speech and writing.) They are typical of announcements, headlines, notices and titles:

2a Open all day Wednesday
2b Encyclopedia Britannica
2c Victoria Station, please
2d The Nook
2e Ticket holders this way
2f No smoking in the store
2g Mother for trial
2h Four in court after bank strike
2i Drying only customers 10p extra

Exercise 17.1
Consider the ways in which the examples in **2** might be associated with their situations of utterance. Given some definite situation of utterance, in what way is the addressee expected to respond to the communication?

Bound clauses are dependent upon free clauses. They have a kind of mood, since the speaker may take up one of various attitudes towards the factuality of the proposition:

3a Unless they submit the report . . .
3b When the report has been submitted . . .
3c . . . that the report has been submitted
3d Having submitted the report . . .

In **3a** the speaker does not profess to know whether they will submit the report; in **3b** he assumes that the report will be submitted; in **3c** he simply encodes the idea of the report being submitted, so that someone's attitude towards the idea can be spoken of, e.g. *He thinks that the report has been submitted*; **3d** envisages the submitting of the report but expresses no attitude whatever about its factuality.

There is quite a variety of speaker-preposition relations in bound clauses; but what makes these clauses different from free clauses is that the addressee is not assigned any role except simply that of addressee. An addressee hearing the clauses in **3** cannot tell how he is supposed to respond to the act of communication. On the other hand, as soon as he can connect them with a free clause he knows whether he is expected to respond as knower, decider, or performer. (See the discussion of mood in Chapters 5–7.) The three dots in the examples in **3** could have a free clause of any mood substituted for them.

There are circumstances, especially in dialogue, where the relation between clauses is rather indirect. For instance:

4A: When's the match?
B: Tomorrow

Speaker B's utterance here is a free clause with declarative mood, but this can only be alleged because of its relation to A's non-polar interrogative. *Tomorrow* is elliptical for *The match is tomorrow*. It is because of the systematic relation between the clauses in **5** that B in **4** can be assigned the features 'free', 'indicative' and 'declarative':

5a When's the match?
5b The match is sometime
5c The match is tomorrow
5d Tomorrow

Ellipsis is a special kind of structural dependence on a linguistic context. Note that none of the clauses in **2** is elliptical. In the dialogue given in **6**, B's utterance is elliptical for *She will get an allowance if she's lucky*:

6A: Will she get an allowance?
B: If she's lucky

So **6**B is a bound clause even though its relation to the free clause **6**A is rather complicated by the fact of ellipsis. It should be noted that ellipsis is meaningful. In dialogue a speaker who does not use elliptical forms is putting a formality and distance between himself and his addressee, as though he were declining to act as responder to what the other has been saying.

Exercise 17.2
Use the structural symbols F (for free clause) and B (for bound

clause). Here are some two-clause sentences with the structure FB. Locate the clause boundary and note the mood of the clause at F.

1 Has he chosen where he wants it?
2 They will always turn up should they be called upon.
3 He's chosen where to put it.
4 Ring if you need me.
5 A pound of apples, please, if they're not too dear.
6 Did you say the stoppage was due to a power cut?
7 He'll ring if you need me.

Exercise 17.3
The following sentences have the structure F B or B F. For each one

(a) find the clause boundary
(b) state the mood of the free clause
(c) say whether F B or B F
(d) say whether the sequence of clauses could be reversed

1 The demonstrators shouted for a long time while the speaker was on his feet.
2 If you'd like a cup of tea help yourself.
3 My aunt had taken a whole suite, which seemed rather unneccessary.
4 Give me a shout when the bell rings.
5 Was the train crowded before you got to Oxford?
6 We asked whether there was a restaurant.
7 While you're away, who's going to feed the cat?

Exercise 17.4
From the evidence of the answers to Exercise 17.3, which of the following statements are true?

1 All the sentences can have the sequence F B.
2 For every F B sequence there is a corresponding B F sequence.
3 Some bound clauses cannot precede the clause they are bound to.

17.2 Binding

Usually bound clauses can be recognized by certain features of their structure, as well as by their being dependent on another clause. There are two chief ways in which the binding of a clause may be signalled: the presence of a binder and/or predicator binding. We will deal first with binders.

Binder is the name given to an element in the structure of bound clauses (though not all bound clauses contain a binder). In **7** the items that function as binders are italicized:

7a I would have always gladly lost my taste for the sonnets of Wordsworth, || *if* I could have bettered my palate for wine
7b It seems to me || *that* we must let her know the truth
7c My thanks are for you, Ischia, || *to whom* a fair wind has brought me rejoicing
7d *When* he came in the house, || he did not turn on the light
7e I like a look of agony || *because* I know || it's true
7f I don't know || *who* you are

The binder is always initial in the clause. Frequently this function is fulfilled by a single word, but this is not always the case (see **7c**). Many of the items that can act as binders, however, can turn up elsewhere with other functions; this is especially true of WH-items like *who*, *at which house*, *when*, *how quickly*, *how*, etc. So while it is possible to recognize a bound clause by the presence of a binder, it is not always a straightforward matter to recognize the binder; to do this we must often look at other features of the clause too. For instance, **7a** is an easy case, since *if* never has any function but that of binder. In the last example, however, the presence of *who* is not conclusive since free clauses can also begin with *who?* (e.g. *Who are you?*). But it is still true that *who you are* must be a bound clause, because if it had been a free clause, the sequence would have been *are you* instead of *you are* (the sequence being determined by the mood system).

Exercise 17.5
Identify all the binders in the following examples:

1 Whether he wanted to or not, he had to pay.
2 However late it gets, don't hurry home.
3 He'll be selected, provided he makes the right impression.
4 The minute he made those remarks, everybody felt offended.

5 Although it's been open for nearly a year, it hasn't been used very much.
6 That situation developed long before the tour ended.
7 He came along to the first performance as if nothing had happened.
8 As soon as it looks right, turn off the heat.
9 They couldn't be rescued until the ice broke up.
10 Since we had that foggy weather, the swans haven't come this way.
11 Seeing he's in hospital, why don't you go and see him?
12 He tells everybody before you can stop him.
13 I'm going to watch it no matter how long it takes.
14 Because he's been swindled, he's very angry.
15 It grew better after we put fertilizer on it.

Exercise 17.6
Write examples in which the items *the minute*, *until*, *seeing*, *since, before* and *after* have some other function than that of binder.

In some types of bound clause a binder is not necessary. Among these are a very common type of reported clause (for reported clauses, see below, and later chapters). For instance:

8 He said *conditions would deteriorate*

The bound, reported clause is italicized. Note that in its own internal structure it does not differ from the free clause in:

9 *Conditions would deteriorate* when times got hard

The italicized clause in **8** is recognized as bound because of the following facts:

1 The binder *that* can be put in at the beginning without disturbing the structure
2 The clause has no primary mood. The same string of words at F, in **9** could be changed from declarative to interrogative: *would conditions deteriorate* . . .? But this cannot happen in **8** without putting in quotation marks and thus altering the structure.
3 The verb *say* in **8** is a *reporting verb*. Such verbs are regularly associated with reported clauses.

17.3 P-bound clauses

There is an important type of bound clause which shows that it is bound by the form of its verbal group. This phenomenon is here called *predicator-binding*, shown in **10**:

10a Finding they had so many pretensions, I had soon had enough of their patriotism
10b Having taken place in December, the Festival had not been well attended
10c They can be thrown out, having served their purpose
10d Giving the responsibility to others, he managed to avoid any further trouble
10e To get enough sleep, you have to retire early
10f He held out his arm to bar the way
10g To be sure of seeing all of them I went over the ground twice

Exercise 17.7
Identify the clauses at F and B in **10**. For each clause, whether free or bound, which item is the predicator?

The predicators in P-bound clauses are non-finite verbal groups (see Chapters 5, 14 and 15 for the technicalities of the distinction finite v. non-finite). Figure 76 shows the range of possibilities, including minor clauses with no predicator at all. (It should be noted that Figure 76 does not allow for phase structures; non-finite verbal groups also occur in phase, whether

	major clause (contains P)		*minor clause (no P)*
	finite	*non-finite*	
free	Bill feels happy	—	happy birthday
bound	if Bill feels happy	feeling happy *(P-bound)*	if happy

Figure 76

the clause is free or bound, e.g. *They want me to phone them tomorrow; wanting me to phone them tomorrow*.)

The P-bound clauses in the examples in **10** happen to have the following characteristics:

1 The first word of the predicator is either the *ing*-form or the *to*-form (e.g. *finding, to get*).
2 There is no subject in the clause.
3 There is no binder in the clause.

None of these features is necessary to the structure of P-bound clauses however.

Exercise 17.8

(a) Identify P-bound clauses in the following examples.
(b) Note any instances of more than one word in the P-binding verbal group.
(c) Note any instances where the first word of the verbal group is not *ing*-form or *to*-form.
(d) Note any instances of a subject in the P-bound clause.
(e) Note any instances of a binder in the P-bound clause.

1 Leaving the boarding house, he set off briskly.
2 With you leaving, I'll have to find someone else.
3 For Bill to have sat opposite her, she would have needed to be there sooner.
4 You make them go sideways by placing a finger across the corner.
5 She wished to be alone, after trying to understand them for so long.
6 His collar twisted half round his neck, he reached for his tie.
7 Presented with such difficulties, they needed to conspire together.
8 With the grass being mown, there's a lot of pollen in the air.
9 Though considered a classic, it has never been popular.
10 To find the answer look in the key.

Exercise 17.9

Which of the binders identified in the preceding exercise can also occur in clauses with finite verbal groups? (e.g. *Before* you

	P	C^o	C^{loc}
he	placed	a finger	across the corner
by	placing	a finger	across the corner

Figure 77

	P	C^o
he	found	the answer
	to find	the answer

Figure 78

	S	P	C^{loc}
	Bill	had sat	opposite her
for	Bill	to have sat	opposite her

Figure 79

throw away the carton, make sure it is empty.) Write examples of such clauses.

In traditional accounts of English grammar the term 'clause' is often withheld from constructions that do not have a subject and a finite verbal group. None of our P-bound clauses would be recognized as clauses. The justification for treating them as clauses shows up in Figures 77–79 which give parallel examples, in which the first is finite and the second P-bound. It is evident that the range of propositional structures in finite and in P-bound clauses is the same.

17.4 Types of bound clause

There are three kinds of structure involving bound clauses. Here the three kinds are merely named and illustrated. The names are suggested by the kind of meaning that these structures have, but the types are structural and are identified by their formal character. We shall study the structures in more detail in later chapters. In the examples, the bound clauses are in italics:

Contingency structures

The bound clause is a contingent clause (symbol B^{cont}):

11a *When you come back*, we'll have a good time
11b I shall certainly dine here, *if my friends turn up*
11c It would be bad for your prospects *now that you're Claude's white-headed boy*
11d Do they tell you things *because you're senior?*
11e *To finish it off quickly*, turn the heat up
11f Finish it off quickly *by turning the heat up*

Adding structures

The bound clause is an adding clause (symbol: B^{add}):

12a You shall carry the flag, *which is a great privilege*
12b It didn't arrive until yesterday, *when it was already too late*
12c He'll be more sympathetic than Harold, *who never seems very worried by anything*
12d Come and see our new centre, *where we serve soup to the needy*

Report structures

The bound clause is a reported clause (symbol: B^{rep}):

13a They told me *that his influence was very great*
13b Remember *that the knife is very sharp*
13c Do you regret *that you handed in your resignation?*
13d The stranger discovered *he was not welcome*
13e I haven't discovered *why the hotel had to close*
13f *What he wanted* I wasn't told
13g I doubt *if he had a happy childhood*

Exercise 17.10
Make lists of the binders that occur in the three types of B

clause illustrated above. Note which items occur in more than one list.

Exercise 17.11
In the following sentences
(a) find the clause boundary;
(b) write the appropriate formula (F B or B F);
(c) although we have not yet studied the structural differences, attempt to decide whether the B clause is adding, contingent or reported;
(d) identify the binder, if any, and add it to the lists started in exercise 17.10;
(e) if B is P-bound, say so

1 I hope you've no complaint about it.
2 There's no place here for private armies, because we're a democratic society.
3 We concluded that he preferred to walk.
4 Without waiting for an order, he mounted the vehicle.
5 We shan't see them again, which is a pity.
6 Holding the knob firmly, turn it anticlockwise.
7 What will you do when the train starts?
8 We saw how they make bread.
9 If I choose, I will.
10 I've just seen the boss, who's in a bad mood this morning.
11 We can't find out who to ask.
12 It must have been raining for the roads to be wet like this.

17.5 Split clauses

So far all the examples we have looked at have the sequence F B or B F. However, it is possible for clauses to be split, i.e. one clause is interrupted and another is enclosed within it, as in **14**:

14 I shall, if the profits are poor, resign the chair

Here, the F clause is *I shall . . . resign the chair*, and a B^{cont} is enclosed within it. This phenomenon is symbolized thus: F ((B^{cont})). (See also the end of section 4.2.)

Exercise 17.12

Identify any cases of clause splitting in the following. What kinds of B clause do the examples contain?

1 In the evenings, when the hotel lounge was full, card playing languished.

2 Don't turn the heat up, even when you're in a hurry.

3 Such people don't seem to understand that there is very great danger.

4 The gates, which are automatically controlled, close as the train approaches.

5 You can, by turning the heat up, finish it off quickly.

6 They tell you things because you're senior, do they?

18 Clause complexes 2

18.1 Joining

We have seen that two clauses may be in the structural relation we have called binding; one clause is dominant and the other is dependent upon it. In a two-clause sentence F is dominant and B is dependent. There is another relation between two clauses, which we will call *joining*. In joined structures neither clause is dominant over the other except in the purely sequential sense that one comes first and the other follows. In a two-clause sentence, both of the clauses joined are F, as in **1**:

1a I've an announcement to make, and I might as well make it now
1b He was innocent, but it was too late then
1c I've just stolen £30,000 from a bank and I've been caught
1d They must have done something naughty, or she wouldn't be angry with them
1e You can't go through the fields; you've got to go along the road
1f I'm looking for the maker's name first of all, and this will establish the place
1g He went to the exhibition; he wasn't impressed, however
1h I went to the exhibition; moreover, I met the Browns there
1i She was going to go there, so I told her the truth
1j Perhaps he was about to tell me; anyway, I knew all about it already
1k You were wrong, but nevertheless you made the right decision
1l Drop your gun, but keeps your hands in the air
1m Haven't they sent a message, and what's happened to Henry?

1n He told you last night, so why are you surprised?
1o You must be tired; would you like to lie down for a bit?
1p Come in and we'll be able to talk
1q Come in or you'll get wet
1r Come in, or would you rather not?

In most of these examples there is at least one element in the structure of the second clause that signals the joining of the clauses; but some of them have no such element, and one of them has two.

Exercise 18.1

(a) For each of the examples in **1**
identify the element or elements, if any, that signal the joining of the clauses;
note the mood of each of the clauses.

(b) Is there any reason for recognizing two kinds of joining elements?

There are four patterns of joining in **1**. Two F clauses may be either listed or not listed, and at the same time either linked or not linked. If they are listed one of the items *and, or, but, so* occurs; and if they are linked there is one of the items *however, moreover*, etc. This analysis gives four possible permutations:

1 listed, linked: e.g. *You were wrong but nevertheless you made the right decision*. (The second clause has the structure A^{+} A^{l} S P C^{o}, where A^{+} = listing adjunct, and A^{l} = linking adjunct)

2 listed, not linked: e.g. *I've an announcement to make and I might as well make it now*. (second clause: A^{+} S P C^{o} A)

3 not listed, linked: e.g. *He went to the exhibition; he wasn't impressed, however*. (second clause: S P C^{i} A^{l})

4 not listed, not linked: e.g. *You can't go through the fields; you've got to go along the road*. (second clause contains neither A^{+} nor A^{l})

In the last type, the two clauses are simply placed in sequence within the same sentence. For this reason they are called *contact clauses*.

18.2 Sentences and clause complexes

Clauses in sequence are related to each other either in the joining relationship, in which the joined clauses are of equal status, or in the binding relationship, in which one clause dominates another. The equal status relation is known as parataxis, and the unequal one as hypotaxis. In **2** there are four clauses and both kinds of relation are exemplified:

> **2** Every summer they had a holiday on a farm ‖ but they were disappointed ‖ when they discovered ‖ that their bungalow was to be sold

If we represent the individual clauses as *a, b, c* and *d*, and the hypotactic relation with an arrow pointing towards the bound member and the paratactic relation with a plus, the structure of **2** is: $a + (b \rightarrow (c \rightarrow d))$. That is to say, *d* is bound to *c*, and both of these together are bound to *b*; finally the whole of this complex is joined to *a*.

The kind of structure that is found in **2** is of a radically different kind from clause structures, such as SPC or SPCA etc. A clause structure is finite; there is a limit beyond which it is not possible to expand the construction any more, even by the addition of adjuncts. Moreover, a clause structure consists typically of several elements, each element performing a different function in the construction of the whole, so that each of the elements is related to each of the others in a different way. The structure of **2**, on the other hand, is infinitely extendable by virtue of adding on more clauses; the same principles of construction can be repeated over and over: joining within joining or binding, and binding within joining or binding; the relations between the parts of the construction vary between the hypotactic and the paratactic, but these same relations are repeated as many times as the speaker wants. This kind of construction is known as a unit complex. It has been illustrated here with a clause complex.

Units below the rank of clause can also be combined in

complexes. A clause in which the subject is not a simple nominal group but a complex of nominal groups in the paratactic relation known as *apposition* is given in **3**:

3 The leader of the train drivers' union, ASLEF, Mr Ray Buckton, said today . . .

Mr Ray Buckton is in apposition to *the leader of the train drivers' union, ASLEF*. Moreover, *ASLEF* is in apposition to *the train drivers' union*. A similar nesting of appositions can be seen in **4**:

4 They fan out from the opening of the body, the openings in its external shell, its exoskeleton (Appendix BI, ll. 18–20)

Another kind of group complex, in which there is the paratactic relation of co-ordination, is found in the subject of **5**:

5 Harold Millstone, Mrs Harbottle and their friends voted against the Government

As with the clause complexes, a complex of groups can be layered (or bracketed); the C^O of the following example is a complex of four nominal groups arranged in two complexes of two each: $(a + b) + (c + b)$.

6 She added potatoes and gravy, brussel sprouts and bread sauce

An example of a hypotactic group complex is provided by the complex adjunct in **7**:

7 She added potatoes and gravy, brussel sprouts and bread sauce, methodically, in a circle, round the slices on her plate

Each of the items in this complex delimits more precisely the meaning of the one before it; *in a circle* is more particular than *methodically*, and *round the slices on her plate* is more particular than *in a circle*. The whole series makes a complex manner adjunct; so the structure of the whole clause is S P C^O A, with complexes at C^O and A.

To return now to clause complexes. The question arises whether a sentence is the same thing as a clause complex. This depends, of course, on how the terms are defined. What is going to be argued here is that what in popular usage is called the sentence is of a different order from the clause complex.

In section 18.1 it was seen that a clause complex can be extended in the paratactic manner without any listers or linkers, by the device that was there called *contact*. Two clauses placed side by side are to be read together, that is, interpreted in the light of each other. Quite often there is some clear structural parallel or antithesis:

8a Don't look at me – I didn't do it
8b I didn't fall; I was pushed

If this is so, then all of the clauses that make up a text can be seen as one clause complex in which the relationship between the parts varies from the very strong connection of binding through the weaker connections of listing and linking, to the weakest connection of contact relation. This means that at the level of grammatical structure the maximum grammatical item is very indeterminate.

The usual sense of 'sentence' is quite different from this. In the first place it is a term that is usually applied only to written text, whereas it is obvious that the notion 'clause complex' is, as a grammatical notion, applicable to text of any kind. In the second place, the sentence is usually held to be that which is delimited by a full stop. Now there is not always a full stop between clauses that are in contact, and, moreover, full stops sometimes occur in other positions. Sometimes at 'contact points' there is only a semi-colon, or even a comma. Sometimes a full stop appears when the following clause is listed, or linked or bound and on occasion a full stop is used in the middle of a clause:

9 They thought it would snow. On the contrary. The sun came out. For hours

Example **9** is grammatically two clauses, but there are four sentences; so it is clear that, in this sense, 'sentence' is not a grammatical term. In fact, it is a term that is normally applied to tactical units of discourse and the full stop is a signal to the reader to react to, or take stock of what has been said. A semi-colon or comma is weaker than a full stop and means 'Do not take stock as yet; suspend judgement until you get to the full stop'. Reaction points that are stronger than the full stop are paragraph boundaries and chapter divisions, etc. In other words the writer superimposes a structure of tactical units onto the complex of grammatical clauses. The smallest tactical units are sentences. There are various conventional norms for locating sentence boundaries according to the types of grammatical relationship between the clauses. For instance, two clauses in a binding or listing relation will normally be treated as belonging to the same sentence. But in spite of these norms the division into tactical units is in principle independent of the grammatical structure. (And, anyway, different norms apply to different kinds of discourse.)

In spoken discourse the reaction points are signalled by various phonological patterns, principally sequences of tone groups and various rhythmical phenomena. Whether it is possible to find a parallel with written discourse sufficiently close to justify the use of the term 'sentence' is a question which there is not space to discuss here.

18.3 Branching

We return now to the topic of clause complexes. An important pattern that occurs in joined clauses is illustrated in **10**:

- **10a** He opened the door and shouted down the passage
- **10b** I'll come to the station but won't wait long
- **10c** The shops are open on Wednesdays but not on Thursdays
- **10d** Bill plays the flute and Mary the harp

The second clause in each of these examples is *branched*. The motive for this term can be illustrated with the simple branched diagram given in Figure 80, which should be self-explanatory.

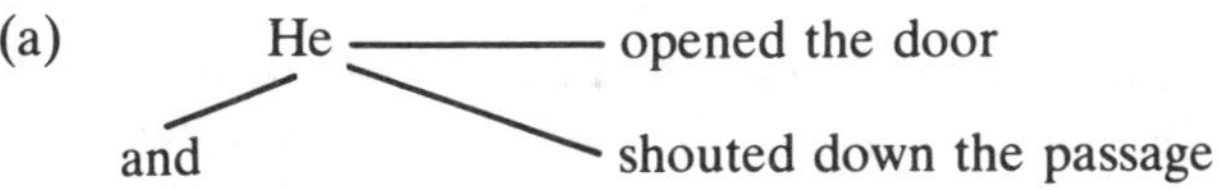

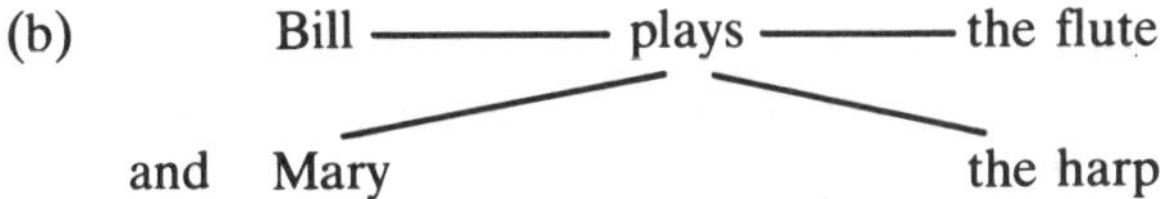

Figure 80

The branched clause is a construction in parallel with the preceding clause, and its structure must be interpreted by reference to its preceding clause:

11 He opened the door || but not the window
S P C^o $A^+ A^{neg}$ C^o

The window is understood as C^o by reference to the functions of *he* and *opened* in the preceding clause. Compare this with **12**:

12 The door was opened || but not the window
S P $A^+ A^{neg}$ S

Branching is a kind of ellipsis (see page 212).

Exercise 18.2
For each of the following sentences
(a) is the structure joining or binding?
(b) if it is joining, is the second clause listed or not, linked or not, and branched or not?
(c) if listed or linked, what item functions as lister or linker?
(d) if branched, explain how the structure of the clause can be interpreted.

1 Mr Millstone was rather late, so wouldn't come in.
2 He didn't want any tea then; he was rather late.
3 However late he is, he can surely manage a cup.
4 He's very late; however, he can surely manage a cup.
5 He went on foot, and in fact carried all his food.
6 He twisted his ankle and couldn't play tennis.
7 The play lasts for four hours but the film only for two hours.
8 I wouldn't have missed it, and besides I've done some shopping.
9 I think that will make it easier for both of us.
10 He might manage to untie himself yet fail to escape through those bars.
11 He was brought to me by a third party, which was very mysterious.
12 The child was very well connected; I should not have taken him otherwise.
13 I paid his fare; I couldn't do otherwise.

14 He couldn't see the rostrum, for he was rather short.
15 Have you signed the form and put a stamp on the envelope?

The words *and* and *or* (and sometimes a few others) can also be used to join units of lower rank than clauses as in **13**:

13 I like bread and butter

This example is not to be analysed as two clauses, the second one branched, but as one clause with a word complex in the nominal group that functions as object. So the structure of the clause is SPC^{O}. Similarly with **14**:

14 Bill and John | met | at the station
S P A

Though the extreme cases of branching, on the one hand, and joining of lower-rank units, on the other, are clearly distinct, it is not always easy to decide which analysis to assign. Consider **15**:

15 I went to London and Birmingham

Is this $SPC^{loc} \parallel A^{+} C^{loc}$, with the second clause branched, or is it SPC^{loc} with *to London and Birmingham* as a single element?

18.4 Varieties of listing

Listed clauses can be divided into five kinds, corresponding to the listers:

or
and
but, yet, and yet
for, 'cos (because)
so, and so

Some of the types are similar to each other in various ways, either semantic or syntactic. We will start by considering the semantic value of the types.

Alternative listing

This type differs from all the others in that in this type the speaker is facing the addressee with a choice.

16 (Either) the train was late, or he missed the bus

In **16** the addressee is expected to accept one of these statements as true, and once he feels able to settle for one of them, he is free to ignore the other. For the function of the item *either*, see below, section 18.5.

17 We've got tickets for the concert tonight, or are you too busy?

In **17** the addressee is offered a choice between consenting to go to the concert and being allowed to excuse himself.

18 Would you like to go for a walk, or shall we stay in?

In **18** the addressee is required to answer 'yes' to one of these polar interrogatives, and to indicate which he is answering 'yes' to.

Despite the striking differences that there are between the remaining types of listing (additive, antithetical, causal), what they have in common is that the addressee is expected to accept and react to both clauses as in **19**:

19a Come in and don't be obstinate (Do both)
19b Do you live here, and travel all that way? (Answer both)
19c He lost his hat and caught a cold (Take note of both)
19d I'd like some tea, but don't put sugar in it, please (Take note of my desire and obey the request)
19e The train was late, so I missed the connection (Take note of both statements)
19f He told you only a moment ago, so why are you surprised? (Accept the statement and answer the question)
19g Why are you surprised? 'Cos he told you only a moment ago. (Answer the question and accept the statement)

Additive listing

This is listing with *and*. The speaker simply lists two clauses without comment on any connection there may be between them. Of course, there usually is some rational connection, but the addressee is left to deduce for himself what it must be:

20a He fell over and broke his leg (Event and consequence, in that order. *He broke his leg and fell over*, would be quite another story)
20b He walked into the town and went into a shop (One event precedes another in a narrative)
20c He has a nice house and owns two cars (The sequence might be reversed, unless it is felt that houses ought to have priority over cars)
20d Sit down and be quiet (Perhaps the speaker thinks of sitting down as a preliminary to being quiet. Otherwise the sequence could be reversed)

Antithetical listing

The uttering of the two clauses is in some way antithetical. Note that the antithesis does not always lie directly in the propositional content of the clauses.

21 We went to Scotland for our holidays, but the weather was wet

There is nothing surprising about having wet weather in Scotland. The antithesis lies in the pleasure of having a holiday, versus the disappointment of having wet weather.

22 Albert is a tax inspector, but he lives in Newcastle

There is no reason why tax inspectors should not live in Newcastle, but perhaps somebody has just said *Albert is a tax inspector and he doesn't live in Newcastle*. In that case the antithesis is between accepting a true assertion and denying a false one.

23 Here he is, but where's his wife?

In **23** the contrast lies in his presence and the absence of his wife.

24 I shan't be very late, but don't wait up for me

In **24** there is a suggestion that you might reasonably wait up for me which contrasts with the request not to do so.

Exercise 18.3

Write notes on the kinds of antithesis between the clauses listed with *but* in the following:

1 I feel it must be English, but I don't know.

2 A: It's a triumph of anarchy over the rule of law.
B: But legally, surely, Mr Millstone has acted properly.

3 A: You can force your way through a hedge or something.
B: Yes, but that's no fun then, is it?

4 There has been a book published on Tompion, which does give numbering, but I cannot find the documentary evidence of where the author got this particular numbering.

5 They were made by his employees, but, of course, they were all of a high standard.

6 Truancy is a problem but one that is coped with well.

7 Now these things are scarce, but they're doubly scarce when they're in colour.

8 It could be an old dial with new works, but the frets are certainly new.

9 I wouldn't hazard a guess at the date, but I think extremely valuable.

Causal listing

This type is listing with *so, 'cos*, etc. Instead of there being an antithesis or incongruence between the clauses listed, there is a congruence, so that uttering one clause is a cause for uttering the other. The causal link may go in either direction:

25a She was going to go there, so I told her the truth
25b I told her the truth, 'cos she was going to go there
25c He told you a moment ago, so why are you surprised?
25d Why are you surprised?, 'cos he told you a moment ago

A more literary style would use *for* instead of *'cos*, but the colloquial language seems to have borrowed *because* from its original binding function. There seems to be no doubt that *because* often has a listing function. Consider **26** where the second clause is obviously free, not bound:

> **26** Don't buy it, 'cos you haven't got room for it, have you?

The result of this, however, is that it is sometimes difficult to decide whether *because* is being used as a binder or a lister. Consider **27**:

> **27** They had to stay in a hotel for a few days, because their new house wasn't ready

There is a clear example of *because* as lister in Appendix BII, l. 17.

Or and *and* can join more than two items as in **28**:

> **28a** He struck the ball, passed the fielders and scored four runs
>
> **28b** He will either declare war, call for a conference, or appeal to the UN

It is optional whether the lister is repeated, or placed only before the last item in the list; but in alternative listings it is usual to give the addressee a clue that this is the type of listing intended, either by using the correlative *either*, or by using *or* repeatedly, or both (as in the list in this sentence). In the examples in **28**, the three clauses listed are of equal status; no two of them are more closely associated with each other than with the third. However, it is possible to have lists within lists as in **29**:

> **29** He declared war and he called for a conference and appealed to the UN

The branched clause coming at the end suggests that the last two clauses are more closely associated with each other than they are with the first. A bracketed formula can be used to illustrate the structure of **29** thus (*a* and (*b* and *c*)). Consider also **30**:

> **30** Either he called for a conference and appealed to the UN, or he declared war

Here there is an additive list within an alternative list, with the structure ((*a* and *b*) or *c*). It is obvious that in a list of three or more items there is scope for a variety of different bracketing. There are several syntactic devices the speaker can use to show the structure of the list. We have already noticed the effect of a branched clause. Correlatives are also important (see section 18.5 below). In **31** the linker *then* has the effect of making a stronger break:

31 He called for a conference and appealed to the UN, and then he declared war

Punctuation is often used to indicate the structure of the list; this usually corresponds to the division of the list into tone groups in speech:

32 // $_{\wedge}$ he called for a conference and appealed to the UN // $_{\wedge}$ and then he declared war //

Exercise 18.4

Suggest a bracketed structure, where appropriate, for the following examples:

1 I would be off tomorrow, but I can no longer lift a heavy suitcase, and there is a distressing lack of porters nowadays.

2 Is that argument really to do with hanging or is it really to do with keeping people shut up and can't we answer it simply?

3 Meanwhile there's something really ugly happening and I lose my temper and I hit.

4 I was in Chepstow and there was this woman in this shop and her accent was the worst accent I've ever heard.

5 Then you stop and get out and talk.

6 I had a real slum of a place and the mice used to come out and play on the carpet.

7 Either the leader will have to resign and a new leader be chosen, or the Party will suffer at the next election, and this fact ought to be recognized.

8 He wrote to his MP and organized a rally but went on hunger strike and alienated public opinion.

9 By the 1770s in England certain liberties already existed which would seem fundamental to stable political regimes: the subject was free from arbitrary arrest; he was tried by jury, not by royal judge alone, and juries frequently flew

> in the face of the law in their dislike of political prosecutions; he was free to criticize the government from a platform or in print; he could report parliamentary debates, and he could travel without passports or special permission – yet the franchise was corrupt, inequitable and inadequate.

Listers other than *and* and *or* do not have the property of listing several items without internal bracketing. For example, if *but* occurs in a list of more than two clauses, the list has to be taken as bracketed so that *but* joins only two parts of the list, e.g. exercise 18.4, number **8**. Consider the oddness of **33**:

33 He called for a conference, appealed to the UN but declared war

This can only be interpreted as it would be if there were an *and* between the first two clauses, i.e. ((*a* and *b*) but *c*). The term 'listing' is suggested by the possibility of an indefinitely extendable list without internal bracketing. In this respect only *and* and *or* are fully listers.

18.5 Correlatives

The listing correlatives are a syntactic device for signalling a listed structure in advance:

34 Either they're trying to make trouble, or they're very tactless

The correlative *either*, not only signals a listed clause to follow, but also tells us what kind of listing it is to be, i.e. alternative. So, if you begin *Either they're trying to make trouble and* . . . it is clear that the clause beginning with *and* is not the anticipated listed clause. The structure might turn out to be (either (*a* and *b*) or *c*) as in **35**:

35 Either they're trying to make trouble and are causing a lot of unneccessary difficulties, or they're very tactless

One of the correlative pairs is *not . . . but*:

36 Albert is not tall, but short

The kind of antithesis in a *but*-listing is different when it is correlated with *not* from when it is not so correlated. In **37** there is no correlation, even though the words *not* and *but* occur in **37b**:

37a Albert is short, but he is strong
37b Albert is not tall, but he is strong

In **36** the antithesis is between *tall* and *short*, which are not compatible with each other: 'not tall; on the contrary – short; he can't be both tall and short'. In **37b** the antithesis is between *not tall* and *strong*: 'not tall is conceded; nevertheless, he is strong'. The difference can be summed up in the use of the expressions *on the contrary* and *nevertheless*.

Exercise 18.5
(a) Which of the examples have correlatives in the first clause?
(b) Make a note of the correlatives, and what they correlate with.
(c) Do the items that function as correlatives appear elsewhere in other functions?

1 The train was both late and crowded.
2 Not only do they keep you waiting, but they don't provide chairs.
3 Both of them said so, but I didn't believe them.
4 Albert doesn't send Christmas cards, but I do.
5 I send Christmas cards, but Albert doesn't.
6 I have neither spoken to him nor heard from him.
7 I spoke to neither of them, and they were offended.
8 Either he will phone up or his wife will come round in the car.
9 Albert isn't well off, but he's sure to help.
10 Albert didn't go to the pub but to the pictures.
11 The students have not only read Bentham and Mill, but written essays on both.
12 They have either read Goethe in the original or Schiller in translation.
13 They haven't read Shakespeare, and they haven't read Spenser either
14 He will either phone up, or come round in the car.

18.6 Summary

A series of joined clauses is not necessarily a simple structure representable as: $a + b + c \ldots$ in which each clause is joined on in the same way as all the others.

There are various kinds of joining, such as listing, linking, both listing and linking together, and contact. In addition there are syntactic devices for indicating bracketed structure; these are branching, correlatives and adjunct linkers. Punctuation and phonological division into tone groups also indicate bracketed structure, even if no syntactic means are used for this purpose.

19 Bound clauses 1

19.1 Clause complexes v. rankshift

In Chapter 17 I named and illustrated three types of binding relationship between clauses:

1a *contingency*: This will disturb you if you are disturbed by politics itself (F B^{cont})

1b *adding*: Aristotle, who took a different view, was more influential (F ((B^{add})))

1c *report*: He claimed that science is inevitably technological (F B^{rep})

In this analysis of English the above constructions are presented as clause complexes. This means they are sequences of two clauses. The relation between the clauses is one of hypotaxis (see page 224); one clause is dominant over the other, which is bound to it.

It is desirable at this point to refer again to the theoretical distinction between a tactic relation of one item to another and a rankshifting of one item into the structure of another. This was first mentioned in Chapter 4. As a reminder, **2** gives some instances of rankshift:

2a Levying a tax on wealth | is | a desperate measure

S P C^i

2b The food which she had eaten | had refreshed | her

S P C^o

In **2a** the entire example is one clause: SPC. But the subject is itself a clause with a predicator (*levying*), and an object (*a tax on wealth*). This is therefore a rankshifted clause. In **2b** the

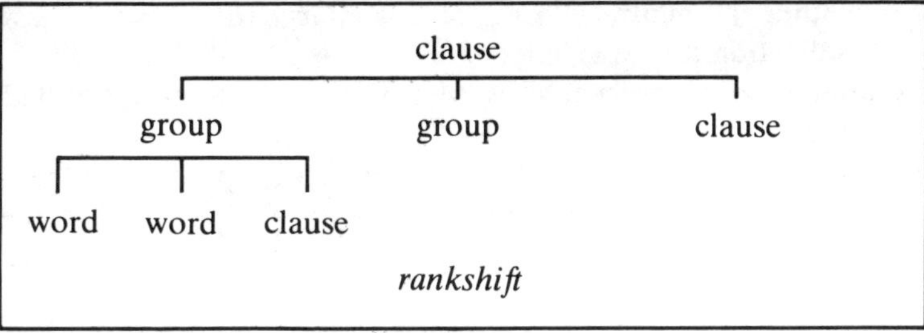

Figure 81

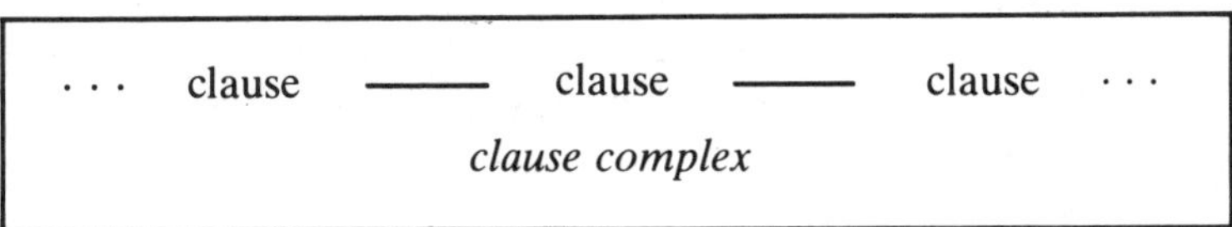

Figure 82

rankshifting goes one stage further. Each of the constituents of this clause is a group, so there is no rankshift at this stage. But the nominal group at S has the structure given in **3**:

3 The | food | which she had eaten
m h q

That is to say, it has a modifier (m), a headword (h) and a qualifier (q). But the qualifier is a clause, a unit of higher rank than the entire structure. The structure of this clause is: WH-C^{O} (*which*) S (*she*) P (*had eaten*).

The two models – rankshifted clause and clause complex – can be displayed in the form of a diagram given in Figures 81 and 82. Both models are needed in describing languages. The question then arises which model is more suitable for examples like **1**. Towards the end of Chapter 4 the kinds of relation between co-present units were spoken of as a scale ranging from parataxis at one end to rankshift at the other. Several independent criteria are used to decide whether to invoke the rankshift model. These include:

1 whether the clause *x* whose status is in question is of higher rank than the other item *y*, as, for instance, in **3**;

2 whether the neutral placing of *x* is after *y* (if so there is less justification for rankshift);
3 whether *x* is replaceable by what is clearly a non-rankshifted element of *y*;
4 whether, if *x* were regarded as an element of *y*, it would be a nuclear or a peripheral one;
5 whether *x* is finite or non-finite (if the latter there is more justification for rankshift).

Needless to say these criteria may point to different conclusions for a single type of construction; so it might become necessary to rate them relative to each other.

It is not my intention to pursue this matter further. What I chiefly want to do is explore the properties of the three kinds of structure exemplified in **1**, however controversial their status as clause complexes.

19.2 Contingent clauses: syntax

The ways of distinguishing one type of bound clause from another come under the headings we have used before: semantics, syntax and componence (see section 3.2).

For contingent clauses the sequential relation between the bound clause and the dominant can be illustrated by the examples in **4**:

4a FB: The book is likely to prove baffling || if we read it in youth
4b BF: If we read it in youth || the book is likely to prove baffling
4c F ((B)) (splitting of F): The book ((if we read it in youth)) is likely to prove baffling

There are often several points at which the dominant clause can be split. The point selected in **4c** is after the subject of F. But the bound clause has no particular syntactic relevance to just the point selected. (There is an important difference here from adding clauses.) The presence of the bound clause is optional; the structure of the dominant clause is not disturbed if the contingent clause is removed.

Exercise 19.1
(a) state whether the sequence is FB, BF or F((B));

(b) if it is F ((B)), note the structural point where the splitting comes;
(c) identify the binder, where there is one.

1 Though this is a less attractive book, it is certainly his most ambitiously planned work.
2 Kipling's work, since he began making money out of it, does not fulfil these conditions.
3 His works might conceivably even be harmful, regarded as a sole guide to life for a young person.
4 They denounce corporations and trusts, as if these things hurt them.
5 As soon as you see cruelty going on before you, you are bound to stop it.
6 You can, if you are not strong enough to face the issue, do nothing for public affairs.
7 Unless we see the evils clearly, contending against them is like fighting an atmosphere.
8 Contending against them, when we do see the evils, is like fighting an atmosphere.
9 As you say this, you see them blench.
10 When you get to the turning, there's a church on your right.
11 He was, when he finally got up, unable to walk without crutches.
12 I must depend for my information on books, never having been in Russia.
13 Amazed, she stood in the doorway.
14 I have no objection, provided you don't stay long.
15 Whatever the cause, the fact remains.
16 Whatever I say, you don't believe me.
17 Moreover, before I read the review, I rushed to get tickets.
18 The ship keeled over three hours before it went down.
19 Turn off the supply by twisting the knob clockwise.
20 In the mornings, however much time you have, it's always a rush.

19.3 Contingent clauses: componence

There are, as the examples in exercise 19.1 show, a great many clause patterns that can function as contingent clauses. Among these are the following:

1 Clause with binder plus finite predicator:

5 Before I read the review

There is a long list of contingent-clause binders, many of which function simultaneously as binder and as adjunct within their clause, e.g. *before, after, if, unless, provided*:

6 Before I read the review
A^b S P C^o

(The symbol A^b stands for *adjunct binder*.) The binder may be some other element if it is also a WH-ever item as in **7**:

7a (Open locks) whoever knocks
WH–S^b P
7b Whatever I say (you don't believe me)
WH–C^b S P
7c Wherever I go (I carry an umbrella)
WH–C^b S P

2 A P-bound clause, with or without binder:

8a Before reading the review (he . . .)
8b On/with reading the review (he . . .)
8c Reading the review (he . . .)
8d The review having been read (he . . .)
8e To read the review (he . . .)

3 A minor clause (no predicator), with or without binder:

9a When famous (he . . .)
9b If Spanish (he . . .)
9c A great orator (he . . .)
9d Always poor (he . . .)

4 A handful of other patterns:

10a Should they leave early . . .
10b Let the wind blow ever so hard (we shall win through)

There is also the type that is borderline between imperative free clause and contingent:

11a *Say that again* and I'll sue you
11b *Give him an inch* and he takes a mile

19.4 Contingent clauses: meaning

A contingent clause modifies or limits the proposition of the dominant clause. There are many types of contingency; the traditional list of eight types of adverbial clause is not exhaustive, nor does it explore the relations there are between some of them. The types, with typical binders, include those given in **12**:

12 *time*: when, as soon as, the moment, until, since . . .
place: where . . .
manner: as, as if . . .
purpose: in order to, so as to, so that . . .
preference: rather than . . .

There is also the important group of related contingencies that might be given the collective name 'conditional', though this term is usually reserved for just the *if*-type. They fall into three groups, here nicknamed (a) *in-any-case*, (b) *nevertheless*, (c) *therefore*. In each of the three there is a distinction between the contingent proposition being (i) presupposed and (ii) not presupposed:

13 Whatever they say, don't believe them
given that they will say something
don't believe them in any case (a, i)
14 Whether they turn up or not, they've got to pay
not given they will turn up
they have to pay in any case (a, ii)
15 Although it's raining, we're going for a walk
given it is raining
adverse condition (nevertheless) (b, i)
16 Even if it rains, we're going for a walk
not given it will rain
adverse condition (nevertheless) (b, ii)
17 Since it is raining, the trip has been cancelled
given that it is raining
congruent condition (therefore) (c, i)

18 If it rains, the trip will be cancelled
not given that it will rain
congruent condition (therefore) (c, ii)

The binders in **13–18** are merely typical of the six types and are not an exhaustive list; there are far more than six binders and several of them appear in more than one type. For instance *since* has both a 'time' and a 'therefore' sense.

Exercise 19.2

(a) Identify any contingent clauses in the following examples, and pick out their binders.
(b) What is the function of the WH-ever items?

1 Wherever you live, you have to register with the police.
2 He listens to whatever they broadcast.
3 Whatever they broadcast he listens to.
4 Whatever they broadcast, he listens.
5 Whatever they broadcast, he listens to it.
6 Don't open the door whoever you hear.
7 I shall buy it, however old it is.
8 Whoever heard of such a thing?
9 Whenever the weather's bad, he takes whatever umbrella he can find.

19.5 Adding clauses: syntax

Clause sequences typical of adding clauses are given in **19**:

19a FB: I saw that film, which wasn't very good
19b FB: I saw that film, which cost me quite a bit
19c F((B)): That film, which wasn't very good, was on last week

The sequence BF is impossible with adding clauses. The point of splitting in F ((B)) is syntactically meaningful, and there is usually no choice; the item that comes immediately before the adding clause is related to the WH-binder:

20a *That film*, which wasn't very good, was on last week
20b I saw *that film*, which wasn't very good
20c In *Wales*, where they have a lot of rain, tourism is growing

20d I want *these letters*, which need stamps on them, to be posted tonight

20e I want you to post *these letters*, which need stamps on them

20f You should avoid *5 o'clock*, when the rush hour is beginning

In all of the examples in **20** there is a nominal group (in italics) that relates to the WH-binder as its antecedent, e.g. in **20e** *these letters* is the antecedent of *which*.

21 Bill, whose coat was torn, was rather angry

22 I saw him in the room behind the kitchen, which has no windows

In **21**, *Bill* is the antecedent of *whose coat*. In **22** the antecedent of *which* could be either *the room behind the kitchen* or *the kitchen*. Both of these items answer the description 'nominal group that immediately precedes *which*'. So **22** is ambiguous.

23a *I saw that film*, which cost me quite a bit

23b *That parcel arrived late*, which was very annoying

In **23** the antecedent of *which* is not a nominal group, but the whole of the preceding clause.

It is also possible to use *when* with such an extended antecedent as in **24**:

24a They said they would invest more capital in the business, when there would be some hope of improving output (*meaning* and then there would be . . .)

24b They poured petrol on the floor, when the whole place burst into flame (*meaning* upon which . . .)

19.6 Adding clauses: componence

In the fullest kind of adding-clause structure there is a WH-item functioning as binder. There are plenty of examples above. Note that the WH-item is not only a binder, but also has another function, shown in **25**:

25 I saw that film, which wasn't very good

WH–S^{b} P C

Exercise 19.3
Assign functions to the WH-items in the adding clauses in examples **20c–24**.

There are also P-bound adding clauses with no binder:

26 These words, taken from the Bible, were quoted by the Prime Minister

Even though there is no binder here, the syntactic relation to *these words* in the dominant clause, is the same as in the type of adding clause we first looked at. The adding clause in fact has an antecedent. Similarly, there are minor clauses with no binder, such as **27**:

27 Bill, a teacher for a few months last year, is now employed by a hospital

P-bound and minor adding clauses have the same internal structure as some P-bound and minor contingent clauses (i.e. when the latter have no subject and no binder). For instance *taken from the Bible* can function as either B^{add} or B^{cont}. Compare the example above with **28**, where the structure is B^{cont} F:

28 Taken from the Bible, this quotation was felt to be particularly apt

It is only the syntax and meaning of the clause, not its componence that distinguishes what type of clause it is. It is therefore not surprising to find instances of ambiguity:

29 This quotation, taken from the Bible, was felt to be particularly apt

In this F ((B)) arrangement, the B clause could be either adding or contingent. The difference in meaning could be expressed as either 'because it was taken from the Bible' (contingent) or 'which, incidentally, was taken from the Bible' (adding).

19.7 Adding clauses: meaning

The adding clause, as we have just seen, supplies extra (incidental) information, quite separate from the proposition of the dominant clause. Quite separate, that is, except that the antecedent happens to be identifiable with an element of the adding clause. For instance, it is as though *That film was on last week* and *That film isn't very good* have been yoked together simply because the speaker happens to be interested in both propositions; he has used the repeated reference to *that film* as a device for binding one clause to the other. This does not mean that it is impossible to read into such an adding construction some rational connection between the two propositions:

30 Bill, who has been out of work since last August, is getting desperate

We may assume that Bill is getting desperate *because* he has been out of work. But the grammatical construction gives no warrant for this assumption; it leaves any causal connection between the propositions quite open. It is up to the addressee to deduce why they are yoked together.

31 Bill, who is my cousin, is getting desperate

In contrast, **31** would not normally be taken to mean that he is getting desperate *because* he is my cousin, but, perhaps, that the speaker is interested in Bill's plight because he is a relative. A similar argument could be advanced about the lister *and*, given in example **32**:

32a Bill has been out of work since last August, *and* he is my cousin
32b Bill has been out of work since last August, *and* he is getting desperate

and does not tell us what the connection is, it only tells us that the speaker has some connection in mind.

19.8 A note on relative clauses

It is important to distinguish between adding clauses and the kind of clause illustrated in **33**, which I shall call a *relative clause*, and which is rankshifted. This kind of clause is traditionally known as a restrictive, or defining, relative clause, because its function is to define or restrict the antecedent:

33a They've had removed from them the penalty *which the law attaches to a breach of trust on the part of a councillor*

33b It's an incitement to people *who refuse to obey the law* . . .

33c . . . and we know from the labwork that they will give off light in the kind of electric fields *which you'd expect to find in these thundery conditions* . . .
(Appendix BI, ll. 59–61)

In **33a** the relative clause provides the answer to the question *What penalty?*, thus identifying the penalty referred to. In **33b** the relative clause provides an answer to *What people?*, restricting the reference of the word *people* by saying what sort of people are meant. In **33c** the relative clause answers the question *What kind of electric fields?*, thus identifying the kind. The relative clause has its own intonational characteristics; broadly, there is an informational unity of the antecedent and the restriction placed on it, which means that one cannot put a Tone 1 or 5 on the antecedent and then bring in a new tone group for the relative clause. That is, one cannot have the intonation pattern shown in **34**:

34 *// *1* . . . the penalty which the // law attaches to a breach of trust . . . //

In fact, very often there is no tonic on the antecedent, and no tone group boundary dividing it from the relative clause, as in **35**:

35 // . . . the kind of electric fields which you'd expect to find . . . //

An adding clause does not define or restrict its antecedent. Instead it adds something which is incidental to it:

36a I'm talking about houses, *which are nothing to do with art* (Appendix BII, ll. 56–7)

36b . . . and so does the Home Secretary, *who said in the election that he supported the rule of law*

36c Nobody got up and took a swipe at one of these UFOs, *which is what they ought to have done* . . . (Appendix BI, ll. 63–4)

In **36a** the adding clause does not specify what sort of houses are meant; the speaker is not talking about the sort of houses that are nothing to do with art. In **36b** the adding clause does not answer the question *What Home Secretary?*; he is already sufficiently identified by his title. In **36c** the antecedent of *which* is the whole of *took a swipe at one of these UFOs*, a sort of propositional antecedent which cannot be restricted by a relative clause.

In their intonation, adding clauses are always informationally divided from their antecedent. There has to be a new tone group for the adding clause as shown in **37**:

37 // : . . . about houses which are // nothing to do with art //

(NB Very often there is a Tone 1 on the antecedent, but this is not always the case, so that sometimes the intonation of relative clauses and adding clauses is not differentiated.) In writing, it is customary to show the informational division of an adding clause from its antecedent by means of a comma, and to put no comma before a relative clause. But there are also other conventions of punctuation, not to mention the inconsistencies of punctuators, which often militate against this practice. (It should perhaps be added that the distinction between adding clauses and relative clauses, which in all the cases discussed so far has been quite sharp, is certainly much less clear after certain kinds of modification of the antecedent, e.g. *There has been passed a special law for them which doesn't apply to other people*.)

Exercise 19.4

In the following passage, find more cases of adding and relative clauses, and say which is which. (There are five altogether.) For the relative clauses write out the entire nominal group within which the relative clause is rankshifted, e.g. for **33b** write: *people who refuse to obey the law*.

A: . . . this law was passed by parliament, and the fact of the matter was that the Labour councillors, who were not entrusted by the public with the task of disobeying the law, but were trustees of public money for their locality, deliberately chose to flout it for party political reasons, and this government has excused them, but not anybody else who chooses to disobey the law for different party political affiliations or reasons, not anybody else, but they've excused them from the consequences which the law, the general law, prescribes for that particular type of conduct, and the fact of the matter is that once you have done that, you have totally undermined the constitutional rule of law.

B: Would you extend your opprobrium to those who have worked in factories and then got government grants?

A: I'm not dealing with anything except the thing which has actually happened, but . . . .

Exercise 19.5

Divide the following passage into its clauses. Assign the labels *free*, *bound*, *listed*, *linked*, *contingent*, *adding*, as appropriate. (There is also a reported clause: *that he has the royal blood of Ireland in his veins*.) Weigh up with special care the status of the final clause, beginning *although*.

Now of course Princess O'Hara is by no means a regular princess, and in fact she is nothing but a little redheaded doll, with plenty of freckles, from over in Tenth Avenue, and her right name is Maggie, and the only reason she is called Princess O'Hara is as follows:

She is the daughter of King O'Hara, who is hacking along Broadway with one of these old-time victorias for a matter of maybe twenty five years, and every time King O'Hara gets his pots on, which is practically every night, rain or shine, he is always bragging that he has the royal blood of Ireland in his veins, so somebody starts calling him King, and this is his monicker as long as I can remember; although probably what King O'Hara really has in his veins is about ninety-eight per cent alcohol.

DAMON RUNYON, *Princess O'Hara*

20 Bound clauses 2

20.1 Reported clauses: syntax

The most commonly found clause sequence is F B:

1 The police say that there is going to be trouble

The reversed sequence, BF, is often possible, but this is not the favoured sequence unless certain conditions are met. In the first place, the free clause must be declarative, so that **2** cannot be reversed to give **3**:

2 Did you think that those tactics would work?
3 *That those tactics would work did you think?

Given a declarative clause, the most favourable conditions for BF sequence are illustrated in **4**:

4a Nobody knows why they paid him (FB)
4b Why they paid him, nobody knows (BF)

Here the reported clause has a WH-binder and the dominant clause is negative. Contrast **4** with **5**:

5a Bill said that I was here (FB)
5b ?*That I was here Bill said (BF)

In this example the binder is *that* and the dominant clause is positive. The BF sequence is, if possible at all, very strongly marked for contrast with something in the context.

Between these two extremes there are intermediate cases, as Exercise 20.1 will reveal. It should first be pointed out that the kind of B^{rep} F structure we are talking about begins with a binder (e.g. *why*, *who* etc.) and has as its normal intonation two tone groups, one for each clause. This is illustrated in **6**:

6 // *4 or 3* Why they *paid* him // *1* nobody *knows* //

The dominant clause has the conclusive Tone 1, while the reported clause has the non-conclusive Tone 3 or 4.

There is quite a different structure shown in **7**:

7 They paid him I suppose

Here there is no binder and the intonation differs as shown in **8**.

8 // *13* they *paid* him I sup*pose* //

This structure will be discussed in Chapter 22.

Exercise 20.1

(a) Identify the binder.

(b) Is the dominant clause negative or positive?

(c) Assess the reversed sequence as acceptable, doubtful or virtually unacceptable.

1 He didn't tell us who fired the gun.
2 I wonder whether they know.
3 He didn't deny that he was the culprit.
4 She never suspected that Bill had done it.
5 I noticed when the postman came.
6 I didn't notice when the postman came.
7 Napoleon regretted that the Russians had abandoned Moscow.
8 Napoleon didn't ask why the Russians had abandoned Moscow.
9 I shan't enquire whether the news is good.
10 He thinks that the military have taken over.
11 You wouldn't believe what I've just seen.
12 They hardly noticed whose car they had stolen.
13 I can't think who would want one.

Reported clauses are dependent on a lexical item in the dominant clause. This is very frequently a verb (a reporting verb) such as *say*, *declare*, *think*, *suspect*, *regret*, *recognize*. Other possibilities than verbs are discussed in Chapter 21.

20.2 Reported clauses: componence

There are three kinds of binding in reported clauses:

1 With binder that *or no binder at all*

9a I suspect that you're deceiving yourself
9b I suspect you're deceiving yourself

2 With binder whether (or not) *or* if

10a I wonder whether this key works (or not)
10b I wonder whether (or not) this key works
10c I wonder if this key works

Reported clauses with *if* should not be confused with contingent clauses, where *if* is also possible, though there it is not interchangeable with *whether*:

11a I'll tell you, if I can (I'll tell you what you want to know, if I can tell you: *contingent clause*)
11b If I can, I'll tell you (*contingent*)
11c I'll tell you if I can (I'll tell you whether I can: *reported clause*)

3 With WH-item as binder

12a They haven't decided who should do it
12b I wonder what reason he'll give

The binders here are *who* and *what reason*. Some reported clauses are P-bound, as in **13**:

13a He won't tell me *whether to apply*
13b I wonder *what reason to give*
13c They haven't decided *when to do it*

These all have *to*-form predicators and the binder must be *whether* or a WH-item. These structures are very close to phase structure. Compare them with **14**:

14a He won't tell me to apply (S P C^{o}/S P)
14b They haven't decided to do it (S P P O)

It is the presence of a binder in examples like **15** that is taken as criterial for treating them as F B^{rep}; and also that under the right conditions F B^{rep} is reversible, while phase-structures fail this test as shown in **16** and **17**:

15 He won't tell me whether to apply

16a Where to apply he won't tell me (B^{rep} F)

16b *To apply he won't tell me

17a When to do it they haven't decided (B^{rep} F)

17b *To do it they haven't decided

Exercise 20.2

(a) Attempt as close a paraphrase as possible of the following examples, using a finite B^{rep} clause, e.g. *He won't tell me whether to apply* (Paraphrase: He won't tell me whether I should apply.)

(b) How did you manage to find an S for your paraphrase?

1 I haven't decided whether to paint it white.

2 They showed me how to turn it off.

3 He can't remember who to tell.

4 Will you find out which figure to believe, please?

5 She mentioned where to park the car.

6 I have forgotten whose certificate to send by post.

20.3 Reported clauses: meaning

It may be thought that the name 'reported' is too restricting for this type of clause. 'Reporting' suggests, first and foremost verbalization, so that the reporting verbs in the dominant clause would be *declare*, *say*, *ask*, *inquire*, etc. However, more than this is intended by the name. Whatever can be said can also be thought and thus reported internally, as it were. So the list of reporting verbs would also include *think*, *suspect*, *know*, *wonder*, *recognize*, etc. The person involved can also perceive and react to facts in the world around him; so there are further reporting verbs, such as *perceive*, *see*, etc. (which have to do with perception) and *regret*, *grieve*, *deplore*, *rejoice* etc. (which have to do with reaction). What all report structures have in common semantically is that they talk about a person's relation to an idea, whether the relation is that of speaker to utterance, cognizant to fact, perceiver to phenomenon or reactor to stimulus.

Exercise 20.3

Identify the clauses in the following passage, and assign the features *free*, *bound*, *major*, *minor*, *listed*, *linked*, *P-bound*, *contingent*, *reported*, *adding*, *branched*, *split*, as appropriate. Identify listers, linkers and binders.

And then there was the difficulty of dress, a subject on which he never offered advice. Desperately in need of information, I asked myself what I was to wear on my head. Stephen had worn some sort of cap last year, but the idea of buying a jockey-cap seemed somehow ludicrous. (I remembered the old brown corduroy one I wore on my first day with the Dumborough.)

On this particular afternoon I had shortened my stirrups by several holes. I had observed, in some steeplechasing photographs in an illustrated paper, that the jockeys rode with their knees ever so much higher than mine. This experiment caused me to feel important and professional but less secure in the saddle. And when Cockbird made a sudden swerve (quite needlessly alarmed by a blackbird that flew out of the hedge) I almost lost my balance; in fact I nearly fell off. Dixon said nothing until we were on our way home, and then he merely remarked that he'd never believed in riding very short. 'They always say that for a point-to-point there's nothing like sticking to the old-fashioned hunting seat'. I took the hint, which was a wise one.

SIEGFRIED SASSOON, *Memoirs of a Fox-hunting Man*

20.4 Clause complexes revisited

In our study of clause complexes we have so far only considered two clauses at a time, whether they are combined in a joining or a binding relationship. We now turn to complexes of three or more clauses.

18 They know, of course, || that they are rich || because others are poor

In one interpretation of this example the final clause is contingent, bound to *that they are rich*, which is therefore dominant to it. But these two clauses are together bound to the first clause as shown in Figure 83. Actually, however, **18** is ambiguous between this interpretation and the one given in Figure 84. It is a question of whether they are rich because others are poor, or whether they know it because others are poor. In the second interpretation the position of clause *c* could

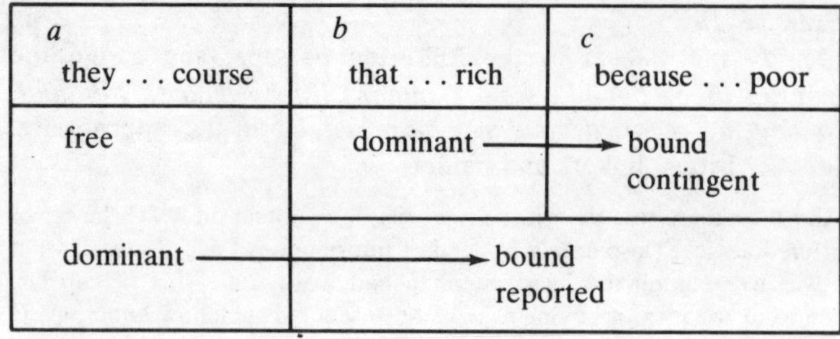

Figure 83

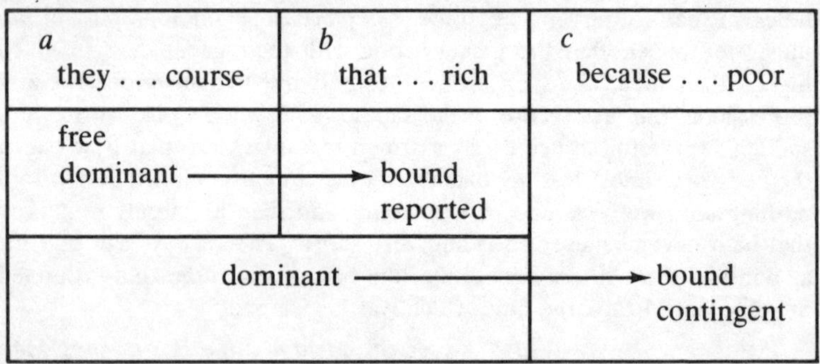

Figure 84

be changed relative to the others to give **19**:

> **19** Because others are poor, ‖ they know, of course, ‖ that they are rich

What is being suggested here is that a complex of more than two clauses may have internal bracketing. We have already seen (sections 18.5–7 and exercise 18.4) that a complex of joined clauses may have such internal bracketing, i.e. that a member of a complex may itself be a complex rather than a single clause. For instance **20** has a structure that can be represented as $(a + b) + (c + d)$.

> **20** They strike lucky ‖ and work feverishly ‖ but there are attacks from bandits ‖ and there is the ordeal of the sun

This structure is illustrated in tabular notation in Figure 85.

a they . . . lucky	*b* and . . . feverishly	*c* but . . . bandits	*d* and . . . sun
joined —	— joined listed branched	joined —	— joined listed
joined —		— joined	

Figure 85

A complex containing bound clauses can be represented in the bracketed linear notation. All we need to do is adopt a convention for distinguishing joining from binding: '+' for joining and '→' for binding, with the arrow pointing away from the dominant member towards the bound. Thus the two interpretations of **18** are represented in **21** and **22**:

21 $(a \rightarrow (b \rightarrow c))$
22 $((a \rightarrow b) \rightarrow c)$

The direction of the arrows ensures that we can tell which clause in such a complex is free: namely, any clause that has no arrow pointing towards it. A slightly more elaborate example with four clauses:

23 He wanted me to promise ‖ that I would write ‖ when I got to London ‖ where the boat was docked

We can see from the structure of **23** given in Figure 86 that it is possible for a bound member of a complex to be itself a complex with a bound member. Every instance of binding can be said to increase the depth of a structure. So in **23** *a* has a depth of 0, *b* has a depth of 1, *c* a depth of 2 and *d* a depth of 3, and this too is shown in Figure 86. It will by this time be clear that the term *dominant* is not synonymous with *free*. A bound clause may be a dominant one.

Exercise 20.4
Analyse the following examples and show the results in tables

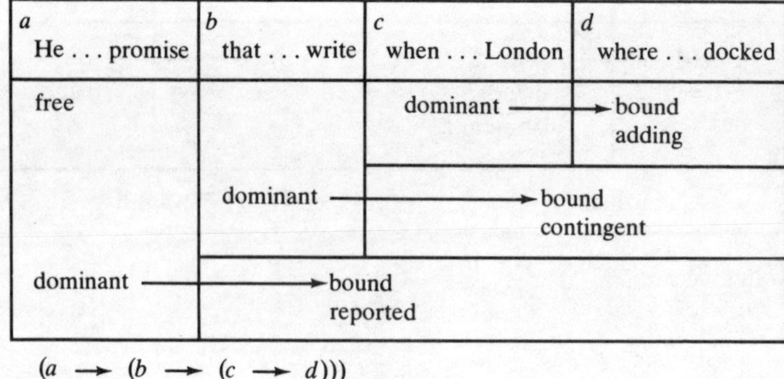

(*a* → (*b* → (*c* → *d*)))
0 1 2 3

Figure 86

and linear diagrams:

1 Have you seen that the factory is closing down when this contract is completed, if we get no more orders.
2 Although she worked so hard, she found the task was beyond her.
3 If you find my coat when they open the cupboard, bring it to me, please.
4 If you find my coat, bring it to me when you come home.
5 I brought in the Christian thing because I think it has had a vast effect on our culture. (Appendix BII, ll. 3–5)

Binding and joining can, of course, both occur in the same clause complex; both relationships are recursive because in a complex of any type one (or more than one) of the members may itself be a complex of any type. When we examined joining relationships in Chapter 18, we looked only at cases where the clauses that were joined were free clauses. But bound clauses may also be joined, as seen in **24** (see also Figure 87).

24 I hate coffee ‖ when it's cold ‖ or when it has no sugar in it

Two clauses that are joined must be of the same depth, and, if

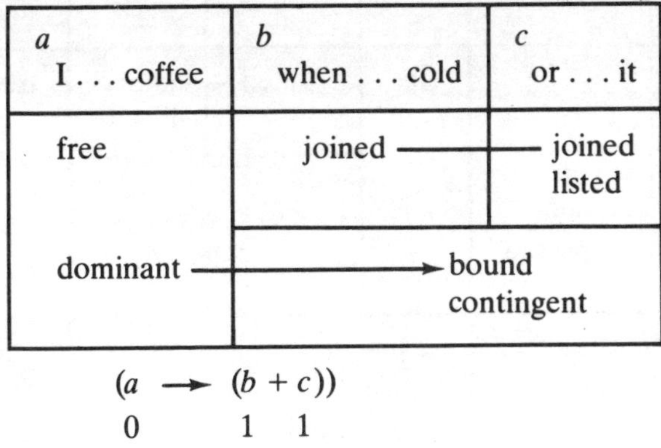

Figure 87

bound, must both be contingent, both adding or both reported. Two further examples of complexes containing joined and bound clauses are given in **25** and **26** (see also Figures 88 and 89).

25 If he simply obeys his party conference, ‖ he's a party hack ‖ and morally quite unjustified

26 *a* Archaeologists must realize ‖ *b* that the world outside their own profession is not entirely populated by

a If . . . conference	*b* he's . . . hack	*c* and . . . unjustified
	free joined ——	—— free joined listed branched
bound ←—— contingent	—— dominant	

(*a* ← (*b* + *c*))
1 0 0

Figure 88

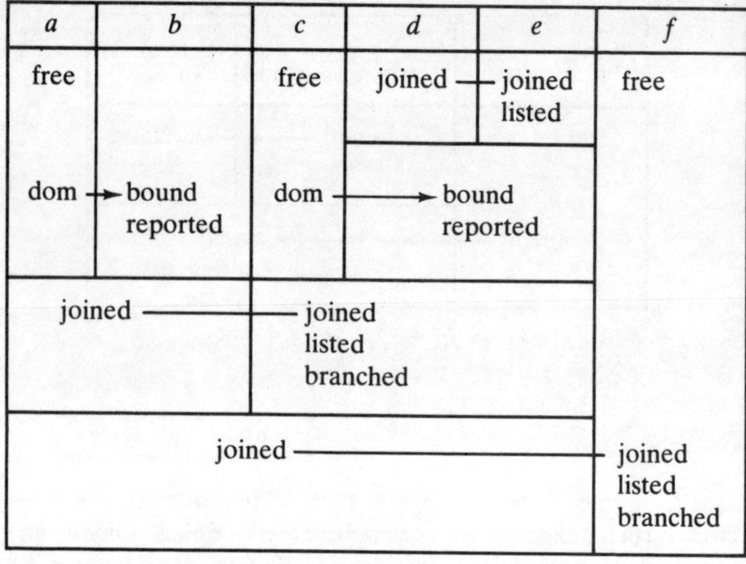

$$(((a \rightarrow b) + (c \rightarrow (d + e))) + f)$$

0 1 0 1 1 0

Figure 89

Philistines ‖ *c* and go all out to explain ‖ *d* what they need ‖ *e* and why they need it ‖ *f* and in that way obtain more financial support from the developers themselves

Exercise 20.5

Analyse the following clause complexes, using both the tabular and the linear notation. The clause boundaries are given thus: ‖.

1 If I battered somebody to death ‖ is it relevant to me ‖ that I'm being used ‖ to deter you from battering somebody else?

2 But, of course, the Clay Cross councillors haven't been given indemnity ‖ because they still have to pay their surcharge of £7000 ‖ and that's not being found out of public funds.

3 They've had removed from them the penalty which the law attaches to a breach of trust ‖ which is that they should be disqualified from acting as councillors again || and thus they are given a privilegium.

4 It was very nice of him || and they had this thing called *A View from Space* || which was films from various satellites || and this in colour was quite fantastic.

5 It's a pity || they can't get the pictures inside the spacecraft clearer || 'cos they're never very clear || they're sort of shady.

6 Of course, the Labour Party Conference did call on the next Labour Government to indemnify these men || so morally do you think || that Mr Crosland is justified in his action?

7 Part of the policy relates to the building of farmworkers' houses in the green belt || which are only permitted || where there is a genuine need for essential accommodation.

8 Once you undermine the rule of law || really what's sauce for the goose is sauce for the gander || and now we find || that at the head of the demonstrators is the Secretary of State for the Environment || and the Attorney General and the Lord Chancellor still remain in the Government || and so does the Home Secretary || who said in the election || that he supported the rule of law.

20.5 Constraints on clause sequence

In discussing the sequence of dominant and bound clauses, we confined our remarks to cases where the dominant clause was free and was not listed. We found that the sequence BF was often possible, as in **27**:

27a When he arrives || we'll tell him the news

B^{cont} F

27b Why I wanted one || he didn't ask

B^{rep} F

We must now reconsider the question of clause sequence.

If the free clause is listed, the bound clause cannot come in front of the lister. In such cases splitting of F is required as in **28**. Example **29** shows cases where the bound clause is in front of the lister.

28a And ((when he arrives)) we'll tell him the news

F ((B^{cont}))

28b But ((why I wanted one)) he didn't ask

F ((B^{rep}))

29a *When he arrives and we'll tell him the news

29b *Why I wanted one but he didn't ask

We know that a dominant clause may itself be bound as in **30**:

30 They feel ashamed ‖ if they are rich ‖ because others are poor $(a \rightarrow (b \rightarrow c))$

The last of these clauses cannot be placed in front of the binder (*if*) of its dominant:

31 They feel ashamed because others are poor if they are rich

This sentence still makes sense, but the *because*-clause is no longer bound to the *if*-clause; it is the other way round. The only possible changes of sequence that preserve the relationship of dominant and bound are **32** when the *if*-clause is split and **33** when both clauses are moved to a position in front of F but their sequence relative to each other is not changed:

32 They feel ashamed if, because others are poor, they are rich

33 If they are rich because others are poor, they feel ashamed

34 If, because others are poor, they are rich, they feel ashamed

In **34** both rearrangements are made together.

This constraint: 'no bound clause before the binder of its dominant', also applies to adding-clause binders, and is illustrated in **35**:

35a Selection is based on banding, which will become illegal if the Bill is passed

35b Selection is based on banding, which, if the Bill is passed, will become illegal

35c *Selection is based on banding, if the Bill is passed, which will become illegal

It is less clear that reported-clause binders have the same effect:

36a He asked why, if I thought them too expensive, I had ordered one

36b ?*He asked, if I thought them too expensive, why I had ordered one

36c He promised that, if I liked them, he would send one round

36d ?*He promised, if I liked them, that he would send one round

This discussion suggests that the neutral sequence of clauses in a binding relationship is dominant–bound. Any departure from this sequence produces a tension in the act of communication; what is uttered creates an expectation that something further is to be uttered, and the tension is not relieved until the expectation is fulfilled. Consider the difference between the examples in **37**:

37a I can't come to the wedding unless I hire a suit

37b Unless I hire a suit, I can't come to the wedding

In **37a** the uttering of the dominant clause creates no expectation of a condition to follow. The speaker might well be afraid that what he says will be taken as a decision not to come to the wedding, as the condition (*unless* . . .) comes too late to save the situation. The lack of tension may thus have a danger. In **37b** the speaker is more cautious. He utters the condition first, thus creating an expectation of a dominant clause to follow and ensuring that he will not be taken as refusing outright to come to the wedding.

On the other hand, a speaker or writer, who began: *If, when, although* . . . would obviously be creating too much tension for an addressee to bear. (But see Appendix BI, ll. 2–5)

The most frequent patterns in clause complexes with a series of bindings are given in **38** and **39**:

38 $(a \rightarrow (b \rightarrow (c \rightarrow d)))$
$\quad 0 \quad 1 \quad 2 \quad 3$

39 $(a \leftarrow (b \rightarrow (c \rightarrow d)))$
$\quad 1 \quad 0 \quad 1 \quad 2$

It can be seen that depth increases mostly towards the right.

21 Reporting clauses

21.1 Reporting clauses

There is a particularly close relation between a reported clause and its dominant. The presence of the reported clause is not optional since the dominant contains a reporting verb such as *think*, *feel*, *suggest*, *say*, etc. We will call the dominant clause in such structures a *reporting clause*.

We noted in section 20.3 the semantic range of the reporting verbs – verbalization (*say*, *deny* . . .), cognition (*believe*, *doubt* . . .), perception (*see*, *hear* . . .), reaction (*regret*, *grieve* . . .). The report structure, consisting of a reporting clause as dominant and a reported clause as bound, expresses a relation between a person and an idea; the bound clause expreses the idea and the dominant the kind of relation. In the examples given in **1** there is a similar range of meanings and a similar syntactic structure.

1a He was confident that she would make up her mind
1b They seemed doubtful who had better go
1c Bill looked surprised that the machine had broken down
1d She is uncertain whether the meat is fresh
1e I'm sorry that he's not more efficient

In these examples the dominant clause has a predicator *be*, *seem*, or *look* and an ascriptive complement of the adjectival type: *confident*, *sure*, *pleased*, *doubtful*, *surprised*, *sorry*, *heartbroken*, *horrified*, *delighted*, *relieved*, *amused*, *curious*, etc; the structure is illustrated in Figure 90.

Syntactically the only difference between the kind of FB^{rep} which has a reporting verb and the examples in **1** is that there is, in each sentence of **1**, a *reporting adjective*. Some of the complements are actually related morphologically to verbs, e.g. *horrified*, *relieved*. These are verbal *n*-forms occurring in complement

She is horrified ‖	that the electricity has been cut off
S P C^i	A^b S P C^{part}
F	B^{rep}

Figure 90

function (see section 13.6). In **2** is an example that further shows the parallel between examples like **1** and the kind of structure that has a reporting verb in the dominant clause:

2 Why the performance didn't continue, he wasn't sure

(For the conditions governing the B^{rep} F sequence, see section 20.1.)

21.2 Various patterns of reporting clause

In the types of report structure we have discussed so far, there has been a person named as subject of the dominant clause, e.g. *He thinks / is sure . . .* This is the person who is in some way cognizant of the idea named in the reported clause. It may, but need not, be the speaker: *I think / I am sure . . . .* There are two kinds of structure in which the cognizant individual need not be specified at all:

3a It is possible that a mass of insects like this would show up on a radar screen (Appendix BI, ll. 45–7)
3b It may be imagined that nobody wants a confrontation

In **3a** the structure of the dominant clause is SPC^i, with *possible* as the complement; in **3b** we have the passive construction that corresponds to the active *S may imagine that nobody wants a confrontation.* In the latter *imagine* is a reporting verb. In these patterns, the subject of the dominant clause is the 'empty' *it*, whose function it is to fill the position of subject and anticipate the presence of a reported clause to follow. The cognizant can be specified, optionally, as in **4**:

4a It is astonishing *to me* that . . . SPC^iC . . .
4b It may be imagined *by the management* that . . . SPC . . .

We can now summarize the types of dominant clause in report

structures:

1 *He expects* (*that* . . .)
SP: S is cognizant; P is an active reporting verb.
2 *He is confident* (*that* . . .)
SPC^i: S is cognizant; P is *be*, *seem* etc.; C^i is a reporting adjective (including *n*-forms).
3 *It is certain* (*that* . . .)
SPC^i: S is *it*; P is *be*, *seem* etc.; C^i is a reporting adjective.
4 *It is expected* (*that* . . .)
SP: S is *it*; P is a passive reporting verb.

Exercise 21.1

(a) Identify the dominant and bound clauses in the following report structures;
(b) Note which of the patterns of reporting clause occurs; (designate them (i) SP (ii) SPC^i (iii) $S^{it}PC^i$ (iv) S^{it} P^{pass}.)
(c) There is *one* example that does not fit any of these types; which is it?
(d) List the reporting verbs and adjectives in four columns, one for each type of reporting clause.

1 Bill didn't notice who led the orchestra.
2 They must have warned her that there was a wolf.
3 I was surprised they didn't let me know.
4 She seemed unsure where she wanted to go.
5 It's true he doesn't mind waiting.
6 It wasn't surprising he backed out.
7 It can be imagined what a sensation it made.
8 It won't be noticed that they haven't painted in that corner.
9 Who put up the money nobody seemed certain.
10 Where the money's coming from, I can't think.
11 It is believed there will be a Liberal landslide.
12 It astonished her that he said such things.
13 It is not very regrettable that the evidence won't be given.
14 They will be pleased they hadn't ordered a taxi.
15 She says there's no hurry.

In the third type of reporting clause (e.g. *It is certain* . . .) it is assumed, unless there is some indication to the contrary, that the speaker is presenting himself as cognizant:

5a It is not certain that the evidence will be given (*meaning* It is not certain to me)
5b It seems doubtful whether it should be called an outrage (*meaning* It seems doubtful to me)

This grammatical structure provides the speaker with a means of supplementing the distinctions made in knowledge modality. When paraphrasing such modalities (see Chapter 8) this structure is useful: *It is possible / conceivable / predictable / certain*, etc. (See also section 8.7 on subjective and objective modality.)

There are other means of supplementing modality. First, the kind of linking adjunct that reflects speaker's attitude, as in **6**:

6 He will *certainly* come

Second, there are some of the semi-auxiliaries (see Chapter 15), illustrated in **7**:

7 He *is likely* to be there

It is not surprising to find that some lexical items occur in more than one of these patterns:

8a He is certain to come (*semi-auxiliary*)
8b Certainly he's coming (*comment adjunct*)
8c I am certain he's coming (FB^{rep})
8d It is certain he's coming (FB^{rep})
(*Compare with the modal*: He must be coming)
9a He is likely to be there (*semi-auxiliary*)
9b It is likely that he's there (FB^{rep})
(*Compare with the modal*: He should be there)

Another detail to note about the third type of reporting clause is that among the reporting adjectives there are words derived from verbs; these are the *ing*-forms: *astonishing*, *surprising*, *pleasing*, *interesting*, etc. For the verbs *astonish*, *surprise* etc. in reporting clauses, see the next paragraph.

There are two further patterns of reporting clause; in addition to those listed on page 266. These are illustrated in examples **10** and **11**.

10 It astonished him that the trains would be running

In this pattern the cognizant is specified, but not as a subject. The subject is, again, the empty *it*. This time there is an object (*him*); obviously, it is 'him' who is the person aware that the trains would be running.

As we would expect, where there is an object there is a passive counterpart:

11 He was astonished that the trains would be running

We are now faced with a familiar problem – that of deciding whether *He was astonished* is SP^{pass} or simply SPC^{i} with an *n*-form as complement. In other words, does this differ from type 2 (page 266): *He was sorry that / disappointed that . . .* ?

21.3 Rankshifted reported clauses

In several of the reporting-clause patterns described above there is an empty subject, *it*. There is a close relation between this *it* and the bound clause that follows, as illustrated in **12**:

12 It is surprising how many people like that kind of bread

In **12** *it* anticipates the presence of the bound clause. There is an alternative structure in which the reported clause is rankshifted into subject position; this is given in **13**:

13 How many people like that kind of bread | is | surprising
S P C

The difference between this type of structure and the FB^{rep} pattern can be explained in terms of textual organization – that is, of the relative prominence given to the constituent parts of the message. From this point of view the rankshifted structure, with the reported clause as subject, is marked. The neutral pattern is the one with anticipatory *it*, and this is the one that occurs most frequently in text. In **14** are further examples of the marked structure:

14a That the evidence will be given is certain
14b That he backed out was surprising
14c That they were not on better terms surprised him

It is relevant to point out that interrogative equivalents of the examples in **14** are scarcely grammatical:

15a *Is that the evidence will be given certain?
15b *Was that he backed out surprising?
15c *Did that they were not on better terms surprise him?

In contrast, interrogative forms with *it* are perfectly acceptable:

16 Is it certain that the evidence will be given?

21.4 Nouns in reporting clauses

Both verbs and adjectives can feature in the structure of reporting clauses. It is an interesting speculation whether nouns can do so, and, if so, to what extent. In raising the question I have supplied an example that begins to answer it:

17 It is an interesting speculation ‖ whether nouns can do so
F B^{rep}

A further example is given in **18**:

18 It is a pity ‖ that I have not time for reading

There is no space to discuss these noun patterns in detail, but **19–21** contain some suggestive parallels between report clauses and constructions involving nouns:

19a We do not know directly that there were actually swarms present
19b We have no direct evidence that there were actually swarms present
19c There is no direct evidence that there were actually swarms present (Appendix BI, ll. 62–3)

20a I suspect that the claim is false
20b I am suspicious that the claim is false
20c I have a suspicion that the claim is false
20d There is a suspicion that the claim is false

21a I don't doubt that he considered the matter gravely
21b I have no doubt that he considered the matter gravely
21c There is no doubt that he considered the matter gravely
21d That he considered the matter gravely, there is no doubt (*or* . . . I have no doubt)

21.5 Theme and report structures

We have now studied several uses of *it* as subject. These sometimes bear superficial resemblances to each other and may be difficult to tell apart. Two of them were introduced in Chapter 12. Here are some notes that will help to keep them distinct:

Postposed theme

It sounded convincing, what he said. What he said could be replaced by a nominal group like *his statement*; *it* has ordinary third person reference like *she* in *she's late again, that typist*; *it* could be replaced by *what he said* to give the neutral thematic form of the clause.

It*–theme*

It was Harold's car that we noticed. It cannot be replaced by any other part of the construction, but it can be eliminated by re-organizing as: *We noticed Harold's car*. The verb *be* is an essential part of the construction and cannot be replaced (e.g. by *seem*).

Report structure

It was astonishing that he had been implicated. It can be replaced by *that he had been implicated* to give a marked organization: *That he had been implicated was astonishing.*

Exercise 21.2
Distinguish the following as postposed theme, *it*-theme or report structure:

1 It's long, what he's written.
2 It isn't known what he's written.
3 It's a very good essay that he's written.
4 It beats me why the insurance company doesn't cough up.
5 It's thought you see the glowing discharge known as St Elmo's fire if you have a swarm of moths like this. (Appendix BI, ll. 8–10).
6 It's incredible that the building has no fire escape.

7 It's a surprise that he's trying.
8 It's the punctuation that I find so erratic.
9 It can't be established what he bought.
10 It can't be dry-cleaned, what he bought.

Exercise 21.3

Sort out the structure of lines 7–10 in Appendix BI, paying special attention to thematic organization and inter-clause relationships. (Comparison with exercise 21.2, number **5** might help.)

22 Reported mood and reported speech

22.1 Reported mood

In Chapter 17 we described free clauses as those in which the speaker indicates the type of communicative act he is performing in speaking. The main grammatical systems that signal the type of act are the mood systems. These are supplemented by intonation (choice of tones), which is to some extent independent of mood.

In bound clauses there is no mood system. But some comment on this claim is necessary, since there is a close parallel between the indicative moods in free clauses and the subtypes of reported clause which are distinguished by the binder:

1 That (or zero); parallel to declarative

1 They know that eggs are going up

2 Whether / if; parallel to polar interrogative

2 They wonder whether eggs are going up

3 WH; parallel to non-polar interrogative

3 They wonder how much eggs are going up

If this system in reported clauses is called *mood*, the term is evidently being used in a secondary or derived sense. *They wonder whether eggs are going up*, has a declarative free clause (*They wonder*) which can be contrasted with the interrogative *Do they wonder . . . ?* ; but *reported mood*, in the bound clause, reflects not the speaker's attitude but the attitude of the cognizant, in this case *they*.

22.2 A type of declarative question

Since the reported mood expresses the attitude of the cognizant, when the cognizant is first person (the speaker himself) the construction FB^{rep} may be used with a force similar to an interrogative, as in **4a**:

4a I wonder whether eggs are going up
4b Are eggs going up?

In other words, **4a** could be interpreted in appropriate circumstances as a question (an utterance which expects an informative response). (NB This does not mean that **4a** is grammatically interrogative; on the contrary, it is grammatically declarative even though it might on occasion be uttered with the intention of stimulating a verbal response.) It is easy to take **4a** as a question asking whether eggs are going up, since the subject of F is *I*, the verb (*wonder*) means that its subject does not know, F is declarative and untagged, there is no attitudinal adjunct present and reference is being made to the time of utterance. The clauses in **5** do not have all of these features and are therefore less easily interpreted as asking the question given in **4b**:

5a He wonders whether eggs are going up
5b I know whether . . .
5c Obviously, I wonder whether . . .
5d Do I wonder whether . . .
5e I wonder whether eggs are going up, do I?
5f Yesterday I wondered whether eggs were going up

22.3 Classes of reporting word

Reported mood is to some extent determined by the sense of the verb or adjective that occurs in the dominant clause. For instance, a number of verbs and adjectives do not allow a WH-binder or *whether/if*:

6a *I *expect* what you want
6b *I *expect* whether you want it
6c *He was *happy* where she wanted to go
6d *He was *happy* whether she wanted to go there

Others allow WH or *whether/if*, but not *that*:

7 *He inquired that the train was late

In general there are three main types of reporting clause:

1 Those allowing any type of binder: *He discovered that/whether/when ....*
2 Those allowing WH or *whether/if*, but not *that*: *He inquired *that/whether/when ....*
3 Those allowing *that*, but not WH or *whether/if*: *He expected that/*whether/*when ....*

The verb *doubt* stands out as allowing *that* or *whether/if*, but not WH:

8a I don't doubt that it will rain
8b I doubt whether it will rain
8c *I doubt /?*don't doubt when it will rain

However, the relationship between reporting clause and reported mood is not merely a matter of classifying the reporting verbs and adjectives. Mood, tense, polarity and modality in the reporting clause may also make a difference, at least to the ease with which a structure is accepted as possible English:

9a ?He revealed when the post had come
9b He didn't reveal when the post had come

10a I wonder what he will say
10b ?*I don't wonder what he will say

11a He blurted out that the post was vacant
11b ?He blurted out whether the post was vacant
11c He always blurts out whether the post is vacant

12a I don't doubt that it will rain
12b ?I doubt that it will rain
12c I doubt whether it will rain
12d ?*I don't doubt whether it will rain

Exercise 22.1

Attempt to classify the following verbs and adjectives according to their potentiality for dominating reported moods. Use the three classes 1, 2 and 3 described above.

reveal, feel, think, observe, ask, wonder, remind (someone), whisper, *hope*, *deny*, *inquire*, *demand*, *investigate*, *discuss*, *find (out)*, *doubtful*, *sorry*, *surprised*, *sure*, *obvious*, *possible*.

(a) Try varying the mood, polarity, tense, etc., of the reporting clause before deciding that a word will not permit some reported mood.

(b) Look out for any sharp shift in meaning that correlates with a shift in reported mood, e.g.

I don't wonder that you don't like it.

(wonder_1 = be surprised)

I wonder why you don't like it.

(wonder_2 = ask oneself)

Treat *wonder* as two homonymous verbs.

22.4 Factive verbs

Some reporting verbs are known as factive verbs since they have the interesting characteristic, when they dominate a reported declarative, that they presuppose the truth of the reported clause. For example, contrast **13** with **14**:

13 He *knew* that it was raining
14 He *thought* that it was raining

In **14** there is no commitment on the part of the speaker as to whether it was raining or not. Thus *He knew that it was raining but it wasn't* is a contradiction, while *He thought that it was raining but it wasn't* is not a contradicition. Presupposing the truth of the reported clause is not the same thing as declaring it. There is a difference between **15** and **16**:

15 He knows that it is raining
16 It is true that it is raining

This difference can be tested by negating the dominant clause as in **17** and **18**:

17 He doesn't know that . . .
18 It isn't true that . . .

We see that the presupposition of truth after *know* is not affected by whether the dominant clause is negative. So anyone who says *He doesn't know that x* is just as much committed to the truth of *x* as if he had said *He knows that x.* But *It isn't true that x* declares the falsity of *x*, while *It is true that x* declares its truth.

Exercise 22.2
Which of the following presuppose the truth of the reported clause? Note which verbs and adjectives have this presupposing sense.

1 He discovered that steam can lift weights.
2 He decided that first thoughts were best.
3 He believes that the world is spherical.
4 He said truthfully that he worked in a bank.
5 He accepted that my statement was true.
6 He realized that my statement was true.
7 He alleged that the remarks were out-of-place.
8 He reminded them that the cost was very high.
9 He is sure that the papers were stolen.
10 He is pleased they have been recovered.
11 He is surprised they have been recovered.
12 It is astonishing that people pay so much for it.
13 It is probable that everybody does so.
14 It was imagined that the trouble was over.
15 I convinced him that there was gold in those hills.
16 I noticed that everybody was tired.
17 He confessed that he had done it.

22.5 Transferred negation

Another peculiarity of some reporting clauses is illustrated in **19**:

19a He thought they were not willing
19b He didn't think they were willing

In the most natural interpretation **19b** is synonymous with **19a**; the negation has been transferred from the reported clause, where it truly belongs, to the dominant. Contrast example **19** with **20** and **21**:

20a He told me that they were not willing
20b He didn't tell me that they were willing

21a He revealed that the mistake had not been made
21b He didn't reveal that the mistake had been made

In these examples it makes a difference which clause is negated. This shows most clearly in **21**, where the verb is factive and the speaker is committed to the truth of the reported clause; but it is also the case in **20**.

Exercise 22.3

Which of the following could have the negation transferred to the dominant clause without change of meaning? Note the verbs and adjectives that allow this.

1 He believes we don't want the others.
2 He discovered we didn't want the others.
3 I imagine he's not very pleased.
4 I assume he's not very pleased.
5 We feel there aren't enough.
6 It's probable he won't come.
7 It's possible he won't come.
8 I expect the ends don't meet.
9 It surprises me they are not on good terms.
10 It is thought that they won't succeed.

Exercise 22.4

1 Comment on the form of the tag in: *I don't think it's going to freeze, is it?*
2 Comment on the following, where *so* and *not* are clause substitutes:

I think not = I don't think so.
I hope not ≠ I don't hope so.

22.6 Pseudo-report structures

We turn now to a structure that was briefly mentioned in Chapter 20 (page 252):

22 It's raining, I think
// *13* ‸ it's raining I think //

(For an explanation of Tone 13 see Appendix A.) The question to be decided is whether this is an instance of B^{rep} F. If so, it is nevertheless clearly very different from cases like **23**:

23 Who said that, I don't remember
// *3* who said that I // I don't remember //

For a description of **23**, which is B^{rep} F, see Chapter 20. The structure illustrated in **22** has no binder, so the first clause, if it is a bound clause at all, does not differ in componence from a free clause. The question is whether its syntactic relation to the other clause is that of bound to dominant.

One relevant fact is that there has to be a congruence between the two clauses such that the second has some modifying effect on the mood of the first. It indicates in what circumstances, from whose point of view, or with what degree of confidence the first clause is asserted. Thus, **24a** and **24b** are well formed, but **24c** and **24d** are not:

24a You're hungry, I expect
24b The price has gone up, he says
24c *The man that wrote it was a communist, I deny
24d *They had spoken to the headmaster, he didn't find out

The fact that he didn't find out they had spoken to the headmaster does not in any way suggest conditions in which the assertion might be made that they had done so. On the other hand, the fact that he has said the price has gone up does explain why it might be safe to make the assertion. All this suggests that the first clause has declarative mood. There would be nothing incongruous about the combination of the clauses in **24c** and **24d** if the relation between them were that of reporting to reported:

25a I deny the man that wrote it was a communist
25b He didn't find out they had spoken to the headmaster

The next stage in the argument is to point out that there are also cases in which the first clause is interrogative. Variability of mood argues for taking these clauses to be free. The clauses in **26** illustrate this point:

26a Has the price gone up, I wonder?
26b Had I seen the others, he asked?

Again, there has to be a compatibility between the second clause and the mood of the first; so those in **27** are unacceptable:

27a *Has the price gone up, I know
27b *Had I seen the others, he didn't ask

Another fact that suggests it would be reasonable to treat the first clause in these problematic structures as free, is that it can be split and the other clause enclosed within it. This arrangement is not characteristic for a dominant-bound relationship; whereas elsewhere we find F ((B)) structures, illustrated in **28**, we do not find B ((F)).

28a Had I, he asked, seen the others?
28b You, I expect, are hungry
28c The curtains, he noticed, were drawn

But if we take the first clause as free, what shall we make of the other one:

29 Has the price gone up || I wonder?
F ?

The fact is that this second clause also shows variation for mood; the only restriction being the compatibility of the two clauses with each other:

30a We have finished the beer, tell them (*declarative + imperative*)
30b I might be late, say (*declarative + imperative*)
30c Are they coming tomorrow, did they say? (*interrogative + interrogative*)
30d He's here, did you know? (*declarative + interrogative*)
30e They're coming tomorrow, they said, didn't they? (*declarative + tagged declarative*)

The conclusion seems to be that this is a special kind of clause relationship involving two free clauses, but different from the co-ordinate relationship of joining. Such structures are used in discourse, for the following purposes:

1 Representing someone else's speech or thoughts in a narrative: *The curtains, he noticed, were drawn.*
2 Representing someone else's speech in journalistic reporting: *Would the government give such assurance, he wondered*?
3 Relaying a message via an intermediary: *I might be late, say*; *He might be late, he says.*
4 Making some adjustment to the expression of the speaker's own attitude: *He's here, I believe.* (i.e. *He's here; or rather, I believe so*.)

22.7 Quoted speech

Some of these uses of what I choose to call pseudo-report structures bring us very close to direct (or quoted) speech:

31a He asked me: 'Have you seen the others?'
(*compare:* He asked me whether I had seen the others; Had I seen the others, he asked me.)

31b 'We assume he is very rich,' they said.
(*compare:* They said that they assumed he was very rich; He was very rich, they assumed.)

31c 'I wonder whether you will give such assurances,' he asked the minister.
(*compare:* He told the minister he wondered whether he would give such assurances; Would the minister give such assurances, he wondered.)

In the direct-speech examples, both clauses have primary mood, and hence are both free clauses, though, of course, it is a rather complicated type of discourse, in which the speaker jumps from one situation to another, from speaking about somebody's utterance, to stating that utterance verbatim.

We can represent the structures we have been discussing as follows:

1 Report (illustrated in Figure 91).

He asked me ‖	whether I had seen the others.
free	
dominant	bound
reporting	reported

Figure 91

2 Quoted speech (illustrated in Figure 92).

He asked me ‖	'Have you seen the others?'
free	free
quoting	quoted

Figure 92

3 Pseudo-report (illustrated in Figure 93).

Had I seen the others, ‖	he asked me.
free pseudo-reported	free pseudo-quoting

Figure 93

The last type is semantically and syntactically poised between the other two, but it is well established as a structure in its own right. In narrative and journalism pseudo-reported clauses frequently occur without a pseudo-quoting clause:

32a The minister said they would try. There was a possibility of success

32b The questioner asked whether the minister had really tried. Had he considered going to the trouble spot himself?

The second sentence in **32a** is understood as stating the minister's opinion, not the journalist's. But it is not quoted speech, which would require the present tense of the verb, and it is not a reported clause, which would not allow interrogative mood, as in **32b**. It is therefore a pseudo-reported clause, though there is no other clause involved in this report structure.

There are certain formulaic expressions which look like pseudo-quoting clauses, and which no doubt may have originated as such, but which have a very different function. These are expressions such as *you see*, *you know*, *I mean* as they occur in **33**:

33a But, I mean, really it's true isn't, surely, that civilization . . . (Appendix BII, l. 24)

33b There aren't very many, you know

33c You see, the shops don't stay open long enough

These expressions are so few and so formulaic that there seems little point in treating them as SP structures. They are best treated *en bloc* as items capable of serving as linking adjuncts:

34 You see, | the shops | don't stay | open | long enough

You see,	the shops	don't stay	open	long enough
A^l	S	P	C^i	A

Exercise 22.5

What types of reporting and/or quoting occur in the following passage from Charlotte Bronte's *Villette*, Chapter 38. Do not be misled by her use of inverted commas, which does not conform to modern practice. What is the literary effect of the grammatical patterns used?

. . . I looked at Madame Beck's face, and into her eyes, for disproof or confirmation of this report; I perused her all over for information, but no part of her disclosed more than what was unperturbed and commonplace.

'This secession was an immense loss to her,' she alleged. 'She did not know how she would fill up the vacancy. She was so used to her kinsman, he had become her right hand. What should she do without him? She had opposed the step, but M. Paul had convinced her it was his duty.'

She said all this in public, in *classe*, at the dinner table, speaking audibly to Zélie St. Pierre.

'Why was it his duty?' I could have asked her that. I had impulses to take hold of her suddenly, as she calmly passed me in *classe*, to stretch out my hand and grasp her fast, and say, 'Stop. Let us hear the conclusion of the whole matter. *Why* is it his duty to go into banishment?' But madame always addressed some other teacher, and never looked at me, never seemed conscious I could have a care in the question.

23 Rankshift

23.1 Subject clauses

The principle of rankshift has been explained and illustrated at various places above (see sections 4.1 and 19.1) The aim of this chapter is to provide further illustrations of rankshift of various kinds, especially of rankshifted clauses. We will begin by reviewing the possibilities of clause-within-clause rankshift.

The examples in **1** show clauses functioning at S within a clause:

1a *Sending that message* was a mistake
1b *For Bill to have sent that message* was foolish
1c *To make a pot of tea* takes only a few minutes
1d *That some are dissatisfied* is admitted

These structures correspond to an alternative with *it* as subject exemplified in **2**:

2 It was a mistake sending that message

There is no space here to explore the differences between the various types of subject clause, but we may note in passing that **1d** is a kind that has been referred to above (pages 268–9) as an alternative organization of a report structure:

3 It is admitted || that some are dissatisfied

F B^{rep}

23.2 Object clauses

Rankshifted clauses also occur in object function, and after a preposition within a complement:

4a I | should appreciate | your sending the goods promptly

S P C^{o}

4b They | blamed | the farmers | for breaking the law at Holyhead

S P C^{o} C^{ob}

4c He | objected | to my being absent last week

S P C^{ob}

The complements in these last two examples are, of course, predicted by the verb; *blame* predicts a *for*-complement, *object* predicts a *to*-complement. Structures like these should be distinguished from those in **5**:

5a They drown the noise || by switching on the vacuum cleaner

F B^{cont}

5b With everybody being late || we couldn't begin on time.

B^{cont} F

Here there is no reason to postulate rankshift; the non-finite clauses are not predicted by the verb of the dominant clause so they need not be seen as part of the structure of that clause.

Exercise 23.1

Decide whether the non-finite clause is rankshifted within a C, or is a separate, P-bound clause.

1 They should be disqualified *from acting as councillors again.*
2 He was hanged *for murdering his wife.*
3 *In turning the corner* I ran over the pavement.
4 I wasn't aware *of your having done anything wrong.*
5 They won't insist *on going by train.*
6 *On going by train*, you don't see that side of the town.
7 We shall have to resort *to using more electricity.*
8 We can save fuel *by using less electricity.*
9 Opera is being ruined *by there not being a notional top.* (Appendix BII, ll. 45–6)

Many of the non-finite clauses that appear in the examples in exercise 23.1 have their predicator in the *ing*-form. When such clauses have a subject, it often appears in the possessive form; for instance *your* and *my* in **6**:

6a Your | having done | anything wrong
S P C^O

6b My | being | absent | last week
S P C A

Two points need to be made about these structures. The first is that the possessive form is unstable in colloquial usage, where it is often dispensed with:

7a I wasn't aware of *you having done anything wrong*
7b He objected to *Bill being absent* (or *Bill's being absent*)
7c I should appreciate *the shop sending the goods promptly* (or *the shop's sending the goods promptly*)
7d They didn't mind *him putting his bicycle on the train* (or *his putting his bicycle on the train*)

Second, these clause structures must be distinguished from a type of nominal group which they rather closely resemble in some respects:

8a The sending of the goods
8b Your telling of the story
8c Bill's singing of the part

The points of difference between the clause and the nominal group are first, that there is an *of* constituent in the nominal group; secondly that in the nominal group the item preceding the *ing*-form could be *the*, *a*, *this*, etc. Third, that an adjectival modifier in the nominal group corresponds to a manner adjunct in the clause, as shown in **9**:

9a Your | prompt | sending | of the goods
m m h q

9b Your | sending | the goods | promptly
S P C^O A

Lastly, the possessive forms *your*, *Bill's*, etc. are not optional in the nominal group:

10a *You telling of the story
10b *Bill singing of the part

23.3 Phase v. rankshift

It follows from some of what has been said above that there is the possibility of ambiguity between a phase structure and a rankshifted clause at C^o.

11a I | didn't notice | you | filling | the tank
S P C^o/S P C^o

11b I | didn't notice | you(r) filling the tank
S P C^o

12a I | can imagine | you | telling | them | that
S P C^o/S P C^{oi} C^{od}

12b I | can imagine | you(r) telling them that
S P C^o

The difference between the meanings of these two structures is admittedly very slight indeed. But it sometimes shows up more sharply, and the structural difference can be brought out by observing that some verbs (like *catch*) do not make any satisfactory sense in the rankshifted C^o-structure, while others do not fit into the phase structure:

13a They caught us walking on the grass (*phase*)
13b *They caught our walking on the grass
14 I appreciated him/his trying (*rankshift at* C^o)

Where the possessive pronoun is impossible, the structure has to be taken as phase. Where both the possessive and the non-possessive are possible, it could be that the two forms are interchangeable. This can be tested by using the passive-voice test. With phase, the C^o/S corresponds to the S of the passive:

15a We were caught walking on the grass
15b *He was appreciated trying

But with the rankshifted structure, the whole rankshifted clause is a single constituent, and thus in the passive the whole clause is the S:

16a *Our walking on the grass was caught
16b His trying was appreciated

Exercise 23.2

Which of the following have a rankshifted clause at C^O and which have a phase structure? Which are ambiguous?

1 I heard them starting the car.
2 I remember you disapproving of them.
3 I regret her throwing them away.
4 I resent Bill always shouting in my ear.
5 I can feel a spider crawling down my neck.
6 I kept them waiting.
7 I don't understand them painting it that colour.
8 I watched you sitting quietly.

23.4 Rankshift in the nominal group

So far we have concentrated on rankshift in the structure of the clause. In clauses there is only one possibility, namely that what is rankshifted is itself a clause, since the clause is the only unit of higher rank than the group. On the other hand, in the structure of groups both clauses and groups can be rankshifted, as in **17**:

17a The question he asked (was interesting)
17b The top of the hill (was visible).

In both these examples the rankshifted unit occurs as part of a nominal group. In **17a** *he asked* (alternatively, *which he asked*) is a clause within the nominal group, and in **17b** *of the hill* is a prepositional group within the nominal group.

The elements of structure in the nominal group are (m . . .) h (q . . .). There is an obligatory head. Preceding the head there may be one or more modifiers, and following it there may be one or more qualifiers. The nominal groups in **17** have the structure given in **18**:

18a	The	question	(which) he asked
	m	h	q

18b	The	top	of the hill
	m	h	q

In these examples the rankshifted units appear at q, and, in fact, this is by far the most frequent position for rankshift in group structure. The next few sections are concerned with clauses, rather than groups, that appear in this position.

23.5 Relative clauses

The kind of clause that is traditionally called the defining (or restrictive) relative clause is a case of clause-rankshift at q in the nominal group. It was introduced above in section 19.8 (pages 247–9), where it was compared with the adding clause (traditionally called the non-defining, or non-restrictive, relative clause).

It should be noted that in relative clauses the WH-function occurs. This is the function that can be described as unspecified element. Thus, (*The question*) *which he asked* has a presupposition 'he asked something' (SPC^{O}); so the structure of this relative clause is that in **19**:

19 Which | he | asked

WH C^{O} S P

The WH-element in a relative clause is often optionally present, though it cannot be omitted from the examples in **20**:

20a The bottle *that fell off the table*
20b The people *who live in that house*
20c The page *to which he referred*
20d The house *where he lives*
20e The party *when he got drunk*
20f The person *whose car they stole*

The conditions for the omission of the WH-element are first, that it is itself nominal rather than adverbial and second, that it comes directly between its antecedent and another nominal group. Thus the examples in **21** are not derivable from **20**:

21a *The bottle fell off the table
21b *The people live in that house
21c *The page to he referred
21d *The house he lives
21e *The party he got drunk
21f *The person car they stole

In **21a** *fell* is not a nominal group, neither is *live* in **21b**. Both **21a** and **b** show that when the WH-element is subject it is impossible to omit it. In **21c** *to* is not the antecedent of *which*. In **21d** *where* is not nominal but adverbial (cf. *The house he lives in*). The same is true of *when* in **21e** (cf. *The party he got drunk at*). In **21f** *car* is not the whole of the nominal group but only part of it.

The words *that* and *whom* require special comment. *That* is fairly freely interchangeable with *which*, *who* or *whom*. *Whom* is a bookish word used when the item is not S:

22a Whom did they speak to?
22b The man whom they spoke to . . .
22c To whom did they speak?
22d The man to whom they spoke . . .

In non-bookish varieties of English *who* is used in place of *whom* in **22a** and **22b**. This would not generally be done in **22c** and **22d**, where a preposition immediately precedes the word in question. On the other hand, putting the preposition first itself tends to be a bookish trait. (It will be observed that these remarks about *whom* apply whether its function is interrogative or relative.)

23.6 Noun complement clauses

The following nominal groups also have a rankshifted clause at q, but it is not a relative clause, since the head noun is not an antecedent to any element in the rankshifted clause:

23a	The |	fact |	that the ground is frozen	
	m	h	q	
23b	The |	question |	why we do this	
	m	h	q	
23c	The |	negative |	proposition |	that we must attack unjustifiable inequalities
	m	m	h	q
				(Appendix B II, ll. 43–4)

There is sometimes a superficial resemblance between these clauses and relative clauses, even resulting in an occasional ambiguity:

24 The question which I asked

If it is synonymous with *The question I asked*, then *which I asked* is a relative clause: 'I asked some question and that's the question I mean'. If it means 'the question: Which of them did I ask?' it is a noun complement clause. Noun complement clauses are very closely related to reported clauses; first, they vary between the *that*, *whether/if* and WH-types, and secondly, they occur as qualifier of nouns like *fact*, *statement*, *question*, *regret*, *news*, *curiosity*, *inquiry*, *belief* – nouns which have the same semantic range as reporting verbs and adjectives. (See also section 21.4.)

23.7 More on relative clauses

The clauses at q in **25** are italicized and are relative clauses in function; they treat the head as an antecedent, but they have no relative WH-element:

25a The glowing discharge *known as St Elmo's fire* (Appendix BI, ll. 8–9)
25b The best thing *to have happened since last April*
25c Students *belonging to this department*

Clauses such as those in **25** can often be paraphrased by using a clearly recognizable relative clause. In **25a** the relation to a relative clause of the central type is simple, since the words *which is* can be inserted, as in **26a**. But in the cases of **25b** and **25c** the differences are greater. These differences are shown in the italicized sections of **26b** and **26c**:

26a The glowing discharge *which is known as St Elmo's fire*
26b The best thing *that has happened since last April*
26c Students *who belong to this department*

23.8 Comparative clauses

These clauses occur in adjectival and adverbial groups as well as in nominal groups. All three possibilities are illustrated in **27**:

1 Adjectival group

27a (This cup is) bigger | than that one is
h Q

2 Adverbial group

27b (Bill runs) faster | than Jack does
h q

3 Nominal group

27c (I've read) longer | books | than that one (is)
m h q

27d (No country in the world has)
such | marvellous | houses | as England has
m m h q
(Appendix B II, ll. 38–9)

23.9 Group rankshift

Example **18b** shows group-within-group rankshift: a prepositional group appears at q. The following are also prepositional groups: *to Bill, under the table, on the last page, on the last page of the book, of the book.* These groups have the structure: preposition + prepositional object (symbolically prep and o). The prepositional object is usually a nominal group, though we have seen in section 23.2 that it could also be a rankshifted clause. It looks then, as though all prepositional groups necessarily have a rankshifted unit functioning as prepositional object. This is illustrated in Figure 94. This analysis might be considered unsatisfactory since, as Sinclair (1972, p. 148) points out, rankshift is normally optional, while here it appears to be obligatory. Since I do not want to enter into a theoretical discussion of this point here, I shall take the orthodox way out and assume obligatory rankshift in prepositional groups.

Example **28** has many layers of rankshift:

28 . . . the back of the shelf over the radiator in the hall of our house . . .

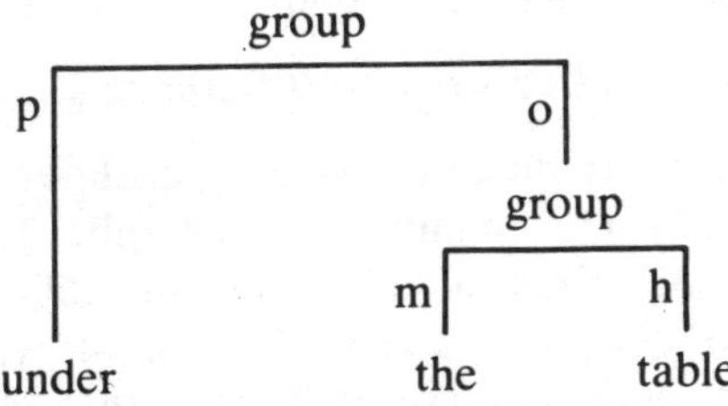

Figure 94

The constituents of the structure are given in **29**:

29	*nominal group*:	Our | house
	prepositional group:	Of | our house
	nominal group:	The | hall | of our house
	prepositional group:	In | the hall of our house
	nominal group:	The | radiator | in the hall of our house
	prepositional group:	Over | the radiator in the hall of our house
	nominal group:	The | shelf | over the radiator in the hall of our house
	prepositional group:	Of | the shelf over the radiator in the hall of our house
	nominal group:	The | back | of the shelf over the radiator in the hall of our house

In spite of the many layers, the structure does not seem very complex. This is because the rankshift occurs in the rightmost constituents, q and o. There is another kind of group rankshift in the nominal group, which occurs in a constituent preceding the head. This results in far greater complexity if there are repeated layers of rankshift. A simple example is given in **30**:

30	The children's |	toys
	m	h

(This example is to be taken in the sense 'the toys belonging to the children' and not as 'the toys of the kind made for children', which has a different structure.) This is a nominal group in which the modifier is not a word, as it would be in *those toys*, but a whole nominal group in possessive form of the type given in Figure 95. If rankshift of this type is repeated for several layers, it soon becomes too complex to follow with comfort:

31 The children's teacher's husband's car

There are many different types of qualifier in nominal groups and it is not my intention to describe them all here. In conclusion, **32** gives a miscellaneous collection of nominal groups with qualifiers, some of them of types not described above. The qualifiers are italicized. In some cases there is rankshift within rankshift; where this is the case the deeper

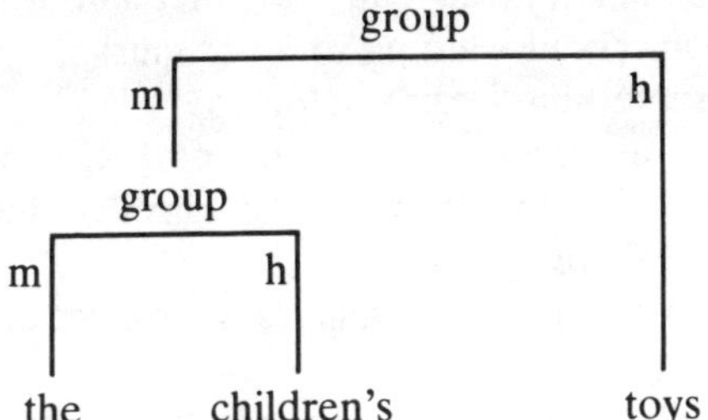

Figure 95

levels are enclosed within brackets:

32a An investigatory reporter *for newspapers and magazines*
32b A writer *of the first rank*
32c The idea *that you are going to change the world*
32d The faces *of the people (who run it)*
32e The flight action *of the animals themselves* (Appendix BI, l. 44)
32f His one-man war *against the system (within which he worked)*
32g An organization *as big as the City Police Department (in New York)*
32h The firm belief *that only when policies (that will guarantee social and economic stability (in the province)) are implemented will a lasting, constructive peace be achieved*
32i The decision *actually to dissect one mummy*
32j A permanent record *of the years that preceded the Jubilee)*
32k A swarm of moths *like this* (Appendix BI, l. 10)
32l A safe journey *into the next world*

Exercise 23.3
(a) Identify the nominal groups in the following. (NB some nominal groups consist of just a pronoun, e.g. the three italicized items in: '*I* gave *them this*.)
(b) Identify the head of each nominal group.
(c) Identify any qualifiers in the nominal groups.
(d) Identify any rankshifted clauses.

1 I don't think any one was bowled over by the fact that there was police corruption.

2 To someone who can't understand, it's very difficult to explain about wanting to write music.

3 It's something I can't help.

4 After an uneventful south-coast childhood and a good many trips to Brighton, he enrolled himself in a drama school there.

5 It was a perfectly straightfaced report of a message to the nation.

6 For all her dreams of living in India, she had failed utterly.

7 Is it possible that a mass of insects like this and of the size you've described would show up on a radar screen? (Appendix BI, ll. 45–7)

Appendix A
English intonation

The following notes are a very compressed explanation of the main principles of the analysis and notation in Halliday 1970a.

There are three sets of systematic choices open to the speaker.

Division of the text into tone groups

The first system serves the purpose of splitting up the text into pieces of message, each of which the speaker regards as being informationally important – though they are not necessarily all equally important. For instance the following text consists of three tone groups, which can also be seen as units of information; the symbol // marks the tone-group boundary.

> // you know all those notes you took // well can I borrow them please // or do you need them this evening //

In general speakers have a great deal of freedom in choosing how to split up the text, but there are conditions in which different divisions correspond to different grammatical structures (e.g. see section 19.8 above).

Each tone group is the field in which two further systems, tonic prominence and tone, operate.

Tonic prominence

Simple tone groups

One syllable – the tonic syllable – is chosen as the focus of attention. It is given phonetic prominence above the other syllables, chiefly by means of a change of direction in the pitch of the voice. The most neutral place for the tonic is, to put it rather crudely, the accented syllable of the last lexical word in the tone group. In the following examples the tonic syllable is underlined:

> // well can I borrow them // or do you want them this evening //

Instead of the neutral placing of the tonic, the speaker may make a marked choice. This has the effect of making the utterance dependent on its context for interpretation, in the way indicated:

(a) // well can I borrow them // (There has already been talk of permission being given for my borrowing *something.*)
(b) // well can I borrow them // (There has already been talk of permission being given for *somebody's* borrowing them.)
(c) // well can I borrow them // (There has already been talk of *whether or not* permission will be given for my borrowing them.)

Compound tone groups

See page 299.

Tone

Among the many ways in which a tone group may be intoned, Halliday distinguishes five main types. The basic form (the primary tone) of each type is, broadly, the one where the speaker is least emotionally involved in what he is saying. I shall not here describe the other forms (the secondary tones).

The choice between the five primary tones reflects the speaker's attitude towards his addressee and his thesis. The definitions given below are rough indications of the expressive range of the tones.

Tone 1 expresses certainty with regard to 'yes' or 'no'.
Tone 2 expresses uncertainty with regard to 'yes' or 'no'.
Tone 3 indicates a dependent or subsidiary thesis, and includes the expression of indifference with regard to 'yes' or 'no'.
Tone 4 expresses reservation in a context where, however, there is something that is certain.
Tone 5 expresses certainty despite a doubt that may have arisen.

In order to describe the phonetic shape of these tones, it is necessary to recognize two main segments of the tone group. First, the tonic segment, which is found in every tone group. It begins with the tonic syllable and, if there are following syllables, continues to the end of the tone group. Second, we must recognize the pretonic segment which occurs only if there are syllables of primary accent (salient syllables) before the tonic. It begins with the first such syllable and continues up to the tonic. In the following illustrations each salient syllable is preceded by a single or double bar line.

// can I / borrow your / notes //

The pretonic segment is *can I borrow your*, and the tonic segment is *notes*. There are three salient syllables: *can*, *bor* and *notes*.

// can I / borrow them //

The pretonic segment is *can I* and the tonic segment is *borrow them*. There are two salient syllables: *can* and *bor*.

// run //

There is no pretonic segment. The tonic segment is *run*. There is one salient syllable.

// here it is //

There is no pretonic segment. The tonic segment is *here it is*. There is one salient syllable: *here*.

// here she / said with/out looking / round //

There is no pretonic segment. Again the tonic segment is the entire tone group. There are four salient syllables: *here*, *said*, *out* and *round*.

Whether or not there is a pretonic segment, the tone group may begin with one or more unaccented syllables. That these are unaccented is shown by placing the symbol ‸ before the first of them:

// ‸well / can I / borrow them //

The pretonic segment is *can I*. There are two salient syllables: *can* and *bor*

// ‸and there was / nothing we could / do //

The pretonic segment is *nothing we could*. There are two salient syllables: *noth* and *do*.

// ∧ and there was / nothing //

There is no pretonic segment. There is one salient syllable: *noth*.

Tone 1 The tonic segment has falling pitch and the pretonic, if any, has a fairly high level pitch:

// *1* ∧ they / showed me the / garden //

Tone 2 The tonic is rising to high; pretonic high:

// *2* can I / borrow your / notes //

// *2* ∧ is / Freddie / coming //

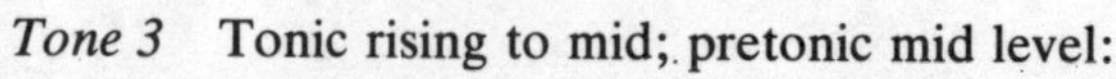

Tone 3 Tonic rising to mid; pretonic mid level:

// *3* ∧ I / shouldn't be sur / prised //

// *3* on the / whole it was // *1* quite a suc / cess //

Tone 4 Tonic falling-rising; pretonic down-stepping:

// *4* ∧ I / don't think it's / necessary to / call him //

Tone 5 Tonic rising-falling; pretonic up-stepping:

// *5* ∧ I / didn't / know they'd / ever / been to / Italy //

There are also two compound tones, occurring in compound (as opposed to simple) tone groups. These are distinguished as compound groups, rather than as a sequence of two tone groups because of the frequency with which Tone 3 occurs after Tone 1 or 5 without an intervening pretonic segment. Compound tone groups, then, have two tonic segments but not more than one pretonic:

Tone 13 // *13* ʌ I'd / taste it / first if / I was you //

No pretonic. Tonic segment with Tone 1: *taste it first if*; tonic segment with Tone 3: *I was you*.

Tone 53 // *53* ʌ I'd / rather / like one if you / feel you can / spare it //

Pretonic: *rather*. Tonic segment with Tone 5: *like one if you feel you can*. Tonic segment with Tone 3: *spare it*.

A note on rhythm

The divisions marked off by single bar lines are called *feet*. It is a characteristic of English rhythm that each foot takes approximately the same length of time to say. The pause that frequently occurs between tone groups falls into this rhythmical sequence as a silent beat. This is the meaning of the symbol ʌ. The silent beat, or rhythmical pause, is often optional:

// *3* on the / whole // *1* ʌ it was / quite a suc/cess //
// *3* on the / whole it was // *1* quite a suc/cess //

In the first of these alternatives there are five feet, the third one having a silence in place of its salient syllable. In the second, the non-salient syllables *it was* are absorbed into the tail of the preceding tone group. There is no rhythmical pause and this version has only four feet.

Appendix B
Passages of spoken text

These texts were broadcast on BBC radio. The first is an interview of an expert by a radio journalist, and the second (which is actually two extracts from the broadcast) is a discussion with a chairman and three guests. The texts were spoken and apparently not rehearsed – at least it is unlikely that the speakers had rehearsed their language to any great extent. In the transcriptions given the punctuation is, of course, editorial. I have underlined tonic syllables. '–' indicates an interruption of structure; '. . .' indicates a silent hesitation, and *em* and *er* voiced hesitations. '. . . ' at the end of an utterance shows that the speaker was interrupted, or that here the transcription ends, though the text continued.

I

A radio journalist (B) is interviewing an expert (A), who has suggested that some unidentified flying objects can be identified as swarms of migrating moths.

A: They are encouraged in their migration by very thundery close conditions, and so when a thunderstorm approaches, or a series of thunderstorms, along a cold weather front, then if this approaches in the evening, they'll start to fly in a large swarm, and it's under these conditions that you get very very strong electric fields set up in the area of the thunderstorms, and it's this electric field which causes the glowing discharge known as St Elmo's fire, which it's thought is what you see if you have a swarm of moths like this.

B: You draw the similarity with St Elmo's fire, which mariners have known for centuries, but how do insects produce light?

A: Well if you take one of these animals and put it between two electrical terminals in a laboratory, and create a strong static electricity field, which doesn't hurt the animal at all, it's perfectly lively and unaffected by it, but it will start to discharge electrons; they fan out from the openings of the body, em the openings in its external shell, its exoskeleton, and there's an avalanche of electrons moving out and knocking into molecules of gas in the air, nitrogen molecules mostly, and these are excited, and because they're excited, they glow, and so each individual insect, gives out rather a weak light, but if you look at it, in a darkened room, you can see this glow fanning out in all directions.

B: But how can light produced in this way be confused with an unidentified flying object?

A: Well, because a swarm of flying insects very often is a a very well-defined object. The insects tend to react to each other, and to stick in a fairly close-knit mat (well not exactly close-knit but the edges are well defined), but it billows and it changes all the time, and so if you can imagine that each insect was glowing – and there are millions and millions of them – some of these swarms of spruce budworm moth can be a hundred kilometres long by fifty kilometres wide.

B: Phew! that's some size.

A: but within that there'll be concentrations, subswarms, and they're all glowing, and the total mass will glow, but the edges will change shape, and you can get dome-shapes, and then cigar-shapes, and of course the whole thing'll be moving, partly with the wind, and partly with the flight-action of the animals themselves.

B: I'm almost convinced, but is it possible that a mass of insects like this and of the size you've described would show up on a radar screen?

A: Well yes; locusts are known to show up on radar screens when they're swarming, and it's quite possible that these could too.

B: And you would say, then, that it is very very possible that there would have been these clouds of insects where UFO's have been seen in the past.

A: Well, we start from the UFO sightings which have been written up in detail – exactly when and where they occurred – and we know that there were infestations of spruce budworm moths in the area during that period; we know that the weather conditions were suitable for them to get up and migrate in swarms; and we know from the labwork that they will give off light in the kind of electric fields which you'd expect to find in these thundery conditions – but there is no direct evidence that there were actually swarms present; you know, nobody got up and took a swipe at one of these UFOs, which is what they ought to have done, with a butterfly net, and come out with moths.

II Broadcast discussion

The participants were Mary Warnock, John Selwyn Gummer and Bernard Crick, with Brian Redhead in the chair. The topic of the discussion was 'Equality'. (Transcribed from *A Word in Edgeways*, 11 October 1975.)

BC: . . . I think there are certain levels beyond which if men rise they begin to . . . act like gods and treat each other not as brothers; I er brought in the Christian thing not as a Christian myself but as a humanist, because I think it has had a vast effect on our culture and that one begins from a position of . . . thinking of brotherhood rather than of hierarchy; now I certainly agree that . . . economic equality is not a direct inference from these previous . . . senses of equality, but I think these previous senses create limitations and that at the moment we've got an idea of the – as em John carefully said we've got an idea of levels below which people shouldn't fall but we don't realise that people don't accept these levels if there are no levels beyond which people should rise.

MW: But then I mean what you're talking about now is equality of power or levels of power beyond which people ought not to rise, aren't you?, because er y- you say they start b-becoming g-godlike or forgetting their brotherhood with other people and this is if they become too powerful; is that what you were saying?

BC: Mm, power, status, income, these are three different types of equality but they do overlap; they are related to each other . . .

MW: But I mean really it's true, isn't it, surely, that civilization depends on some degree of inequality; . . . I mean, nobody – em, isn't this right, you can't have . . . b-buildings or any of the important, essential things of civilization unless you have people with either money or power . . . [here several speak at once]

JSG: . . . the equality of Beethoven always seems to me to be the problem here, isn't it?, I mean . . .

MW: You're right . . . .

MW: My original point was that if people had not at one time had em inequality of income, for instance, there wouldn't be – er a whole number of art forms . . . wouldn't exist, and the most important one in my eyes is the er art form of country houses for instance, of which er I-I mean, no country in the world has such marvellous houses as England has . . .
BC: Well . . .
MW: And that essentially depends on inequalities of income.
BC: What yes but relative inequalities; em I am – I am arguing the negative proposition that we must attack unjustifiable inequalities; I'm not arguing for pure inequality[*sic*]; now take the case of opera, which is being ruined by there not being a notional top, whereas the theatre is very healthy, on the whole, because great stars in the theatre haven't got this ruinously extravagant expectation of the great stars of opera.
MW: Yes, but you see I think that you're talking – you keeped[*sic*] on talking about the arts, which in a way are frightfully difficult to bring in to this argument.
BC: Not me, not me; you and John started the arts.
MW: Well, you were talking about opera.
BC: I was talking about economics.
MW: I'm talking about houses, which are nothing to do with art, or at least only indirectly; they are to do with the way people live; and er I think that if the present policy of equalizing incomes go on, then all the houses – er that all the country houses, not enormous country houses but ordinary smallish beautiful country houses, will actually fall down, and I regard this as . . . terrible; I mean, I really can't talk about it without crying I find it so terrible . . . .

Notes and suggestions for further reading

There are many introductions to linguistics, the scientific study of language. Crystal (1971) is quite short, and Bolinger (1975) is much longer and more wide-ranging. Lyons (1968) is aimed at a more academic readership. Any of these would help the reader to understand modern attitudes, aims and methods in the study of linguistic structure.

Chapter 1

Gimson (1970) provides a thorough grounding in English pronunciation. The system of intonation analysis used in the present book is that of Halliday (1970a). For a general introduction to the study of discourse see Coulthard (1977).

Chapter 2

Introductory studies of grammatical units and systems can be found in the general works referred to at the head of these notes. Halliday, McIntosh and Strevens (1964) gives an introduction to an early version of systemic grammar, at that date known as scale and category grammar. A more academic treatment of the same is Halliday (1961). For a detailed and up-to-date introductory account of systemic grammar see Berry (1975–7). Fawcett (1974–6) is a short discussion of the model, with suggestions for some modifications.

Chapters 3 and 4

The most compendious, up-to-date reference grammar of English is Quirk *et al.* (1972). It presents a large amount of material, but is sometimes inexplicit on theoretical issues. Muir (1972) is an introductory description of English made in systemic terms, but is not very comprehensive. Sinclair (1972) is similar but covers more ground. The present book is much indebted to Sinclair's.

Chapters 5 and 6

There is a brief discussion of the lack of 'fit' between mood categories and discourse in Huddleston (1976, ch. 9) as well as in Sinclair and Coulthard (1975). Davies (1979), using the term 'literal mood meaning', deals in detail with the moods of the clause as making a constant contribution to the significance of discourse acts. Her method includes a theory of *roles* in acts of communication. Langendoen (1970, ch. 2) provides an amusing account of an investigation into the structure of mood tags (and also discusses the question of acceptability). For readings on theme and related matters see the notes to Chapter 12, below.

Chapter 7

Bolinger (1977) has two papers on the imperative which survey the scene and pursue the topic to deeper levels: 'Is the imperative an infinitive?' and 'Imperatives are imperatives and *do* is *do*'.

Chapter 8

The difficulty with recommending readings on modality is that elementary discussions tend to be superficial and fragmented. Perhaps Leech (1971) contains the most satisfactory treatment at this level. Halliday (1970b) Lyons (1977, ch. 17) and Palmer (1974) are at a higher academic level. Halliday and Palmer are concerned specifically with English, and Lyons with the general theory of modality.

Chapters 9, 10 and 11

The question of the ways in which the predicator, the 'pivotal' element of propositions, is complemented has been a major area of study for some time. Quirk *et al.* (1972, pp. 343–4) gives an inventory of the structural patterns. For discussion of theoretical issues and description of the English system see Halliday (1967–8) and also Halliday's 'Types of process' in Kress (ed.) (1976). Fillmore (1968) treats this topic from a transformational point of view, and Langendoen (1970, chs. 3 and 4) from a transformational point of view at a more elementary level.

Chapter 12

See Halliday (1973, especially chs. 1 and 2) and (1970c) on the notion of functional components. Leech and Svartvik (1975, pp. 12–13, 41–185) also work with functional components but slightly different ones from Halliday's (and they do not use the term *functional component*). For a first approach to Halliday's theory of theme in English see Halliday

(1967). A much fuller treatment is included in Halliday (1967–8, pt. 2). Another source of writings on thematic organization is the Linguistic School of Prague; a major contributor, writing on what he calls *functional sentence analysis* (later, *functional sentence perspective*) is Firbas (1964). Other topics connected with the textual function of language are covered in Halliday and Hasan (1976).

Chapter 13

Mentions of voice are found throughout the literature on linguistic theory and the description of English. Discussions of its meaning are, however, relatively few. For this see Quirk *et al.* (1972) and Halliday (1967–8).

Chapters 14, 15 and 16

The description of verbal group structure given in these chapters is very similar to that in Sinclair (1972), where, however, the notation is more detailed. Halliday's description can be found in Kress (ed.) (1976, ch. 10). There are discussions of tense and aspect in very many books. Leech (1971) is short and easy; Palmer (1974) is a full-scale study of the subject. (Both these also deal with modality.) Lyons (1968, ch. 7 and 1977, ch. 15) has useful general treatments of tense and aspect.

Chapters 17 and 18

Some of the ideas on the sentence I owe to suggestions made by Sinclair (private communication). A discussion of the semantic types of linkage between clauses and sentences can be found, among much else, in Halliday and Hasan (1976) under the heading of *conjunction*. They have much to say on the functions of the elements that are in this book called connective adjuncts.

Chapters 19, 20, 21 and 22

The theory of bound clauses given here is essentially that of Sinclair (1972) though modified and extended in certain ways. In particular the categories *contingent*, *adding* and *reported* are taken from that source. My category of *pseudo-reports* is virtually the same as *represented speech* in Jespersen (1924).

Chapter 23

See Halliday, McIntosh and Strevens (1964) on rankshift, and Lyons (1968) on embedding.

References

BERRY, M. (1975–7), *An Introduction to Systemic Linguistics*, vol. 1: *Structures and Systems* (1975); vol. 2: *Levels and Links* (1977), London: Batsford

BOLINGER, D. (1975), *Aspects of Language*, 2nd ed., New York: Harcourt, Brace, Jovanovich

BOLINGER, D. (1977), *Meaning and Form*, London: Longman

CRYSTAL, D. (1971), *Linguistics*, Harmondsworth: Penguin

COMRIE, B. (1976), *Aspect: an introduction to the study of verbal aspect and related problems*, Cambridge: Cambridge University Press

COULTHARD, R. M. (1977), *An Introduction to Discourse Analysis*, London: Longman

DAVIES, E. C. (1979), *On the Semantics of Syntax*, London: Croom Helm

FAWCETT, R. P. (1974–6), 'Some proposals for systemic syntax', pts 1, 2 and 3, *MALS Journal*, nos. 1 and 2

FILLMORE, C. J. (1968) 'The case for case', in E. Bach and R. T. Harms (eds.), *Universals of Linguistic Theory*, New York: Holt, Rinehart & Winston

FIRBAS, J. (1964), 'On defining the theme in functional sentence analysis', in *Travaux Linguistiques de Prague*, no. 1

GIMSON, A. C. (1970), *An Introduction to the Pronunciation of English*, 2nd ed., London: Edward Arnold

HALLIDAY, M. A. K. (1961), 'Categories of the theory of grammar', *Word*, no. 17 (An extract appears in Kress (ed.) (1976))

HALLIDAY, M. A. K. (1967), *Some Aspects of the Thematic Organisation of the English Clause*, Santa Monica, California: Rand Corporation (An extract appears in Kress (ed.) (1976))

HALLIDAY, M. A. K. (1967–8), 'Notes on transitivity and theme in English', pts 1, 2 and 3, *Journal of Linguistics*, nos. 3 and 4

HALLIDAY, M. A. K. (1970a), *A Course in Spoken English: Intonation*, London: Oxford University Press

HALLIDAY, M. A. K. (1970b), 'Functional diversity in language, as seen from a consideration of modality and mood in English', *Foundations of Language*, no. 6

HALLIDAY, M. A. K. (1970c), 'Language structure and language function', in J. Lyons (ed.), *New Horizons in Linguistics*, Harmondsworth: Penguin

HALLIDAY, M. A. K. (1973), *Explorations in the Functions of Language*, London: Edward Arnold

HALLIDAY, M. A. K., and HASAN, R. (1976), *Cohesion in English*, London: Longman

HALLIDAY, M. A. K., McINTOSH, A., and STREVENS, P. D. (1964), *The Linguistic Sciences and Language Teaching*, London: Longman

HOCKETT, C. F. (1958), *A Course in Modern Linguistics*, New York: Macmillan

HUDDLESTON, R. D. (1976), *An Introduction to English Transformational Syntax*, London: Longman

JESPERSEN, O. (1924), *The Philosophy of Grammar*, London: Allen & Unwin

KRESS, G. (ed.) (1976), *Halliday: system and function in language*, London: Oxford University Press

LANGENDOEN, D. T. (1970), *Essentials of English Grammar*, New York: Holt, Rinehart & Winston

LEECH, G. N. (1971), *Meaning and the English Verb*, London: Longman

LEECH, G. N., and SVARTVIK, J. (1975), *A Communicative Grammar of English*, London: Longman

LYONS, J. (1968), *Introduction to Theoretical Linguistics*, Cambridge: Cambridge University Press

LYONS, J. (1977), *Semantics*, 2 vols., Cambridge: Cambridge University Press

MUIR, J. (1972), *A Modern Approach to English Grammar: an introduction to systematic grammar*, London: Batsford

PALMER, F. R. (1974), *A Study of the English Verb*, 2nd ed., London: Longman

QUIRK, R., GREENBAUM, S., LEECH, G. N., and SVARTVIK, J. (1972), *A Grammar of Contemporary English*, London: Longman

SINCLAIR, J. McH. (1972), *A Course in Spoken English: grammar*, London: Oxford University Press

SINCLAIR, J. McH., and COULTHARD, R. M. (1975), *Towards an Analysis of Discourse: the English used by teachers and pupils*, London: Oxford University Press.

Key to exercises

1.1 (page 7)

(a) **1** interrogative
2 imperative
3 moodless
4 interrogative
5 declarative

(b) For instance in a keep-fit class, i.e. in a situation where touching one's toes is an expected activity. Note that it has to be the instructor who says it, i.e. the one who has authority to give the word. In most other circumstances the utterance would be taken as a request for information, e.g. if it was not the instructor who said it, or if the sentence is uttered in a telephone conversation to a friend who is known to have injured himself.

(c) This is advice if it is the addressee who stands to gain from the action e.g., spoken to someone who has just received faulty goods from a shop. It is a command if it is the speaker who stands to gain, and if he has authority to issue the instruction, e.g. a boss speaking to his warehouseman.

(d) This would be an instruction to act if uttered to a taxi driver by someone getting into his taxi. It would be an announcement if uttered by a bus conductor on approaching the place named.

(e) This might be a protest if somebody has assumed that the speaker wants to go for a walk; e.g. by saying 'When we go for our walk . . . .' It could be a request for information if uttered by an organiser of activities at a holiday camp. Alternatively, it could be an invitation if uttered by somebody who is known to be about to set out on a walk.

(f) This could be a threat if it is understood that the addressee does not want the police to be called. The sentence could equally be uttered as a promise, if the addressee is the victim of a burglary. In itself it is neither.

1.2 (page 10)

He needs detailed knowledge of the social context in which the utterance takes place; this includes knowledge of the social relations holding between himself and the speaker and of the activity to which the utterance is supposed to be a contribution. He also needs a knowledge of the linguistic system. Only then can he understand the implications of the proposition that has been uttered and the intentions that the speaker has with regard to how he should respond.

1.3 (page 10)

// When the / weather was / fine we // went for / walks in the / fields //

2.1 (page 17)

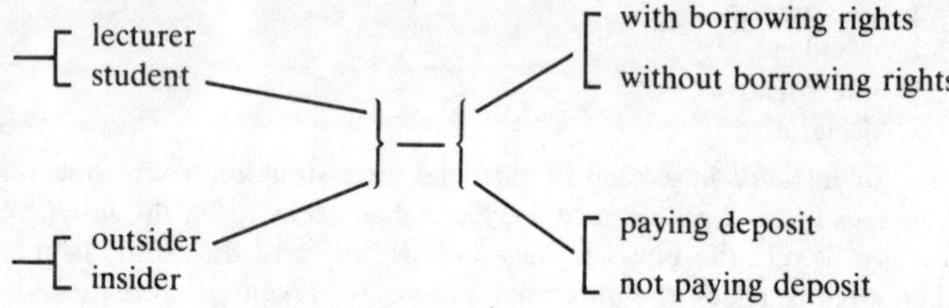

(Only the relevant part of the network is included in this key; the other parts remain unchanged.)

2.2 (page 19)

Each word has four features, e.g. 'adjective', 'masculine', 'nominative', 'singular'; or 'adjective', 'neuter', 'dative', 'singular'. ('Adjective' is just as much a classificatory feature as the other features. However, it would be perfectly natural to interpret the question as not meaning the one feature that all the words have in common, in that case the answer is three.)

2.3 (page 21)

12 *Run*: imperative, intransitive, non-intensive
13 *Be careful*: imperative, intransitive, intensive
14 *He ran*: indicative, declarative, non-modal, intransitive, non-intensive
15 *Did he run?* indicative, interrogative, non-modal, intransitive, non-intensive
16 *He is careful*: indicative, declarative, non-modal, intransitive, intensive
17 *Is he careful?* indicative, interrogative, non-modal, intransitive, intensive

18 *He would run*: indicative, declarative, modal, intransitive, non-intensive

19 *Would he run?* indicative, interrogative, modal, intransitive, non-intensive

20 *Mend the tyre*: imperative, transitive, non-intensive
Make the box big: imperative, transitive, intensive

21 *He must be careful*: indicative, declarative, modal, intransitive,
22 intensive

23 *Must he be careful?* indicative, interrogative, modal, intransitive, intensive

24 *He is mending the tyre*: indicative, declarative, non-modal, transitive, non-intensive

25 *Is he mending the tyre?* indicative, interrogative, non-modal, transitive, non-intensive

26 *He would mend the tyre*: indicative, declarative, modal, transitive, non-intensive

27 *Would he mend the tyre?* indicative, interrogative, modal, transitive, non-intensive

28 *He is making the box big*: indicative, declarative, non-modal, transitive, intensive

29 *Is he making the box big?* indicative, interrogative, non-modal, transitive, intensive

30 *He would make the box big*: indicative, declarative, modal, transitive, intensive

31 *Would he make the box big?* indicative, interrogative, modal, transitive, intensive

3.1 (page 25)

Left-handedness is abnormal
Left-handedness may be abnormal
Perhaps left-handedness is abnormal
If left-handedness were abnormal . . .
If left-handedness is abnormal . . .
Since left-handedness is abnormal . . .
For left-handedness to be abnormal . . .
With left-handedness being abnormal . . .
Is left-handedness abnormal?
Left-handedness is not abnormal
and so on.

3.2 (page 27)

(a) **1** The cat was chased by the dog.
2 That house is going to be bought by somebody.

3 The crowd was addressed by Harold.
4 The chickens can be smelt by the fox.

(b) 1 The goats ate some of the grass.
2 Another firm must have finished the job.
3 Their regular correspondents probably wrote these articles.
4 The inspector didn't notice the marks in the corner.

3.3 (page 27)

Object complements: **1, 2, 5, 6, 8, 10.**
Intensive complements: **3, 4, 7, 9.**

3.4 (page 30)

1 *still*: A; *their surcharge of £7000*: C.
2 *deliberately*: A; *the law*: C.
3 *a bad law*: C.
4 *similar incitements*: C; *on this precedent*: A.
5 *it*: C; *for party political reasons*: A.
6 *normal*: C.
7 *obviously*: A; *in a hurry*: A.
8 *suddenly*: A; *overcast*: C.
9 *The clover*: C; *next month*: A.

3.5 (page 36)

all these conditions: C^o (nominal group);
irreproachable: C^i (adjectival group);
from this point of view: A (prepositional group);
For a man of a bookish turn of mind: A (prepositional group);
very satisfactory: C^i (adjectival group);
throughout the whole of the waking hours: A (prepositional group)
In this respect: A (prepositional group);
on the whole: A (superficially a prepositional group but the expression is highly formulaic so that its structure is a 'fossil');
in the case of women whose work is in the home: A (prepositional group)
natural: C^i (adjectival group);
the office: C^o (nominal group)
a new mood: C^o (nominal group;
in this respect: A (prepositional group)
almost as much as those who work at home: A (adverbial group).

4.1 (page 42)

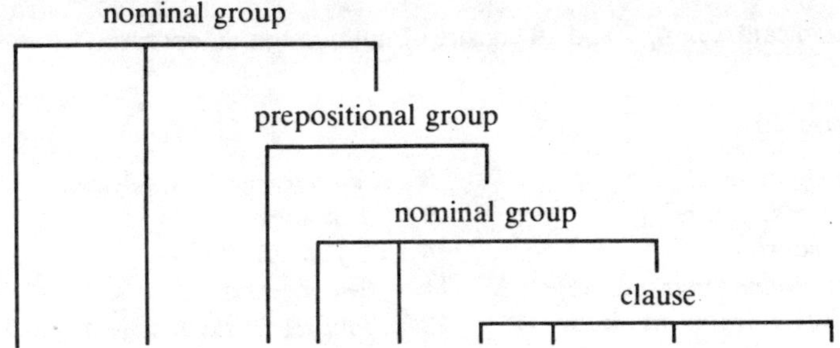

4.2 (page 42)

1. *whose work is in the home* (included in the nominal group: *women whose work is in the home*).
2. *who work at home* (included in the nominal group: *those who work at home*).
3. *who treats everything as a matter of principle* (included in the nominal group: *the man who treats everything as a matter of principle*).
4. *we are in* (included in nominal group: *the situation we are in*).
5. *that rational planning is prevented by the intrusion of politics* (included in the nominal group: *the view that rational planning is prevented by the intrusion of politics*).
6. *their destroying an established order* (included in prepositional group: *of their destroying an established order*, which in its turn is included in the nominal group: *the possibility of . . . order*).
7. *that a valuable distinction was lost* (this is not part of the structure of a nominal group, but is the subject of the clause in which *was not noticed* is P).
8. *what's wrong in one case* (this is S; *must be* is P, *wrong* is C^i and *in every case* is A.)
9. *your preferring such expressions* (this is the C^o to the P: *can't understand*, and S: *I*.)

5.1 (page 48)

Operators in italics:

1. *are* encouraged
2. causes
3. *do* produce
4. *is*
5. *will* start (to discharge)
6. glow
7. *is*
8. *are* glowing

9 start
10 *is*
11 *have* known

(The predicators in **4, 7** and **10** consist of nothing but an operator.)

5.2 (page 50)

1 *she's*: neutral
2 *Peter's*: neutral
3 *I*: neutral
4 *shorthand*: marked, object
5 *all this winter*: marked, adjunct
6 *who*: neutral
7 *what work*: neutral
8 *at dinner*: marked, adjunct
9 *I'll*: neutral
10 *are you*: neutral
11 *when*: neutral
12 *all those*: marked, object
13 *nowadays*: marked, adjunct
14 *a merry old soul*: marked, intensive complement.

5.3 (page 54)

1 A
2 S
3 C^o
4 C^i
5 WH–C
6 WH–C^o
7 WH–S
8 WH–C^i
9 WH–A
10 WH–S
11 WH–C^o
12 WH–A

(for a discussion of **5** see Chapters 9 and 10.)

5.4 (page 56)

1 P(S); P = *did . . . become*
S = *he*
Indicative, interrogative, polar, neutral theme.

2 SP; S = *it*
P = *is*
Indicative, declarative, neutral theme.

3 P^{op} S; P^{op} = *is*
S = *that*
Indicative, interrogative, polar, neutral theme.

4 WH P(S); WH = when
P = *will . . . be*
S = *you*
Indicative, interrogative, non-polar, not-S-questioned, neutral theme.

5 PS; P = comes
S = the bus
Indicative, declarative, marked theme, C^{loc} theme, with S-arrest.

6 WH–S P; WH–S = who
P = would have believed
Indicative, interrogative, non-polar, S-questioned, neutral theme.

7 WH–S P; WH–S = what
P = can
Indicative, interrogative, non-polar, S-questioned, neutral theme.

8 P^{op} S; P^{op} = is
S = it
Indicative, declarative, marked theme, negative theme.

9 P^{op} S; P^{op} = are
S = they
Indicative, interrogative, polar, neutral theme.

10 SP; S = this creed
P = has accepted
Indicative, declarative, neutral theme.

11 WH P(S); WH = which of the examples
P = haven't . . . analysed
S = you
Indicative, interrogative, non-polar, not-S-questioned, neutral theme.

12 SP; S = what you're talking about now
P = is
Indicative, declarative, neutral theme.

13 P; P = go
Imperative, neutral theme.

5.5 (page 56)

1 *has* is main verb and operator. (cf. *He hasn't a new coat; Has he a new coat?*)
2 *has* is main verb but not operator. (cf. **He hasn't dinner at his digs;* **Has he dinner at his digs?*)
3 *have* is not a main verb (*gone* is the main verb); nor is it an operator (*may* is the operator).
4 *has* is operator but not main verb.
5 *had* is main verb but not operator.

(NB In most varieties of American English main verb *have* is not an operator; in these varieties the interrogative of **1** is *Does he have a new coat?* For further comment on main verb *have* see section 15.2.)

6.1 (page 63)

1 checking	**4** checking	**7** copy
2 checking	**5** copy	**8** checking
3 copy	**6** checking	

(Note that the proposition in **6, 7** and **8** is negative; this could be tested by constructing sentences on the pattern, e.g.:

He doesn't like it and *nor/neither* do I. (negative)

He likes it and *so* do I. (positive)

Nothing matters and nor does this (. . . * and so does this).

Few people have seen one and nor have I (. . . * and so have I).

In **4** and **5**, howevever, the proposition is positive.

Another way of testing for copy tags is that copy tags cannot have falling tone on the tag. **5** and **7** must be copy tags by this test; conversely **4**, **6** and **8** must be checking.)

6.2 (page 63)

(a) The proposition must be positive.

(b) The proposition must *either* contain no operator, e.g.

Briggs remembered . . . , *or*

the operator in the proposition must be *do, does* or *did* (respectively), e.g.

Briggs did remember . . .

(c) *don't* and *doesn't* occur when the tense of the proposition is present, and *didn't* occurs when the tense of the proposition is past. The variation between *don't* and *doesn't* depends on the person and number of the tag subject, e.g. *don't they; doesn't she.*

6.3 (page 67)

All of the types go with declaratives. Only type 2 can be used in responding to interrogatives.

6.4 (page 67)

Types 1, 2 and 3 all have P^{op} and S^{pron} in their structure, and are thus like mood tags; moreover the items that realize these elements are determined by concord with the proposition that is being responded to, just as tags have their P and S determined by the proposition onto which they are tagged. Type 1 also has the same sequence of elements as tags, viz. $P^{op}S$. Types 2 and 3 differ from tags in the sequence S P^{op}. Type 1 has the same polarity as the proposition. So does type 3, though there is some doubt about the acceptability of negative responses of this type, some speakers seeming to accept 'Neither/nor they do' and others having no negative form at all. The polarity of type 2 is not predetermined by the proposition, so in this respect type 2 is not like mood tags. (See also answer to question 6.5).

Type 4 has the structure $P^{op}S$, and the P is determined, like tags, by concord with the proposition, but the S does not have to be a pronoun, e.g. *So is the one I was talking about yesterday*), and moreover, the S must not be coreferential with the S of the proposition, e.g. A: *She's looking much better*; B: *So is he.*

6.5 (page 67)

Speaker A is treating B as one who does not know. Speaker B either rejects this treatment by responding with the declarative form (i) ('I knew already'), or he accepts it by using the interrogative form (ii) ('that's news to me'). In both cases speaker B accepts the proposition that 'they went to Spain'. The intonation of (i) must be falling; a rising tone would only be appropriate if he was disagreeing with the claim that they went to Spain (*No, they didn't*). The intonation of (ii) can be either rising or falling; if rising, this shows interest: 'that's news; what more is there to tell?'; but if falling: 'that may be news, but I don't want to know any more'. The falling tone might well be taken as a 'conversation stopper'.

7.1 (page 78)

1 jussive inclusive
2 jussive exclusive
3 jussive exclusive
4 subjunctive
5 declarative
6 jussive inclusive
7 declarative
8 interrogative
9 declarative
10 jussive exclusive
11 optative
12 declarative
13 subjunctive
14 jussive exclusive
15 declarative
16 declarative
17 jussive exclusive
18 jussive exclusive
19 ambiguous: (a) declarative; (b) jussive exclusive
20 Declarative (This is, strictly, ambiguous in the same way as **19**, but the imperative interpretation is highly improbable with the verb *like*.)
21 optative (Strictly, this is ambiguous, and could be taken as jussive exclusive, but in the well-known historical context it is clearly optative.)
22 jussive exclusive
23 jussive exclusive
24 interrogative
25 jussive exclusive
26 declarative
27 interrogative
28 jussive exclusive
29 ambiguous: (a) optative; the meaning is similar to that of **30**; (b) jussive exclusive; the meaning is similar to that of **31**.
30 declarative
31 jussive exclusive
32 jussive exclusive
33 optative

8.1 (page 82)

(a) If they were modal auxiliaries they would be operators and could be used to form negatives and interrogatives as follows:

*They needn't more paper (cf. They don't need more paper)
*Need they more paper? (cf. Do they need more paper?)
*He needs not to find new digs (cf. He doesn't need to find new digs)
*Need he find new digs? (cf. Does he need to find new digs?)
*He dared not to publish libellous material (cf. He didn't dare to publish libellous material)
*Dared he to publish libellous material? (cf. Did he dare to publish libellous material?)

(b) If they were modal auxiliaries they could not be preceded by another auxiliary (since modal auxiliaries are always initial in the verbal group); but in fact they can:

They may need more paper
They are needing more paper
He will need to find new digs
He is needing to find new digs
He had dared to publish libellous material
He would dare to publish libellous material

(c) If they were modal auxiliaries they would not be variable for concord with the subject; but in fact they are:

They need/he needs more paper
He needs/they need to find new digs
He dares/they dare to publish libellous material

8.2 (page 85)

1 *Knowledge*: It is possible that Bill works for the BBC. Perhaps Bill works for the BBC.
Influence: Bill is allowed to work for the BBC; I say so. I give permission for Bill to work for the BBC.

2 *Knowledge*: The inescapable conclusion is that Rosemary paints in oils. It is certainly true that Rosemary paints in oils.
Influence: Rosemary is compelled to paint in oils; I say so.

3 *Knowledge*: It is highly likely that Jack is asleep (if all has gone according to plan).
Influence: It is highly desirable for Jack to be asleep. (Send him off to bed now.)

4 *Knowledge*: (If I haven't misjudged the matter) it is likely, almost certain, that he has wound up the clock.
Influence: It was obligatory for him to wind up the clock (but he didn't). He was in duty bound . . .

8.3 (page 90)

1 *Knowledge* most likely. (The influence interpretation would not make good sense, since it would be unusual to give someone permission to be an MP.)
2 *Influence*: ability. (It is possible for us to read; we are able . . . .)
3 *Influence* most likely. (But it is possible to devise a context where the knowledge interpretation would be unavoidable, for instance 'The people round here don't respect Beethoven very much. After this concert Beethoven should be respected more', i.e. It is likely he will be respected more.)
4 *Knowledge.*
5 *Ambiguous*: (a) knowledge: it is certain that there is some restriction; (b) influence: it is necessary to introduce some restriction.
6 *Knowledge.*
7 *Influence*: it is only possible for it to be construed as . . . (It is only able to be construed as . . .).
8 *Knowledge.*
9 *Influence* (not willing to).
10 *Ambiguous*: (a) knowledge: it is not certain that she hid/has hidden/will have hidden the key; (b) influence: she was not compelled to hide the key (though she did).
11 *Knowledge*: it is likely that you are . . . . (Without the context supplied it would be natural to take this as meaning 'you are obliged . . .').
12 *Knowledge*: (assuming a past time reference) it is certain that I acted on your guidance. (A future time reference, for some reason, does not spring so readily to mind, but it is possible, especially if the personal pronouns are reversed, e.g. 'By the time you reach that stage of the work, sometime next year, you must have acted on my guidance for at least some of the time'. This is influence, compulsion.)
13 *Knowledge.*
14 *Influence.*
15 *Influence*: you are permitted not to (or you are not compelled to).

8.4 (page 93)

1 Negating the possibility gives 'it is not possible that there is . . .': *There can't/couldn't be a lot of expense involved.* Negating the proposition gives 'It is possible there is not . . .': *There needn't be a lot of expense involved.* Negating both gives 'It is not possible there is not . . .': *There must be a lot of expense involved.*

2 Negating the permission gives 'It is not permissible for them to . . .': *They mustn't/can't/may not walk on the grass.* Negating the proposition gives 'It is permissible for them not to . . .': *They needn't walk on the grass.* Negating both gives 'It is not permissible for them not to . . .': *They must walk on the grass.*

8.5 (page 96)

Subjective: **2, 3, 4, 8, 9.** Objective: **1, 5, 6, 7, 10.**
(In **6** the expression *it's possible* may be subjective, but it is the use of *will* that we are talking about.)

8.6 (page 97)

1 Democracy can be intolerant of minorities (influence)
2 Democracy may/could be intolerant of minorities (knowledge)
3 (He said) he would be the happiest man in the world (knowledge)
4 They wouldn't be very pleased/they wouldn't/won't have been very pleased (knowledge)
5 I can't live for long without some kind of luxury (influence)
6 It won't/wouldn't be too late to change, will/would it? (knowledge)
7 He must agree (knowledge)
8 He must agree (influence)
9 You can't/mustn't/may not give them food (influence)
10 There should/ought to be some tickets available (knowledge)
11 The Second Coming must be at hand (knowledge)
12 It will/must be Harold that fetches the crowds (knowledge)
13 Harold will mow the lawn (influence)
14, 15, 16 He may/could have been delayed (all knowledge)

8.7 (page 98)

(a) *had better* is a unitary item to the extent that each of the words is highly restricted when it occurs in this combination; *had* never varies for tense or concord (**has better*, **have better*, **is having better*), and *better* does not contrast with *good* and *best* (**had good*, **had best*).
(b) On the other hand *had better* is analysable into two units on account of the tag forms, negatives and interrogatives, i.e. *better* does not function as part of the operator (**had bettern't*, **bettern't we*, **had better we*). The operator is *had* by itself.
(c) Considered, now, as a unitary whole, *had better* cannot be preceded by modal auxiliaries (**may have better*, **could have better*), but it can be followed by non-modal auxiliaries (*we'd better be standing there, he'd better have gone*). Auxiliaries that cannot be preceded by modal auxiliaries, and can be followed by non-modal auxiliaries are themselves modal auxiliaries. Therefore, to the extent that *had better* is a unitary item it is a modal auxiliary.

(d) In meaning *had better* is like an influence modal of the compulsion type; compare with *we ought to go; we must go.*
(e) *had* is in origin a past tense form, but *had better* in present-day English does not function as a past tense; consider *we'd better go tomorrow*; **we'd better go yesterday.*
CONCLUSION: *had better* is more like a modal auxiliary than it is like anything else, but it has the peculiarity of consisting of two words only the first of which functions as operator. (It is interesting to note that children are sometimes reported to say things like 'You better be careful, bettern't you?' It is easy to see how this arises: the/d/of *you'd better* is usually inaudible, and this would produce the tag form *you better be careful, hadn't you*, which would be anomalous.)

9.1 (page 100)

(a) *political*: C; *nevertheless*: A.
(b) *the roof*: C; *at the moment*: A.
(c) *slowly*: A; *the curtain*: C.
(d) *Bill*: C; *a scholarship*: C; *for his excellent work*: A.
(e) *busy*: C; *tomorrow*: A.

9.2 (page 102)

1 *conceivably*: linking (comment)
2 *however*: linking (connective)
3 *purposely*: not linking
4 *clearly*: not linking
5 *conveniently*: not linking
6 *clearly*: linking (comment); *conveniently*: not linking
7 *conveniently*: ?linking (comment) (but see end of section 9.8)
8 *anyhow*: not linking
9 *anyhow*: linking (connective);
10 *though*: linking (connective):
11 *thus*: not linking;
12 *thus*: linking (connective);
13 *equally*: not linking;
14 *equally*: linking (connective).

The clause in which *anyhow* is not a linking adjunct (it is a manner adjunct) is normally spoken as one tone group: // ∧ they / laid the / table / anyhow //. The other has two tone groups, and hence two tonic syllables: // ∧ they / laid the / table / anyhow //. (NB Not all linking adjuncts require a separate tone group, but at least we can say that they cannot receive the only tonic, so that // ∧ he / spoke / clearly // has a manner adjunct, while // ∧ he / spoke / clearly // has a linking adjunct.)

9.3 (page 104)

1 *in an old sock*: inherent
2 *in an old sock*: inherent
3 *in the evening*: ?circumstantial
4 *at five o'clock*: inherent
5 *last week*: circumstantial;
6 *in the Government*: inherent
7 none
8 none
9 *at eight o'clock*: ?circumstantial
10 *on the bus*: circumstantial
11 *to the right*: inherent
12 *by the gate*: circumstantial

9.4 (page 106)

1 what . . . for
2 who . . . for
3 who . . . to
4 what . . . on (*also possibly* where)
5 where
6 where
7 how
8 when
9 where *or* what . . . on
10 what . . . with

9.5 (page 109)

1 S P C^i A
2 S P C^o
3 A^l S P A C
4 C^o S P C
5 S P C^o
6 S A P C C
7 S P A
8 A S P
9 S P C A
10 S P C^o C
11 S P C^o C
12 S P C A
13 S P(A) C^o C
14 S P A C
15 S P C^i

16 I | call | him | by his first name
S P C^o C

17 They | arrived | at the apartment door
S P C

18 She | had changed | her costume | some time before
S P C^o A

19 He | regarded | her | intently | with his head on one side
S P C^o A A

20 She | lowered | her voice | again
S P C^o A

21 You | were | crazy about him | for a while
S P C^i A

22 The bottle of whisky | was | in constant demand
S P C

23 It | pulled | me | into my chair
S P C^o C

24 On Mondays | eight servants | toiled | all day | with mops
A S P A ?C?A

25 A tinkling sound | was made | intermittently | by the band
S P A ?C

26 They | looked | a little hungry
S P C^i

27 They | talked | in earnest voices
S P A

28 He | was | a German spy | during the war
S P C^i A

29 It | was making | me | uneasy | that night
S P C^o C^i A

30 As a matter of fact | they | 're | absolutely real
A^1 S P C^i

31 He | smiled | understandingly | for an instant
S P A A

32 Then | she | answered | me | with a wan smile
A^1 S P C^o A

33 He | drifted | coolly | out of nowhere
S P A C

34 She | filled | the pause | with gasping, broken sobs
S P C^o C

35 One of the girls in yellow | was playing | the piano
S P C^o

36 They | harshly | confined | the prisoners | to their cells
S A P C^o C

9.6 (page 114)

manner: **1, 2, 6, 9;** action: **3, ?4, 5, 7, 8, 10, ?11.**

9.7 (page 116)

1 place
2 action
3 time
4 linking, comment

5 action
6 intensifying
7 time
8 linking, connective
9 action
10 time
11 manner
12 manner

10.1 (page 120)

ascriptive: **1, 3, 5, 6, 7, 10, 11, 13**;
equative: **4, 8, 12**;
neither: **2, 9** (these are both transitive and have C^o).
(NB **13** has a marked thematic organization: C^i P S.)

10.2 (page 127)

(a) S P: **6, 7, 11** (b) S P C^o: **1, 2** (c) S P C^{oi} C^{od}: **10**

(d) S P C^o C^{ob}: **4, 8, 9** (e) S P C^{ob}: **3, 5, 12**

10.3 (page 131)

Transitive, intensive: **3, 4, 7, 9** (with C^{loc}), **11**.

Double transitive: **1, 2, 5, 6, 8** (with C^o C^{ob}), **10, 11, 12** (C^o C^{ob}).
Note that **11** is ambiguous: 'I found her to be a good secretary', v. 'I found a good secretary for her'.

10.4 (page 133)

Adverb particles: **1, 2, 4, 6, 7.**
Prepositional groups: **3, 5, 7, 8, 9, 10, 11.**
It will be seen that No. 7 is ambiguous: (a) He ran through it = he played it, perhaps cursorily; (b) He ran it through = he passed it through the playback machine.

10.5 (page 135)

1 S P C^x (C^x = *along with us*)
2 S P C^i A^{time} (C^i = *our recommendation*)
3 S P C^o A^{time} (C^o = *its ups and downs*)
4 S P C^{part} A^x (C^{part} = *out*)
5 A^l S P C^i (A^l = *on a brighter note*, C^i = *over*)

6 S P C^{ob} (C^{ob} = *for further talks*)

7 A^{l} S P C^{i} (C^{i} = *a wise move*)

8 S P(A^{time}) C^{ob}(P = *will lead*)

9 S P C^{ob} A^{time} (C^{ob} = *into trouble of this magnitude*)

10 S P C^{part} C^{ob} (P = *has come*, C^{part} = *up*)

11 S P A^{x}

12 S P A^{x}

13 S P(A^{x}) C^{o} (P = *could stand*)

14 S P C^{part} C^{o}

15 S P C^{i} (S = *what they get*, C^{i} = *more than 5%*)

16 S P C^{i} (C^{i} = *the primary target*)

17 S P(A^{x}) A^{time} (P = *may be defeated*)

18 S P C^{ob}(C^{ob} = *into a November election*)

19 S P C^{o} C^{ob}

20 S P C^{i}

21 S P C^{o} (C^{o} = *the whole atmosphere in which the Government is functioning*)

22 S P C^{ob}

23 S P C^{loc} A^{man} (C^{loc} = *through*)

24 S P C^{o} (C^{o} = *a pretty full statement*)

25 S P(A^{x}) C^{loc} (P = *has returned*)

26 S P C^{i} (C^{i} = *the largest open-air school in the world*)

27 S P C^{o} C^{ob} (C^{o} = the camp)

28 A^{l} S P A^{int} C^{loc} (A^{int} = *almost entirely*)

29 S P A^{x} S^{x} C^{loc} A^{x} (S = *there*, S^{x} = *young mothers with babies*, C^{loc} = *there*)

30 S P C^{ob} A^{man} (S = *most of them*, C^{ob} = *in the liberation struggle*)

31 A^{x} S P C^{i}(C^{i} = *the fighters of next year or the year after*)

32 S P S^x C^{loc} (S^x = *white curtains*)

33 S P C^o

34 S P C^o A^{place} A^{time} (C^o = *a little reunion*)

35 S P C^{ob} (C^{ob} = *for me*)

36 S P C^{loc} (C^{loc} = *onto the stage*)

37 S P C^o C^{loc} (C^o = *it*, C^{loc} = *into the audience*)

38 S P C^o A^x (C^o = *a great deal*)

39 S P C^o C^{loc} (C^o = *us*)

11.1 (page 140)

decide
We decided to leave at once. (*to*-form)
This decided us to leave at once. (C^o/S, *to*-form)
remember
We remembered to close the door. (*to*-form)
I remember him to have been keen on sport. (C^o/S, *to*-form)
We remember hearing a bang. (*ing*-form)
We remember you falling over. (C^o/S, *ing*-form)
escape
They escaped being arrested. (*ing*-form)
see
I saw you arrive. (C^o/S, base-form)
I saw you arriving. (C^o/S, *ing*-form)
I saw you robbed. (C^o/S, *n*-form)
?I saw the door to be solid. (C^o/S, *to*-form)
manage
We managed to reach the top. (*to*-form)
?*I can't manage eating any more. (*ing*-form)
continue
They continued to hold talks. (*to*-form)
They continued holding talks. (*ing*-form)
(But see section 15.3 on semi-auxiliaries).
postpone
I shall postpone seeing them. (*ing*-form)
hear: (like *see*)

deny:
They denied having crossed the line. (*ing*-form)
?They denied us to have got there soon enough. (C^o/S, *to*-form)

11.2 (page 142)

1, 2, 5 and **7** are phase structures:

1 S P C^o/S P A
2 S P C^o/S P C^{ob}
5 S P C^i P C^o/S P C^{ob}
7 S P C^o/S P C^{part} A

2 is ambiguous; in the sense that is like **3** it is not phase, but two clauses. **4** could be paraphrased 'I read it in order to be prepared', or 'To be prepared, I read it'. This is not phase but two clauses. **6** has only the most superficial resemblance to phase, arising from the verb-like appearance of the noun *painting*.

11.3 (page 143)

1 None possible.
2 They were heard opening the door.
I heard the door being opened.
The door was heard being opened.
3 The guards were commanded to bring in the prisoners.
The captain commanded the prisoners to be brought in.
The prisoners were commanded to be brought in.
4 They were caught stealing apples.
NB *not* *I caught apples being stolen.
5 I was kept waiting.
6 Telegrams keep being sent.
7 None possible.

6 differs from the others in that *keeps sending* is made passive as a whole; there are no forms: **Keeps telegrams being sent*, or **Telegrams are kept being sent*. (See also section 15.3: complex verbal groups.)

11.4 (page 143)

1 . . . the weather conditions | were | suitable | for them |
S P C^i C/S
to get up . . .
P

2(a) . . . you | 'd expect | to find | such electric fields | in these conditions . . .

S P P C^O A

(b) . . . which | you | 'd expect | to find | in these conditions . . .

WH–C^O S P P A

12.1 (page 149)

1 We're having *fish* for dinner. (*fish* = C^O)
2 We're having fish *for dinner.* (*for dinner* = A)
3 *We*'re having fish for dinner. (*we* = S)
4 We travelled *by train.* (*by train* = A)
5 *The typist* does all the work. (*the typist* = S) (This sentence is ambiguous in the way mentioned, and in fact the other interpretation is required in **6**.)
6 *The typist that does all the work* sits at that desk. (*The typist . . . work* = S)
7 They announce the results *on the radio.* (*on the radio* = A)
8 *Bill* makes the mistakes. (*Bill* = S)
9 I can't stand *the food.* (*the food* = C^O) (This is also ambiguous.)

12.2 (page 153)

1 Postposed theme; *What he bought was a forgery.*
2 *It*-theme; *He bought a watercolour.*
3 None.
4 Identification; *He bought the Mona Lisa.*
5 It-theme; *Julius Caesar said 'I came, I saw, I conquered.'*
6 None.
7 It-theme; *You have to look out for television aerials.*
8 It-theme; *With inexpressible concern I now find myself under the necessity of adding to the above description.*
9 Identification; *They're going to Tenby for their holidays this year.*
10 Identification: *We chiefly need a loaf of bread.*
11 Identification: *Tom rang for the waiter.*
12 Postposed theme: *That social worker is terribly late.*
13 Postposed theme: *They sent what was written at the last session by post.*
14 None.

12.3 (page 154)

(a) . . . *it's under these conditions that you get . . . thunderstorms* . . . This is *it*-theme for: . . . *under these conditions you get . . . thunderstorms* . . . (*under these conditions* = A).

(b). . . *it's this electric field which causes the glowing discharge known as St Elmo's fire* . . . This is *it*-theme for: . . . *this electric field causes the glowing discharge known as St Elmo's fire* . . . (*this electric field* = S)

(c) . . . *nobody got up and took a swipe at one of these UFOs, which is what they ought to have done,* . . . This is relatable to: *what they ought to have done is get up and take a swipe at one of these UFOs* . . . This is an identification structure for: *they ought to have got up and taken a swipe at one of these UFOs* . . .

12.4 (page 154)

Leaving out the introductory items (*but then I mean*), the identification structure is:

(a) *what you're talking about now*	*is*	*equality of power or levels of power beyond which people ought not to rise* . . .
S	P	C^i

The unmarked form is:

(b) *now you are talking about equality of power or levels of power beyond which people ought not to rise* . . .

The interesting point about the checking tag is that the form that actually occurs is the form that is oriented to (b), *you are . . . aren't you?*, rather than the form that is oriented to (a), *it is . . . isn't it?*

12.5 (page 157)

Explicitly given material in italics:

1 . . . but how do insects *produce light*
2 . . . which doesn't hurt *the animal*
3 . . . and because *they're excited*
4 . . . gives out rather a weak *light*

13.1 (page 159)

1 *wouldn't be encouraged* (passive); *wouldn't encourage* (active)
2 *should be paid* (passive); *should pay* (active)
3 *has been built* (passive); *has built* (active)
4 *isn't going to allow* (active); *isn't going to be allowed* (passive); *to write* (active); *to be written* (passive)

5 *is ruining* (active); *is being ruined* (passive)
6 *is being offered* (passive); *is offering* (active)
7 *have given* (active); *have been given* (passive)
8 *could construe* (active); *could be construed* (passive); *to disregard* (active); *to be disregarded* (passive)
9 *were entrusted* (passive); *entrusted* (active)

13.2 (page 162)

The following can appear in all three patterns: *sit, rattle, store, waken, fill, march, mend, play, stand, stretch, drop, shine* and *work*. For instance:

That piano plays beautifully.
That piano is played beautifully.
He plays that piano beautifully.

Work has two senses, both of which appear in all three patterns:

(a) That machine doesn't work.
That machine isn't worked.
We don't work that machine.

(b) He works hard.
He is worked hard.
They work him hard.

13.3 (page 166)

The ones that are clearly passive predicators are in the following lines:

1 *are encouraged*;
9 *is thought*;
27 *can . . . be confused*;
45 *am . . . convinced*;
48 *are known*;
53 *have been seen*;
54 *have been written (up)*.

The ones with PC^i are in lines:

22 and 24 *are excited*;
32 *are well-defined*.

The only one to cause some hesitation is 17: *is . . . unaffected by it*, where the agentive expression occurs. On the other hand there is no verb **to unaffect* (cf. *to unfasten*) and the *n*-form *unaffected* is joined to the adjective *lively*. This, therefore seems to be the intensive complement structure.

14.1 (page 168)

Have been given; suppose; will foot; 've had; removed; attaches; is; should be disqualified; acting; are given; is; to say; doesn't apply; break;

ø	d	n
tread	trod	trodden
win lose sell	won lost sold	
beat		beaten
come	came	
	put split	

Figure 96

did call; took; came; to indemnify; do . . . think; is. (I take *justified* to be at C^i.)

14.2 (page 169)

With the verbs listed, it is only the way the *d*- and *n*-forms vary from the base-form that is of interest. The *to*-, *s*- and *ing*-forms are quite regular. We can distinguish five types according to whether ø, d and n are all different, or all the same, or two are the same and one different, as shown in Figure 96. We can also classify the verbs according to the type of phonological differences between one form and another: vowel change, consonant change and suffix.

Vowel change

/ tred / v. / trɒd /
/ wɪn / v. / wʌn /
/ kʌm / v. / keɪm /

Suffix

(a) *d*-form + suffix: / trɒd / v. / trɒdn /
(b) base(=*d*-form) + suffix: / bit / v. / bitn /

Vowel change and suffix

/ sel / v. / səʊld /

Vowel change and consonant change and suffix

/ luz / v. / lɒst /

14.3 (page 171)

```
 ø     n     n          ø          ø    ø      ø   n
have been given;   suppose;   will foot;   've had;
 fa     a      v          fv          fa    v      fa    v

   n               s          s      ø      ø        n
removed;   attaches;   is;   should be disqualified;
   bv              fv         fv       fa     a          v

  ŋ        are      n         s          t             s          ø
acting;   are given;   is;   to say;   doesn't apply;
  bv       fa        v        fv        bv             fa          v

  ø        d    ø         d          d                  t
break;  did call;   took;   came;   to indemnify;
  fv       fa     v        fv         fv                 bv

ø    ø        s
do  think;   is
fa     v       fv
```

14.4 (page 176)

```
1  present:   s      n
              has been
               fh      v

2  present:    s       ŋ
               is  exciting
               fc      v

3     ø    ø     n       ŋ
   could have been arguing
      fm     h     c        v

4  present:    ø          d     ø          t
              take;   should try;   to think;
                fv         fm      v         bv

   present:    s
              looks
                fv
```

5 t n ø ø n
to have seen; must have had
bh v fm h v

6 *past*: d^2 ŋ
were saying
fc v

7 *past*: d^1 n
was published;
fp v

present: ø
think;
fv

past: d n n
had been translated
fh p v

past: d n
had passed
fh v

15.1 (page 181)

1(a) d
Seemed
fv

Finite, no polar emphasis, non-modal, past, non-perfect, non-continuous, active.

(b) d ø
Should be
fm v

Finite, no polar emphasis, modal, ?past, non-perfect, non-continuous, active.

(c) d n
Had discussed
fh v

Finite, no polar emphasis, non-modal, past, perfect, non-continuous, active.

2(a) ø t n
Oughtn't to be taken
fm neg p v

Finite, polar emphasis, modal, present, non-perfect, non-continuous, passive.

(b) ø n n
Have been warned
fh p v

Finite, polar emphasis, non-modal, present, perfect, non-continuous, passive.

(c) ø ø
Do bring
f v

Finite, polar emphasis, non-modal, present, non-perfect, non-continuous, active.

15.2 (page 181)

Doesn't apply; did call; do think. The emphatically positive one is *did call*. The speaker is suggesting in defence of the Labour Government that they have acted in obedience to the Labour Party Conference. 'It is not as though the Party Conference had not called upon them to take the action.' (Note the two negatives in this gloss.)

In Appendix B, II, l. 22 *do overlap* is emphatically positive. If power, status and income are three different types, one might perhaps suppose that they are totally different. The speaker is countering this supposition by pointing out that it isn't that they don't overlap.

15.3 (page 185)

1 It may be able to be sent next week.
2 These cups are liable to be broken.
3 They are likely to have been seen.
4 It would by now have been beginning to be built.
5 Our feelings tend to be disregarded.

15.4 (page 187)

1 Complex verbal group. The verbal construction *is sure to serve* cannot be divided by supplying a separate subject for *to serve*, e.g. **She is sure for you to serve the dinner soon.* On the other hand the whole construction can be rendered passive: *The dinner is sure to be served soon.* Note also that *sure* does not have the meaning associated with ordinary complements. Although *She is sure* (= 'she feels certain') is a possible clause, that is not the meaning of *sure* in our example.

2 Phase. *am keen* and *to read* can be separated by supplying a separate subject for *to read*, e.g. *I am keen for you to read that book*; *I am keen for that book to be read.*

Further, *keen* is interpretable as a complement to the subject: *I am*

keen. (NB It would be possible to construct examples like
(a) I am keen to interview that applicant
(b) That applicant is keen to be interviewed
But this does not prove the unity of the construction *be keen to interview*, since (b) is not the passive counterpart of (a) – a different person is described as being keen.

3 Phase. cf.
We agreed for their complaints to be heard.
**Their complaints agreed to be heard.*

4 A doubtful example. It depends whether *The bell started being rung* is acceptable. If so, this is a complex verbal group.

5 Phase. cf.
We remembered the bell being rung.
**The bell remembered being rung.*

6 Phase. cf.
**He is trying to be dismissed by the manager.*
(Of course, this is possible, but it is not the passive counterpart of the example being analysed.)

7 Complex verbal group. cf.
The bucket appears to have been filled.

8 Complex verbal group. cf.
The solution may fail to be found.
(Some speakers hesitate to accept this; for such speakers *fail to . . .* is not a semi-auxiliary.)

9 Complex verbal group. cf.
The tango is likely to be done.

10 Phase. cf.
**You are happy to be invited.* (not passive counterpart)
They are happy for you to be invited.
They are happy for me to invite you.

11 Complex verbal group: cf.
Electrons will start to be discharged.

15.5 (page 189)

1 There is a very clear difference of meaning. In (a) I first remembered, then posted the letter — so the remembering had the posting in prospect. In (b) I first posted the letter and subsequently remembered doing so; so the remembering did not have the posting in prospect.

2, 3 These forms are more or less interchangeable. Some speakers, however, claim that they sense a distinction. e.g. you say **2**(a) if you have not yet started writing, and **2**(b) while you are actually writing. Similarly, you say **3**(a) if you did not manage to get here early and **3**(b) if you succeeded.

16.1 (page 196)

Past non-perfect: was passed; was; were not entrusted; were; chose. *Present perfect*: has excused; have excused; have done; have undermined; have worked; (have) got; has happened.

The speaker is differentiating between past events which preceded the present situation, and past events which created the present situation. The election of the councillors and their flouting of the law are the prelude; the present situation has been created by the Government's pardoning the offence and thus weakening the constitutional rule of law.

16.2 (page 199)

1 He should/ought to have told her by tomorrow. (influence)
2 He needn't have told a lie. (influence)
3 He needn't/may not have told a lie. (knowledge)
4 He needn't/might not have told a lie. (knowledge)
5 He could have changed his job. (influence)
6 He could/may have changed his job. (knowledge)
7 He could/may have changed his job. (knowledge)
8 The door should/ought to have been locked. (influence)
9 The door must/should/ought to have been locked (by tomorrow evening). (influence)
10 They must have been asked to avoid a confrontation. (knowledge)

16.3 (page 200)

1(a) It is highly probable that the road was/has been/will have been repaired. (knowledge)
(b) It was obligatory/desirable for the road to be repaired (but it wasn't). (influence)
(c) It is obligatory/desirable for the road to have been repaired (by some time in the future). (influence)
2(a) It is possible that he was/has been/will have been killed. (knowledge)
(b) It was possible for him to be killed (but he wasn't). (influence)
(c) It was permissible for him to be killed (but he wasn't). (influence)

16.4 (page 200)

Must and *can't* as influence modals cannot occur with *have* in reference to past time. (Compare with reference to future time: *They must have moved to another house by the time I return*.) Contrast with the non-modal *have (to)*: *They had to move to another house last year*; and with the past tense modal *could: They could have taken mine yesterday.* ('They were permitted to, but didn't'.)

16.5 (page 209)

Almost every clause in this passage is habitual in aspect. The speaker is generalizing so naturally he is talking about what characteristically happens on repeated occasions. In most clauses it would be possible to insert a frequentative adjunct such as *usually, often, always, normally* (one of them already has *very often*), e.g. *The insects normally tend to react to each other.* The modal verbs *can* and *will* are used in the generalizing senses of 'sometimes' and 'usually', e.g. *some of these swarms . . . are sometimes a hundred kilometres long* . . . . The clauses which are not habitual in aspect are *if you can imagine* and *that's some size.* (It should be noted that the clauses with continuous aspect are also habitual.)

Continuous aspect occurs in *was glowing, are glowing, will be moving.* This feature tends to stress the simultaneity of the glowing and the moving in order to explain how the swarm can be mistaken for a UFO. The speaker understandably fluctuates between viewing the make up of the swarm for its own sake, and for the sake of the appearance it presents to a witness.

16.6 (page 209)

In the course of a discussion it is customary for the speakers to explain what they mean (and to ask for explanations) by using such verbs as *say, argue, talk (about)* in continuous aspect, e.g. *I am arguing* . . .; *I'm not arguing* . . . . The notion of simultaneity is inherent in this: 'in saying x, I am arguing y', or 'in saying x, are you saying y?'.

In lines 45–6 *is being ruined* has a different explanation. This is an event 'happening now', simultaneously with the utterance (though, of course, there is still a sense of giving an explanation of things that are not visibly present to the addressee).

17.1 (page 211)

Several of these are likely to be written notices actually fixed to the thing being talked about:

Open all day Wednesday (fixed to a shop), *The Nook* (fixed to a house), *Encyclopaedia Britannica* (fixed to a book), *Ticket holders this way* (fixed to a door, or doorway), *No smoking in the store* (fixed to the store), *Drying only customers 10p extra* (fixed to a launderette).

St Paul's Cathedral next stop: uttered by the bus conductor while the journey is in progress.

Victoria Station, please: uttered by someone as he gets into a taxi.

Mother for trial and *Four in court after bank strike* are likely to be printed in large bold type at the head of a news article.

Most of the utterances, as described here, would require the addressee simply to take note of the information imparted; the speaker is not expecting a particular action as response. However, (c), (e), (f) and (i) do require an action response. The fact that the actions are suggested here by means of imperative clauses does not mean that the examples being analysed are to be seen as imperatives: *Take me to Victoria* (c), *Step this way if you are an addressee of this notice* (e), *Extinguish cigarettes* or *Refrain from lighting up* (f), *Pay 10p extra if you are an addressee of this notice* (i).

17.2 (page 212)

1	. . . chosen ‖ where . . .	interrogative
2	. . . up ‖ should . . .	declarative
3	. . . chosen ‖ where . . .	declarative
4	Ring ‖ if . . .	imperative
5	. . . please ‖ if . . .	moodless
6	. . . say ‖ the . . .	interrogative
7	. . . ring ‖ if . . .	declarative

17.3 (page 213)

1	. . . time ‖ while . . .	declarative; FB; reversible
2	. . . tea ‖ help . . .	imperative; BF; reversible
3	. . . suite ‖ which . . .	declarative; FB; not reversible
4	. . . shout ‖ when . . .	imperative; FB; reversible
5	. . . crowded ‖ before . . .	interrogative; FB; reversible
6	. . . asked ‖ whether . . .	declarative; FB; not reversible
7	. . . away ‖ who's . . .	interrogative; BF; reversible

17.4 (page 213)

Statement 1 is true; all the sentences that are not already FB can be reversed to give FB.

Statement 2 is false; sentences **3** and **6** have non-reversible FB sequences.

Statement 3 is true for the same reason that 2 is false.

17.5 (page 214)

1	whether (or not)	**3**	provided
2	however late	**4**	the minute

5 although
6 long before
7 as if
8 as soon as
9 until
10 since
11 seeing
12 before
13 no matter how long
14 because
15 after

17.6 (page 215)

The minute is up.
I'm not leaving until tomorrow.
He is seeing them tonight.
I haven't been there since the war.
I've never seen it before.
He takes after his father.

17.7 (page 216)

Predicators underlined:

(a) Finding ‖ they had so many pretensions ‖ I had soon had . . . patriotism; BBF
(b) Having taken place in December ‖ the Festival had not been well attended; BF
(c) They can be thrown out ‖ having served their purpose; FB
(d) Giving the responsibility to others ‖ he managed to avoid . . . trouble; BF
(e) To get enough sleep ‖ you have to retire early; BF
(f) He held out his arm ‖ to bar the way; FB
(g) To be sure of seeing all of them ‖ I went over the ground twice; BF

17.8 (page 217)

1 *leaving the boarding house*
2 *with you leaving*: S = *you*: binder = *with*
3 *for Bill to have sat opposite her*: P = *to have sat*; S = *Bill*; binder = *for*
4 *by placing a finger across the corner*: binder = *by*
5 *after trying to understand them for so long*: binder = *after*
6 *his collar twisted half round his neck*: P = *twisted* (*n*-form); S = *his collar*
7 *presented with such difficulties*: P = *presented* (*n*-form)
8 *with the grass being mown*: P = *being mown*; S = *the grass*; binder = *with*
9 *though considered a classic*: P = *considered* (*n*-form); binder = *though*
10 *to find the answer*

17.9 (page 217)

after: after she had tried to understand them
though: though it is considered a classic

17.10 (page 219)

Contingent	*Adding*	*Reported*
*when	who	that
*if	*when	why
now that	which	what
because	where	*if
by		

(Items that occur in more than one column are starred.)

17.11 (page 220)

1	. . . hope ‖ you . . .	FB; reported; no binder
2	. . . armies ‖ because . . .	FB; contingent; binder = *because*
3	. . . concluded ‖ that . . .	FB; reported; binder = *that*
4	. . . order ‖ he . . .	BF; contingent; binder = *without*; P-bound
5	. . . again ‖ which . . .	FB; adding; binder = *which*
6	. . .firmly ‖ turn . . .	BF; contingent; no binder; P-bound
7	. . . do ‖ when . . .	FB; contingent; binder = *when*
8	. . . saw ‖ how . . .	FB; reported; binder = *how*
9	. . . choose ‖ I . . .	BF; contingent; binder = *if*
10	. . . boss ‖ who . . .	FB; adding; binder = *who*.
11	. . . out ‖ who . . .	FB; reported; binder = *who*; P-bound
12	. . . raining ‖ for . . .	FB; contingent; binder = *for*; P-bound

Contingent	*Adding*	*Reported*
without		how
for		*who

17.12 (page 221)

1 Split: *In the evenings . . . card playing languished.* The enclosed B clause is adding. (Strictly this is ambiguous; the B clause could be contingent, but this is not the most natural interpretation of the example, cf. *When the hotel lounge was full, in the evenings card playing languished*. In this case the B clause must be contingent.)

2 No splitting; B^{cont}
3 No splitting; B^{rep}.
4 Split: *The gates . . . close as the train approaches.* The enclosed B clause is adding.
5 Split: *you can . . . finish it off quickly*. The enclosed B clause is contingent.
6 Split: *they tell you things . . . do they?* The enclosed B clause is contingent.

18.1 (page 223)

(a) **1a** *and*; both declarative
1b *but*; both declarative
1c *and*; both declarative
1d *or*; both declarative
1e no overt joining element; both declarative
1f *and*; both declarative
1g *however*; both declarative
1h *moreover*; both declarative
1i *so*; both declarative
1j *anyway*; both declarative
1k *but, nevertheless*; both declarative
1l *but*; both imperative
1m *and*; both interrogative
1n *so*; declarative + interrogative
1o no overt joining element; declarative + interrogative
1p *and*; imperative + declarative
1q *or*; imperative + declarative
1r *or*; imperative + interrogative

(b) One kind of joining element has to be initial in its clause: *and, but, or, so*. . . . The other kind is variable in position: *however, moreover, nevertheless*. . . . If both occur at the beginning of the clause the fixed initial kind comes first.

18.2 (page 228)

1 Joining; listed, not linked, branched; lister = *so*; the structure of the second clause is: A^{+} P C^{loc} The subject of the preceding clause functions also as subject of this one.
2 Joining; not listed, not linked, not branched.
3 Binding.
4 Joining; not listed, linked, not branched; linker = *however*.

5 Joining; listed, linked, branched; lister = *and*; linker = *in fact*; structure $A^{+}\ A^{l}\ P\ C^{o}$, by reference to S in the previous clause.
6 Joining; listed, not linked, branched; lister = *and*; structure: $A^{+}\ P\ C^{o}$, by reference to S in the previous clause.
7 Joining; listed, not linked, branched; lister = *but*; structure: A^{+} S A C, by reference to P in the previous clause.
8 Joining; listed, linked, not branched; lister = *and*; linker = *besides.*
9 Binding.
10 Joining; listed, not linked, branched; lister = *yet*; structure: A^{+} P P A. The branched structure is more complex here since it is not only the S of the previous clause that is relevant but also the operator = *he might*.
11 Binding.
12 Joining; not listed, linked, not branched; linker = *otherwise.*
13 Joining; not listed, not linked, not branched.
14 Joining; listed, not linked, not branched; lister = *for*.
15 Joining; listed, not linked, branched; lister = *and*; structure: $A^{+}\ P\ C^{o}\ C^{loc}$ by reference to operator and S of the previous clause (*have you*). Note that both clauses are interrogative.

18.3 (page 232)

1 In the first clause the speaker's intuition leads him to think 'it must be', while in the second his lack of knowledge suggests 'it may not be'.

2, 3 In each case speaker B concedes the point A has just made, at least ostensibly, and then goes on to make an objection. The antithesis can be summarized thus: 'what you say is true but objectionable (irrelevant, inappropriate etc.); what I say is true and to the point'. This is a very common conversational tactic, even when you don't think what the other says is true.

4 The first clause suggests 'there is evidence for the numbering', while the second suggests 'there is no evidence for the numbering'. The antithesis is based on the assumption 'if it were true, I would have been able to corroborate it'.

5 There is an assumption that if they were made by his employees they would not be of a high standard. The antithesis is therefore 'not of high standard' v. 'of high standard'.

6 It is in the nature of problems to defy solution; the expectation would therefore be that the problem is not coped with well.

7 The first clause leads one to suppose they are all equally scarce; the second declares they are not all equally scarce. This is a rhetorical trick to emphasize the scarcity of the object being talked about.

8 The antithesis is between 'possibly partly old' and 'certainly partly new', i.e. possibly v. certainly, and old v. new.

9 The contrast is 'Don't know one thing' v. 'do know another'.

18.4 (page 234)

1 (*a* but (*b* and *c*)). Note that there must be bracketing, for two reasons: first, because *but* opposes each of two items to the other, so where there are three or more items some of them must be bracketed together; second, because any string of clauses that has a mixture of different types of listing (e.g. a mixture of *ands, buts, ors*, etc.) must have bracketing — a list can only be extended to three or more items if they are all related to each other in the same way.

There are two possible bracketings for example **1**: the one given above, and ((*a* but *b*) and *c*). Syntactically there is no evidence to guide us; we must rely on the meaning. Perhaps both interpretations make sense, but I feel that the one I have given is slightly more satisfactory.

2 ((*a* or *b*) and *c*) . Again there must be bracketing, because there is a mixture of alternative and additive listing. The choice of this bracketing rather than (*a* or (*b* and *c*)) is guided only by the meaning, and might be disputed. (Note that if the sentence occurred in spoken text, the intonation would probably settle the matter.)

3 (*a* and *b* and *c*) . Syntactically there is no need for any bracketing. Nor does the meaning strongly suggest any brackets here.

4 (*a* and *b* and *c*) . There is no reason to suggest any brackets here.

5 (*a* and *b* and *c*) . Possibly one might favour (*a* and (*b* and *c*)) but we really need evidence of intonation.

6 (*a* and (*b* and *c*)). There is syntactic evidence here since the third clause is branched with the second, while the second is not branched with the first. (Contrast with **5** where both of the last two clauses are branched.) There is also the meaning to help in the decision, and the strong collocational tie between *mice* and *play* and *come out* and *play*.

7 (((*a* and *b*) or *c*) and *d*) . There obviously must be brackets because of the mixture of *and* and *or*. The first clause must be bracketed with the second because the first begins with the correlative *either*; everything that comes before we get to the anticipated *or* must be in brackets. Moreover, (b) is branched. This would still leave us with the possibility of ((*a* and *b*) or (*c* and *d*)). Only the meaning can help us in rejecting this interpretation.

8 ((*a* and *b*) but (*c* and *d*)). Syntactically, there must be brackets, but the only reason to choose the above rather than (*a* and (*b* but *c*) and *d*) is the meaning.

9 ((*a* (*b*((*cd*) and *e*) *f g* and *h*)) yet *i*). The evidence is, again, partly syntactic and partly semantic, though the punctuation certainly helps in the interpretation of the meaning.

The first clause (down to the colon) is a generalization; there is then a list of five items that justify the generalization:

(i)	the subject . . . arrest	*b*
(ii)	he was tried . . . prosecutions	(*cd*) and *e*
(iii)	he was free . . . print	*f*
(iv)	he could . . . debates	*g*
(v)	and he . . . permission	and *h*

This is an additive list with *and* appearing only before the last item. However, the second item is a complex of three clauses with internal bracketing: ((*cd*) and *e*).

The final clause is an antithesis to the whole of the rest of the passage.

18.5 (page 236)

1 correlative; *both . . . and*
2 correlative; *not only . . . but*
3 no correlative; *both* is here part of the nominal group subject *both of them*
4 no correlative
5 no correlative
6 correlative; *neither . . . nor*
7 no correlative; *neither* is here part of the nominal group *neither of them*
8 correlative; *either . . . or*
9 no correlative
10 correlative; *not . . . but*
11 correlative; *not only . . . but*; note that *both* is here not a correlative but a nominal group as prepositional object
12 correlative; *either . . . or*
13 no correlative; but it is interesting to note that there is a close relation to the correlative pair *neither . . . nor* in the paraphrase: 'They have read neither Shakespeare nor Spenser'.
14 correlative; *either . . . or*

19.1 (page 240)

1 BF; binder = *though.*
2 F ((B)); F is split after S; binder = *since.*
3 FB; no binder.
4 FB; binder = *as if.*
5 BF; binder = *as soon as.*

6 F ((B)); F is split after S + operator; binder = *if.*
7 BF; binder = *unless.*
8 F ((B)); F is split after S; binder = *when.*
9 BF; binder = *as.*
10 BF; binder = *when.*
11 F((B)); F is split after S + operator; binder = *when.*
12 FB; no binder.
13 BF; no binder.
14 FB; binder = *provided.*
15 BF; binder = *whatever.*
16 BF; binder = *whatever.*
17 F((B)); F is split after A^1; binder = *before.*
18 FB; binder = *three hours before.*
19 FB; binder = *by.*
20 F((B)); F is split after A; binder = *however much time.*

19.2 (page 244)

1. *Wherever you live*; binder = *wherever*; WH–C^{loc}.
2. No contingent clause; *whatever they broadcast* is a nominal group, prepositional object to *to*; WH–C^{o}.
3. This is the same as **2** except that *whatever they broadcast* has been brought to the front (i.e. made thematic).
4. *Whatever they broadcast* is here a contingent clause; binder = *whatever*; WH–C.
5. Same as **4**.
6. *Whoever you hear* is a contingent clause; binder = *whoever*; WH–C.
7. *However old it is* is a contingent clause; binder = *however old*; WH–C.
8. No contingent clause; *whoever* is here functioning in its interrogative sense, initial in a free clause; WH–S.
9. *Whenever the weather's bad* is a contingent clause; binder = *whenever*; WH–A. Note that *whatever* is a modifier in the nominal group *whatever umbrella he can find*; headword = umbrella.

19.3 (page 246)

20c *where*: WH–A
20d *which*: WH–S
20e *which*: WH–S
20f *when*: WH–C^{loc}
21 *whose coat*: WH–S
22 *which*: WH–S
23a *which*: WH–S
23b *which*: WH–S
24a *when*: WH–A
24b *when*: WH–A

19.4 (page 249)

(a) . . . who were not entrusted by the public with the task of disobeying the law, but were trustees of public money for their locality . . . (Adding. This is actually a complex of two joined clauses, with the lister *but* to connect them and the second one branched.)
(b) . . . anybody else who chooses to disobey the law for different party political affiliations or reasons . . . (Relative clause beginning at *who chooses*. . .)
(c) . . . the consequences which the law, the general law, prescribes for that particular type of conduct . . . (Relative clause beginning at *which the law* . . .)
(d) . . . those who have worked in on factories and then got government grants. (Relative clause — or rather complex of clauses — beginning at *who have worked*. . . .)
(e) . . . the thing which has actually happened . . . (Relative clause beginning at *which has*. . . .)

19.5 (page 250)

1 Now of course Princess O'Hara is by no means a regular princess: *free, linked*
2 and in fact she is nothing but a little redheaded doll, with plenty of freckles, from over in Tenth Avenue: *free, listed, linked*
3 and her right name is Maggie: *free, listed*
4 and the only reason she is called Princess O'Hara is as follows: *free, listed*
5 She is the daughter of King O'Hara: *free*
6 who is hacking along Broadway with one of these old-time victorias for a matter of maybe twenty-five years: *bound, adding*
7 and (. . .) he is always bragging: *free, listed*
8 ((every time King O'Hara gets his pots on: *bound, contingent*
9 which is practically every night, rain or shine)): *bound, adding*
10 that he has the royal blood of Ireland in his veins: *bound, reported*
11 so somebody starts calling him King: *free, listed*
12 and this is his monicker: *free, listed*
13 as long as I can remember: *bound, contingent*
14 although probably what King O'Hara really has in his veins is about ninety-eight per cent alcohol: *free, listed, linked*

20.1 (page 252)

The judgements of acceptability in the following answers are, of course, mine, not yours.

1 binder = *who*; negative; acceptable.
2 binder = *whether*; positive; unacceptable.
3 binder = *that*; negative; doubtful.
4 binder = *that*; negative; doubtful.
5 binder = *when*; positive; unacceptable.
6 binder = *when*; negative; acceptable.
7 binder = *that*; positive; unacceptable.
8 binder = *why*; negative; acceptable.
9 binder = *whether*; negative; doubtful.
10 binder = *that*; positive; unacceptable.
11 binder = *what*; negative; acceptable.
12 binder = *whose car*; negative; acceptable.
13 binder = *who*; negative; acceptable.

If the above judgements of acceptability are acceptable, it appears that the condition on the binder (that it must be WH) can be relaxed more readily than the condition on the polarity of the dominant clause (that it must be negative).

20.2 (page 254)

1 I haven't decided whether *I* should paint it white.
2 They showed me how *you* turn it off.
3 He can't remember who *he* should tell. (*or* . . . who *one* should tell.)
4 Will you find out which figure *one* is to believe, please?
5 She mentioned where *one* should/can park the car.
6 I have forgotten whose certificate *I* am to send by post.

The subject in the paraphrase is either the same as the subject in the dominant clause, or is of an indefinite nature — expressible as *one* or *you*.

20.3 (page 255)

1 *And then . . . dress*: free, major, listed, linked; lister = *and*; linker = *then*.
2 *a subject . . . advice*: bound, minor, adding.
3 *Desperately . . . information*: bound, minor, contingent.
4 *I . . . myself*: free, major.
5 *what . . . head*: bound, major, reported; binder = *what.*
6 *Stephen . . . last year*: free, major.
7 *but the idea . . . ludicrous*: free, major, listed; lister = *but*.
8 *I remembered . . . Dumborough*: free, major.
9 *On this . . . holes*: free, major.
10 *I had . . . paper*: free, major.

11 *that . . . mine*: bound, major, reported; binder = *that*
12 *This experiment . . . saddle*: free, major. (NB possibly *but less secure in the saddle* might be taken as a separate clause, free, major, listed, branched.)
13 *and (. . .) I almost lost my balance*; free, major, split, listed; lister = *and*.
14 ((*when . . . swerve*: bound, major, contingent; binder = *when*.
15 *quite needlessly . . . hedge*)): bound, major, contingent, P-bound.
16 *in fact . . . off*; free, major, linked; linker = *in fact*.
17 *Dixon . . . nothing*: free, major
18 *until . . . home*; bound, major, contingent; binder = *until*.
19 *and then . . . remarked*: free, major, listed; lister = *and*.
20 *that . . . short*: bound, major, reported; binder = *that*.
21 *They . . . say*: free, major.
22 *that . . . seat*: bound, major, reported; binder = *that*.
23 *I . . . hint*: free, major.
24 *which . . . one*: bound, major, adding; binder = *which*.

20.4 (page 257)

1

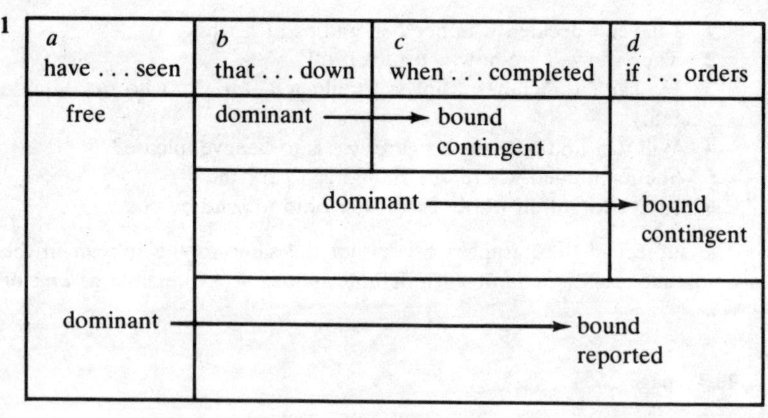

$(a \rightarrow ((b \rightarrow c) \rightarrow d))$
0 1 2 2

2

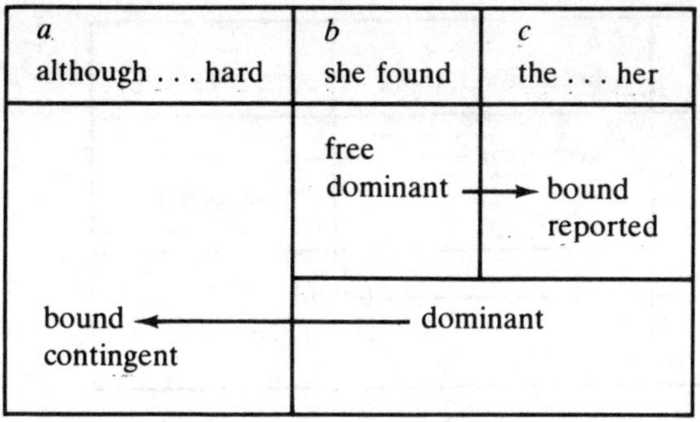

a although . . . hard	*b* she found	*c* the . . . her
	free dominant →	bound reported
bound ← contingent	dominant	

$(a \leftarrow (b \rightarrow c))$

1 0 1

3

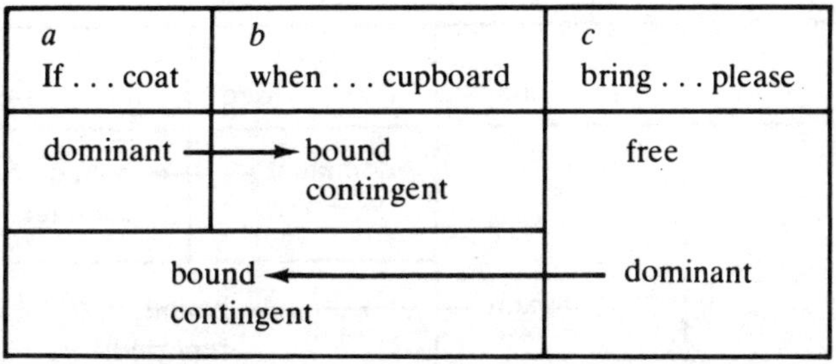

a If . . . coat	*b* when . . . cupboard	*c* bring . . . please
dominant →	bound contingent	free
bound ← contingent		dominant

$((a \rightarrow b) \leftarrow c)$

1 2 0

4

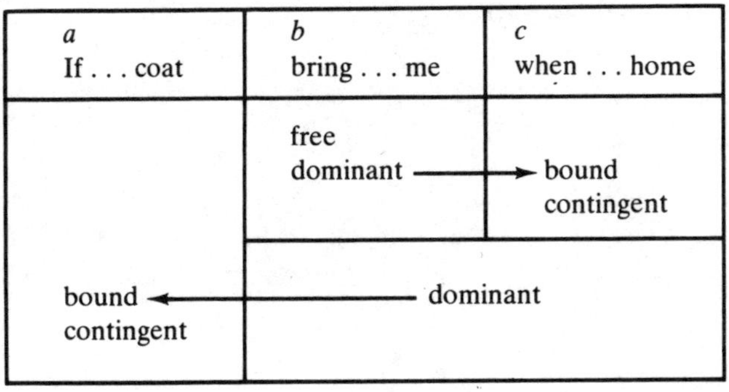

a If . . . coat	*b* bring . . . me	*c* when . . . home
	free dominant →	bound contingent
bound ← contingent	dominant	

$((a \leftarrow (b \rightarrow c))$

1 0 1

5

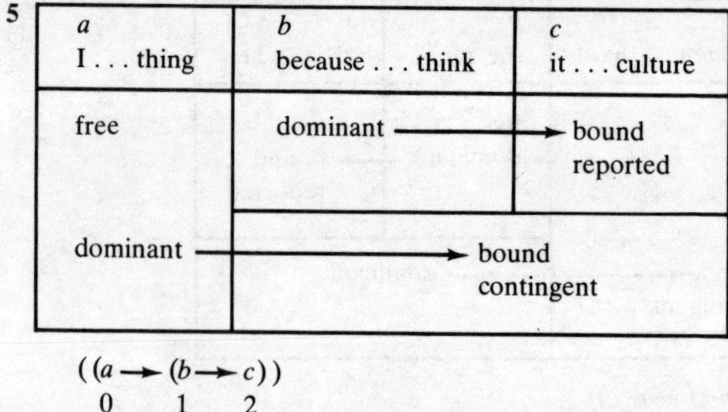

$((a \rightarrow (b \rightarrow c))$
0 1 2

20.5 (page 260)

1

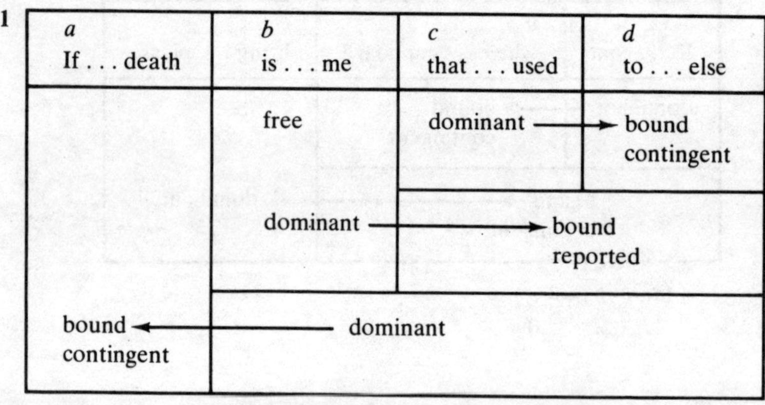

$(a \leftarrow (b \rightarrow (c \rightarrow d)))$
1 0 1 2

2

a But . . . indemnity	*b* because . . . 7000	*c* and . . . funds
free	free joined ——	—— joined listed
joined ——	—— joined listed	

$(a + (b + c))$

3

a They've . . . trust	*b* which . . . again	*c* and . . . privilegium
free dominant ——	——→ bound adding	free
joined ——		—— joined listed

$(a \rightarrow b) + c$

0 1 0

4

a It . . . him	*b* and . . . space	*c* which . . . satellites	*d* and . . . fantastic
free	free dominant ——	——→ bound adding	free
joined ——	—— joined listed ——		—— joined listed

$(a + (b \rightarrow c) + d)$

0 0 1 0

5

a It's . . . pity	*b* they . . . clear	*c* 'cos . . . clear	*d* they . . . shady
free dominant →	bound reported	free joined —	free joined contact
joined —		—	joined listed

$(a \rightarrow b) + (c + d)$
0 1 0 0

6

a Of . . . men	*b* so . . . think	*c* that . . . action
free	free dominant →	bound reported
joined —	joined listed	

$(a + (b \rightarrow c))$
0 0 1

7

a Part . . . belt	*b* which . . . permitted	*c* where . . . accommodation
free	dominant →	bound contingent
dominant →	bound adding	

$(a \rightarrow (b \rightarrow c))$
0 1 2

8

a	*b*	*c*	*d*	*e*	*f*	*g*	*h*
	free	free				dominant →	bound reported
					dominant →	bound adding	
			joined +	joined listed +	joined listed		
bound ←	dominant	dominant →	bound reported				
joined —		joined listed					

$$((a \leftarrow b) + (c \rightarrow (d + e + (f \rightarrow (g \longrightarrow h)))))$$

1 0 0 1 1 1 2 3

21.1 (page 266)

The dominant clause is written out:

1 Bill didn't notice: SP
2 They must have warned her: SP
3 I was surprised: SPC^{i}
4 She seemed unsure: SPC^{i}
5 It's true: $S^{it}PC^{i}$
6 It wasn't surprising: $S^{it}PC^{i}$
7 It can be imagined: $S^{it}P^{pass}$
8 It won't be noticed: $S^{it}P^{pass}$
9 nobody seemed certain: SPC^{i}
10 I can't think: SP
11 It is believed: $S^{it}P^{pass}$

12 It astonished her: this is the one that does not fit into any of the four types given so far: $S^{it}\ P\ C^{o}$

13 It is not very regrettable: $S^{it}\ P\ C^{i}$

14 They will be pleased: $S\,P\,C^{i}$

15 She says: SP

SP	*SPC*^{i}	*S*^{it} *PC*^{i}	*S*^{it} *P*^{pass}
notice	surprised	true	imagine
warn	unsure	surprising	notice
think	certain	regrettable	believe
say	pleased		

21.2 (page 270)

1 Postposed theme (neutral: *What he's written is long*)
2 Report (meaning 'We are ignorant of what he's written')
3 *It*-theme (neutral: *He's written a very good essay*)
4 Report (meaning 'I don't understand why . . .')
5 Report (cf. the active: *People think that you see . . .*)
6 Report (cf. *One wouldn't believe that . . .*)
7 Ambiguous: (a) Report (meaning: 'I'm astonished that he's trying'); (b) *It*-theme (neutral: *He's trying a surprise*)
8 It-theme (neutral: *I find the punctuation so erratic*)
9 Report (meaning 'We haven't been able to find out what he bought')
10 Postposed theme (neutral: *What he bought can't be dry-cleaned*)

21.3 (page 271)

This is a complicated structure built up out of isolatable pieces. We can simplify the explanation by substituting *x* for the cumbersome nominal group *the glowing discharge known as St Elmo's fire.*

1 *You see x* dominant
2 *if you have a swarm of moths like this* contingent

1 can be subjected to thematic identification:

3 *what you see is x* ‖ *if . . .*, or
4 *x is what you see* ‖ *if . . .*

The whole of **4** can be treated as a reported complex:

5 *it is thought* ‖ *(that) x is what you see* ‖ *if . . .*

But there has been previous mention of *x*:

6 *This electric field causes x*

and **6** has been subjected to *it*-theme treatment in respect of its subject:

7 *It is this electric field which causes x.*

If we now juxtapose **7** and **5** we have the basis for an adding structure in which x is the antecedent for the WH-binder:

7 *It is this electric field*
which causes x
↕
5 *which it is thought is what you see if . . .*

22.1 (page 274)

1 (any binder): reveal, observe_1 (=notice), remind, whisper, find(out), sure, obvious.
2 (WH, *whether/if*): ask_1(=inquire), wonder_1(=ask self), inquire, demand_1(=inquire), investigate, discuss, doubtful.
3 (*that*): feel, think observe_2(= say), ask_2(= request action), wonder_2(= be surprised), hope, deny, demand_2(= command), sorry, possible, ?surprised.

22.2 (page 276)

The following presuppose the truth of the reported clause: **1, 6, 8, 10, 11, 12** and **16**. The verbs and adjectives are: *discover, realize, remind, be pleased, be surprised, be astonishing, notice.*

22.3 (page 277)

1 *believe*
3 *imagine*
5 *feel*
6 *probable*
8 *expect*
10 *think*

22.4 (page 277)

1(a) From the meaning, this can be identified as a checking tag. For instance it could be used as a request for acknowledgement.
(b) Phonologically also it is identifiable as a checking tag: the intonation on the tag could be Tone 1 (falling). This rules out the possibility that it is a copy tag, which could only have a rising tone.
(c) As a checking tag in this context *is it* has two peculiarities:
(i) the tag is modelled not on the free clause *I don't think* (which would give: *do I*?) but on the reported clause: *it's . . . is it.* This modelling of the tag on the reported clause is possible in very

restricted circumstances:

**He thinks it will freeze, won't it?*
I imagine he's rather pleased, isn't he?
I believe they're here, aren't they?
**I imagined he was rather pleased, wasn't he?*
**He believes you're rather pleased, aren't you?*

The subject has to be *I*, and the tense has to be present. In these circumstances, obviously, the speaker's attention is more on the truth of the reported clause than on the truth of the dominant.

(ii) the tag does not have the opposite polarity to that of the proposition on which it is modelled:

it's . . . is it? (both positive)

This fact is easily explained, however, by reference to the phenomenon of transferred negation. *I don't think it's going to freeze* is an alternative to *I think it's not going to freeze*. In the second of these alternatives the reported clause is negative. The tag in our example is constructed as though the reported clause were negative — which, in a sense, it is.

2(a) *Think* is a verb allowing transferred negation. The negation can come before or after the verb. Compare with other verbs of this kind: *I don't believe so = I believe not*; *He didn't imagine so = He imagined not.*

(b) *Hope* is not one of these verbs, so the alternative placings of negation are not equivalent. Compare with *He didn't say so* which is not equivalent to *He said not.*

22.5 (page 282)

Grammatical analysis

First paragraph: no report or quoting structures.
Second paragraph:

1 *This secession . . . to her*: free, pseudo-reported.
2 *she alleged*: free, pseudo-quoting.
3 *she did not know*: free, pseudo-reported, dominant, reporting.
4 *how . . . the vacancy*: bound, reported.
5 *She was . . . right hand*: free, pseudo-reported.
6 *what . . . without him*: free, pseudo-reported, interrogative.
7 *She had . . . the step*: free, pseudo-reported.
8 *but M. Paul . . . her*: free, pseudo-reported, dominant, reporting.
9 *it was his duty*: bound, reported.

Third paragraph: no reporting or quoting.
Fourth paragraph:

10 *Why . . . duty?* free, pseudo-reported.

11 *I could . . . that*: free.
12 *I had impulses . . . and say*: free (an elaborate structure containing some paratactic complexes; the last part — *and say* — is quoting.)
13 *Stop*: free, quoted, imperative.
14 *Let us . . . matter*: free, quoted, imperative.
15 *Why . . . banishment*: free, quoted, interrogative.
16 *But . . . teacher*: free.
17 *and never . . . me*: free, branched.
18 *never . . . conscious*: free, branched, dominant, reporting.
19 *I could . . . question*: bound, reported.

The pseudo-reported clauses are syntactically distinguished by
(a) the selection of pronouns, e.g. *she, her* (instead of *I, me, my*)
(b) past tense, e.g. *was, did not know* (instead of *is, do not know*)
The interrogative clause **6** does not ask a question, but represents a question asked by Madame Beck. Indeed the whole of the second paragraph (with the exception of clause **2**) is represented speech and contrasts with the narrator's first-hand discourse and the quoted speech in the fourth paragraph. The fourth paragraph begins with a pseudo-reported clause — note the past tense *was*. But clauses **13–15** are quoted clauses. The tense of the verbal groups suddenly switches to present, and there are imperative clauses, which would not fit easily into the represented speech since imperatives have no past tense forms.

Literary effect

It is noticeable that the only words that are actually uttered — by Madame Beck — are not addressed to the narrator and are not given direct in quoted clauses but in pseudo-reports. Thus Madame Beck's ignoring the narrator is depicted by the grammatical form in which her words are represented. On the other hand the quoted clauses in the last paragraph are not actually spoken; they are imagined speech and even the lively imperatives are articulated silently to herself as the narrator conceals her agitation. In these ways the narrator is made to seem isolated from her companions and the grammatical structures are symbolic of the meaning of the passage.

23.1 (page 284)

Rankshifted within C: **1, 4, 5, 7, 9**
P-bound clause: **2, 3, 6, 8.**

23.2 (page 287)

Rankshifted clause at C^O: **2, 3, 4, 7.**
Phase: **1, 2, 5, 6, 8.**

2 is ambiguous:

(a) I remember the fact of your disapproving of them (*rankshifted clause*)

(b) I remember you and you were disapproving of them (*phase*)

23.3 (page 293)

The nominal groups are listed and the head is in italics. Qualifiers are placed after a bar line.

1 *I; anyone*; the *fact* | that there was police corruption; police *corruption.*
Rankshifted clause: that there was police corruption.

2 *someone* | who can't understand; *it*; *music.*
Rankshifted clauses: (i) who can't understand; (ii) to explain about wanting to write music; (iii) wanting to write music.

3 *It*; *something* | I can't help; *I*.
Rankshifted clause: I can't help.

4 an uneventful south-coast *childhood*; a good many *trips* | to Brighton; *Brighton*; *he*; *himself*; a drama *school* | there.

5 *It*; a perfectly straightfaced *report* | of a message to the nation; a *message* | to the nation; the *nation.*

6 all her *dreams* | of living in India; *India; she.*
Rankshifted clause: living in India.

7 *It*; a *mass* | of insects | like this and of the size you've described; *insects*; *this*; the *size* | you've described; *you*; a radar *screen.*
Rankshifted clause: you've described.

Index

Numbers in bold type indicate pages where brief explanations or illustrations of technical terms are to be found.